Culturing the Child, 1690–1914

Essays in Memory of Mitzi Myers

Edited by Donelle Ruwe

THE CHILDREN'S LITERATURE ASSOCIATION
AND
THE SCARECROW PRESS, INC.
Lanham, Maryland • Toronto • Oxford
2005

SCARECROW PRESS, INC.

Published in the United States of America
by Scarecrow Press, Inc.
A wholly owned subsidiary of
The Rowman & Littlefield Publishing Group, Inc.
4501 Forbes Boulevard, Suite 200, Lanham, Maryland 20706
www.scarecrowpress.com

PO Box 317
Oxford
OX2 9RU, UK

British Library Cataloguing in Publication Information Available

Library of Congress Cataloging-in-Publication Data

Culturing the child, 1690–1914 : essays in memory of Mitzi Myers / edited by
Donelle Ruwe.
    p. cm.
"Bibliography of Mitzi Myers' scholarly works" : p.
Includes bibliographical references and index.
ISBN 0-8108-5182-2 (pbk. : alk. paper)
    1. Children's literature—History and criticism. 2. Children—Books and
reading—History—19th century. 3. Myers, Mitzi. I. Ruwe, Donelle Rae, 1965– .
II. Myers, Mitzi.
  PN1009.A1C85 2005
  809'.89282—dc22
                                        2004021252

$\circledinfty^{TM}$ The paper used in this publication meets the minimum requirements of
American National Standard for Information Sciences—Permanence of Paper
for Printed Library Materials, ANSI/NISO Z39.48-1992.
Manufactured in the United States of America

Contents

Acknowledgments   v

Introduction by Donelle Ruwe   vi

Part 1: Creating the Contexts of Children's Literature

1 The Book on the Bookseller's Shelf and the Book in the
   English Child's Hand   3
   Ruth B. Bottigheimer

2 Virtue in the Guise of Vice: The Making and Unmaking
   of Morality from Fairy Tale Fantasy   29
   Karen E. Rowe

3 "Delightful Task!": Women, Children, and Reading in the
   Mid-Eighteenth Century   67
   Julia Briggs

Part 2: Reading the Rational Dames

4 Mother of All Discourses: Anna Barbauld's *Lessons
   for Children*   85
   William McCarthy

5 Gender, Nationalism, and Science in Hannah More's
   Pedagogical Plays for Children   113
   Marjean D. Purinton

6 "A Conservative Woman Doing Radical Things":
   Sarah Trimmer and *The Guardian of Education*   137
   M. O. Grenby

Part 3: The Politics of Pedagogy and the Child

7   The Making and Unmaking of a Children's Classic:
    The Case of Scott's *Ivanhoe*   165
    Bruce Beiderwell and Anita Hemphill McCormick

8   Heroism Reconsidered: Negotiating Autonomy in
    St. Nicholas Magazine (1873–1914)   179
    Susan R. Gannon

9   Worlds of Girls: Educational Reform and Fictional Form
    in L. T. Meade's School Stories   199
    Mavis Reimer

Part 4: Remembering Mitzi Myers

10 Mitzi Myers: A Memoir (9 October 1939 to
    5 November 2001)   221
    Patsy Myers

11 The Scholarly Legacy of Mitzi Myers   227
    Gillian Adams with Donelle Ruwe

12 A Bibliography of Mitzi Myers's Scholarly Works   241
    Donelle Ruwe

Index   254
About the Contributors   265

Acknowledgments

$\mathscr{I}$ gratefully acknowledge the encouraging letters and notes from the many friends of Mitzi Myers. U. C. Knoepflmacher, Andrea Immel, Octavio Olvera, Patsy Myers, and James Leve in particular must be recognized for their assistance during different stages of this project. I thank Eastern Illinois University for providing a research leave of absence during the editing of this project, and I appreciate the Northern Arizona University Cline Library staff for helping me to obtain numerous publications by Mitzi Myers. The Children's Literature Association Publications Committee and its chair, Raymond E. Jones, made this project possible, and I thank Millicent Lenz and Elizabeth Lennox Keyser for recommending me to the ChLA committee as editor of the collection.

It is impossible to imagine what scholarship on eighteenth- and nineteenth-century children's literature would be without Mitzi Myers. Her dedication, brilliance, generosity, and joy are an example to us all. This volume, a tribute to her research and an attempt to carry on her work, is dedicated to her.

Introduction

Donelle Ruwe

I might say that I first came to the study of children's and young adults' literature from an historical perspective; I was and still am working in late-eighteenth-century literature for young readers, when realistic fictions were called "moral tales," so I've always been especially concerned with what kind of moral possibilities stories present. Moral then didn't mean piously moralistic, but concerned with social manners and the possibilities of juvenile agency: how shall I live my life, what's important, what values do I embrace? The central injunction of these Enlightenment writers is that you must "think for yourself," that there are no easy answers and that you can't rely on pat rules. (Mitzi Myers, "'No Safe Place to Run to'" 448)

In August of 2000, Mitzi Myers's home was destroyed in a catastrophic fire. Although she escaped the sudden blaze, she sustained serious burns and suffered from smoke inhalation, for she reentered her burning home again and again in an attempt to rescue her research and her books, many of them rare and all of them annotated. Her books were like children to her, all 35,000 of them, and in the end she not only dedicated her life to them, she gave her life for them. Her health never fully recovered, and after recurring bouts of pneumonia and general weakness, she died on 5 November 2001.[1]

She left behind multiple legacies, only one of which was her record of brilliant critical publications in the field of women's studies and children's literature. As Gillian Adams notes in her overview of Mitzi's scholarly legacy, she reshaped the field of historical children's literature with her compelling arguments on behalf of early female didactic writers and by her conviction that scholars of children's literature must learn the lessons of New Historicism and integrate text with sociohistorical context.

Most importantly, Mitzi inspired a cadre of scholars whose work she not only encouraged but often edited and published. For many of us it seemed incomprehensible that Mitzi's voice—vibrant, polemical, erudite, and visionary—could be silenced. In the months following her death, tributes to Mitzi were printed in children's literature journals; a Modern Language Association special session was offered in her honor; journal issues, essay collections, and conferences were dedicated to her; and a library fellowship in her name was established at the UCLA Children's Literature Special Collection.[2] This festschrift joins with those tributes in carrying forward the legacy of Mitzi Myers.

   Culturing the Child, 1690–1914: Essays in Memory of Mitzi Myers continues Mitzi's lifelong project of bringing smart feminist, New Historicist, and cultural studies critiques to early children's texts. The first part of this collection, "Creating the Contexts of Children's Literature," takes on large sociohistorical issues in the study of children's literature from the long eighteenth century. Part 2, "Reading the Rational Dames," continues Mitzi's advocacy of Georgian-era female pedagogues. The third section, "The Politics of Pedagogy and the Child," uses the critical paradigm of cross-writing, which Mitzi developed with U. C. Knoepflmacher, to explore how the dual audience of child and adult affects the political, nationalistic, ideological, and literary messages of children's books.[3] The final section of this festschrift, "Remembering Mitzi Myers," includes a memoir of Mitzi's early days written by her sister Patsy Myers, an extensive introduction to Mitzi's scholarship by Gillian Adams and Donelle Ruwe, and a comprehensive bibliography of Mitzi's scholarship, beginning with her dissertation in 1969 and concluding with a posthumous essay on Mary Wollstonecraft's literary reviews.

   Prior to Mitzi's work in eighteenth-century children's literature, most of what passed for scholarship in historical children's literature was what Beverly Lyon Clark has described as broad historical surveys listing categories of books, a type of scholarship produced by and for librarians interested in catalogue issues but not necessarily appealing to literary scholars. Ironically, the opening essay of *Culturing the Child* returns us to where we began: the necessity of creating good catalogues. Ruth B. Bottigheimer's "The Book on the Bookseller's Shelf and the Book in the Child's Hand" asks scholars to work together to create a comprehensive catalogue of early children's books—not a positivist survey of the progress of early children's books but, rather, a catalogue set up for the rigorous demands of literary–historical scholarship. Children's literature scholars need something special in their catalogues, Bottigheimer argues, if they are to attend to what Mitzi felt was an essential part of the childhood reading experience: "rips, dirt, spills, uncensored comments, drawings and scribbles, rude jokes and missing pages—in these 'defacements' we discover the hidden history of childhood" (qtd. in McClellan). How can we truly apply the concepts of cross-writing and crossover reading to our discussions of early children's books if we have no systematic way of identifying who purchased books for whom? New Historical scholarship requires, at the very least, a good catalogue of early children's books. Such a catalogue might include, for example, information about handwritten dedications that would tell scholars not only who purchased the book but also how long the book sat on a bookseller's shelf before finally reaching its reader.

The other essays in Part 1, "Creating the Contexts of Children's Literature," cover the same crucial, formative period for children's literature described in Bottigheimer's essay, the Enlightenment through the early Romantic era. These essays focus on the ways in which gender, Lockean ideas, morality, and debates about pleasure versus utility are articulated in texts for and about children. In the long eighteenth century, children were first recognized as a distinct group and, further, as a particular reading public that could be marketed to. At the same time women were becoming increasingly important as educators, for the growing cult of domesticity recognized the importance of children to the family as well as the importance of mother–teachers, who were responsible for the early inculcation of moral sensibilities. Karen E. Rowe's "Virtue in the Guise of Vice" tracks the relationships between morality, utility, pleasure, and gender in the discourse of fairy tales from Perrault to Sarah Trimmer. Pre-Romantic authors understood that morality was best taught through pleasure, that imagination was an aid to reason, not an enemy. Rowe shows how Perrault's framing narratives and prefatory materials reconstellate the family as an educative domain or literary "academy," with Perrault himself as a benevolent paternal figure who oversees a fictionalized nursery (complete with a lower-class housemaid, Mother Goose). The fairy tale within a literary academy was imported to England along with French governesses in the eighteenth century; it reappeared in texts such as Sarah Fielding's *The Governess; Or, Little Female Academy*; and it was eventually co-opted by the publisher Tabart for his lurid fairy tale chapbooks, which were excoriated by a different sort of female governess, Sarah Trimmer. Julia Briggs's "'Delightful Task!': Women, Children, and Reading in the Mid-Eighteenth Century" also examines the female academy and its mixture of pleasure and moral instruction. According to Briggs, when we analyze popular figures of the female educator, such as Goody Two-Shoes, Richardson's Pamela, and Sarah Fielding's Mrs. Teachum, we discover that mothers and female pedagogues were largely responsible for disseminating a re-envisioned Lockean educational ideal throughout England. Women, for example, emphasized instructional toys. The Lockean understanding that education was environmental, or dependent upon outside influences, meant that mothers had important roles in the formative years of children's intellectual and moral growth. At the same time, dame-school teaching became a respectable form of employment, and it presented the single adult life of women as morally admirable while allowing women to participate in the economic exchange of knowledge.

By the end of the eighteenth century, the figure of the strong, rational mother–pedagogue who controls the educational environment of children had reached its zenith. The second group of essays, "Reading the Rational Dames," takes its title from Mitzi Myers's award-winning essay, "Impeccable Governesses, Rational Dames, and Moral Mothers: Mary Wollstonecraft and the Female Tradition in Georgian Children's Books." Women writers and education reformers found a "genuine vocation" in children's books and created a didactic literature that emphasized "the instructive and intellectual potential of narrative" (33). They also created the "educating heroine," a new and powerful figure of "enlightenment domesticity" (34). William McCarthy, M. O. Grenby, and Marjean D. Purinton's essays on late-eighteenth-century female pedagogues continue Myers's work in recuperating women's didactic texts by providing nuanced readings of the sociocultural work undertaken by these pedagogical writers and their educating heroines. They also extend one of Mitzi's most important insights about the construction of children's literary history. She condemned the way in which this history has been written according to the precepts of masculinist Romanticism. In the Romantic version of childhood, children are written *about* rather than *for*—they are not "actors in the present, doers," but, rather, objects of nostalgia, memory, and innocence ("Introduction" 161). From this fundamentally "masculinist high Romantic discourse" ("Reading" 44) arises an anti-feminine and anti-eighteenth-century metanarrative of children's literary history. This metanarrative assumes, for example, that Lewis Carroll and other male fantasy writers rescued children's literature from the dungeon of didacticism and created a golden age of children's literature. As long as we cling to the Romantic ideology of the child, we will continue to dismiss the innovations of the eighteenth-century moralists, those authors who believed that children should learn to think for themselves and who understood that morality required juvenile agency and understanding of social rules and manners. "The Romantic child is our foundational fiction, our originary myth," wrote Mitzi, and we must move beyond it ("Reading" 45).

The essays in Part 2 of this book, thus, are not about the child of nature but about "culturing" the child. William McCarthy's "Mother of All Discourses" is explicit in its recognition of how damaging the Romantic ideology of childhood has been to the reputations of early female pedagogical writers such as Anna Laetitia Barbauld, whose *Lessons for Children* is pedagogically and artistically innovative. McCarthy applies contemporary understandings of how children learn in order to prove that Barbauld's texts were not only prescient, but well deserving of the high esteem in which they were held throughout the Georgian era. Because the history of children's literature has been corrupted by an ongoing reinscription of Wordsworth's androcentric myth of the natural boy, actual socializing agents, like Barbauld, have been dismissed. Marjean D. Purinton applies Mitzi's approach to reading women's educational texts to Hannah More's pedagogical dramas. Purinton demonstrates how More's sacred dramas, which are often dismissed as simple didactic retellings of the Bible, actually use gender to articulate nationalism, imperialism, the supernatural, and science. Because these dramas present a powerful relationship between the governance of the nation and the governance of the passions, More's dramas are simultaneously moral and political enactments. In effect, they turn theater into a pedagogical site. More, like the eighteenth-century writers whom Rowe and Briggs discuss, feels no compunction in using folk, fairy tale, and myth in adapting Bible stories. She conflates the secular and the sacred with ease and understands that creating pleasure and magical power intensifies children's appreciation of the Bible. M. O. Grenby recognizes the centrality of Sarah Trimmer's *The Guardian of Education*, the first journal dedicated to reviewing children's literature, in establishing literary criticism of children's books and in defining the genre of children's literature. He wishes to move away from futile discussions of whether or not Trimmer was conservative or secretly subversive. Instead, he recognizes that Trimmer is the first author who systematically politicized children's literature. To write for children is a political act, and women, pedagogical writers, therefore, had access to the public sphere.

The third section of this collection, "The Politics of Pedagogy and the Child," extends Myers's project of examining the historical contexts of didactic works to the latter half of the nineteenth century and early twentieth century. These essays take Mitzi's precept for good historical children's scholarship as their guiding principle: they "demonstrate how a work of historical children's literature not only reflects its period's concerns, but how it comments on its social and intellectual milieu, how it tries to answer its era's questions about childhood . . . how it functions as a cultural critique of contemporary educational practice and gender definition" ("Socializing" 52). These essays also explore how adult concerns, such as nationalism and patriotism, cross from adult writers to child readers. For example, issues of pedagogical reform might be written into a children's school-story book with a dual purpose: to show adults that such reforms are possible while entertaining the child through comfortingly formulaic school stories. Other essays explore what happens to a text when it crosses from its intended audience of adult readers to an audience of children, what Mitzi termed "crossover reading." In "The Making and Unmaking of a Children's Classic," Bruce Beiderwell and Anita Hemphill McCormick demonstrate what happens to an adult "classic" once it becomes a classic school text and enters into what John Guillory has called the teaching or pedagogical canon. Once a text is "tainted" as a pedagogical work, it loses cultural capital and is considered to have lesser intellectual and aesthetic merit than texts from the adult canon. Beiderwell and McCormick's reception history of Sir Walter Scott's *Ivanhoe* tracks the novel's declining cultural capital over the nineteenth century. After the British Education Act of 1870, *Ivanhoe* shifted from a high-status historical novel to a frequently required reading for working-class children. It was used to reinforce Victorian and Edwardian values of Anglo Saxon heroism and British patriotic sentiments throughout the empire, but in so doing it became linked to teaching and middlebrow literature and lost its status as high art. Today's scholars who recuperate Scott for academic audiences resent its association with children's literature and, in fact, see themselves as rescuing it from the hands of teachers and children. Mitzi would have recognized this all too familiar rhetoric of the adult—and masculine—rescue fantasy: male Romanticists riding to the rescue of *Ivanhoe*, a text that must be saved from the pedagogues. Susan R. Gannon also considers the teaching function of heroic tales, in her case American hero stories from *St. Nicholas Magazine*. These formulaic stories did, indeed, pass on traditional values, just as did Scott's *Ivanhoe*. However, as Gannon notes in "Heroism Reconsidered," *St. Nicholas Magazine* expected not only classic heroes but also women and children to behave heroically, and often independently, from the guidance of husbands, parents, or other socially sanctioned authorities. In short, *St. Nicholas Magazine* required young readers to think for themselves about heroism, within moral and ethical contexts. With similar attention to the pedagogical subtexts of formulaic fiction, Mavis Reimer's "Worlds of Girls" reconsiders late nineteenth-century girls' school stories by L. T. Meade and outlines recurrent motifs in women's debates about education. Reimer places these stories within contemporary debates about educational reform, proving that the supposedly formulaic and conservative girls' stories are actually full of rich and complicated interactions between girls and between girls and society. L. T. Meade replaces the standard school story plot, which opposes age and youth, with a plot that opposes society administered by men to a society headed by women. Girls struggle between the two societies and, in the resolution of the stories, are fully integrated into a world defined by girls. L. T. Meade is her era's Rational Dame, the female pedagogue whose "absolute assurance" never failed in its advocacy of "new pedagogical techniques and goals" ("Impeccable Governesses" 34).

This final essay brings us back to Mitzi and her life's work: scholarship that recognizes the complexities of women's pedagogical literature and works for children. Authors who wrote for children participated in a long tradition of children's literary forms, but they also reflected their period's particular concerns. Didactic literature, fairy tales, formulaic texts, school stories, and heroic tales partake in a rich discourse about the nature of childhood, education, and society itself. If scholars do not immerse themselves in the discourse of education and childhood as it is manifested in each historical moment, they cannot truly appreciate the work of early children's writers or understand those long-gone child readers. In the epigraph that opens this Introduction, Mitzi remarked that she was always interested in juvenile agency, and that the central message of her favorite Enlightenment writers was to "'think for yourself,' that there are no easy answers and that you can't rely on pat rules" (448). We are all fortunate that Mitzi saw through pat rules and critical commonplaces and led the way into a new world of children and their books.

NOTES

1. Maureen O'Connor's Introduction to a special issue of *Women's Studies* on Maria Edgeworth discusses Mitzi's final year. She describes how Myers was with "amazing few real qualms . . . reinventing herself and her career" after the traumatic fire, and excerpts Mitzi's last, unfinished essay, "'Miss Edgeworth's Naughty Girl'; Or, The Importance of Being Rosamond."

2. Journals publishing tributes include *The Lion and the Unicorn* (Goodenough et al.), *Children's Literature Association Quarterly* (Adams), and *Women's Studies* (O'Connor). Events and publications dedicated to Mitzi include the 2003 Cotsen Children's Library conference, a special session at the 2002 MLA, Claudia Johnson's *Cambridge Companion to Mary Wollstonecraft*, and several volumes of Pickering and Chatto's *Works of Maria Edgeworth*. For full citation information about these tributes, see "The Scholarly Legacy of Mitzi Myers" (Adams and Ruwe) at the end of this collection, especially endnotes 10 and 13.

3. Cross-writing explores the ways in which adult writers choose children and childhood as their subject and sometimes as their audience; a second, related concept called "crossover reading" examines what happens when children appropriate books written for adults. Mitzi provides a general introduction to these concepts in "Literature for Children," her rather erudite encyclopedia entry for *Encyclopedia Americana*. She explains that crossover reading and cross-writing "are in fact built into the very idea of children's literature: the authors are adult, the buyers and readers (at least for young audiences) are adult, and always the writer aiming at a young readership must simultaneously inhabit two positions" (562). A more complete analysis of cross-writing can be found in "From the Editors: 'Cross-Writing' and the Reconceptualizing of Children's Literary Studies" (Myers and Knoepflmacher).

WORKS CITED

Clark, Beverly Lyon. "Kiddie Lit in Academe." *Profession* (1996): 149–57.

Guillory, John. *Cultural Capital: The Problem of Literary Canon Formation*. Chicago: U of Chicago P, 1993.

McLellan, Dennis. "Mitzi Myers, 62: Literary Scholar." *Los Angeles Times* 13 Nov. 2001: Bll.

Myers, Mitzi. "Impeccable Governesses, Rational Dames, and Moral Mothers: Mary Wollstonecraft and the Female Tradition in Georgian Children's Books." *Children's Literature* 14 (1986): 31–58.

————. "Introduction: Here's Looking at You, Kid: or, Is Culturing Childhood Colonizing Casablanca." *Nineteenth-Century Contexts* 21 (1999): 157–67.

————. "Literature for Children." *Encyclopedia Americana*. International Edition, 2000. 561–79.

————. "'No Safe Place to Run to': An Interview with Robert Cormier." *Lion and the Unicorn* 24 (Sept. 2000): 445–64.

————. "Reading Children and Homeopathic Romanticism: Paradigm Lost, Revisionary Gleam, or '*Plus ça Change, Plus C'est La Même Chose*'?" *Literature and the Child: Romantic Continuations, Postmodern Contestations*. Ed. James Holt McGavran. Iowa City: U of Iowa P, 1999. 44–84.

————. "Socializing Rosamond: Educational Ideology and Fictional Form." *Children's Literature Association Quarterly* 14.2 (1989): 52–58.

Myers, Mitzi, and U. C. Knoepflmacher. "From the Editors: 'Cross-Writing' and the Reconceptualizing of Children's Literary Studies." *Children's Literature* 25 (1997): vii–xvii.

O'Connor, Maureen. "Introduction: Our Debt to Mitzi Myers." Special Issue of *Women's Studies* (*The Politics of Reading: Maria Edgeworth*) 31 (2002): 289–97.

Part 1

CREATING THE CONTEXTS
OF CHILDREN'S LITERATURE

The Book on the Bookseller's Shelf and the Book in the English Child's Hand

Ruth B. Bottigheimer

*M*itzi Myers loved the Georgian writings of women like Sarah Fielding, Ellenor Fenn, Anna Letitia Barbauld, Mary Wollstonecraft, and above all, Maria Edgeworth. The scholarly oeuvre that grew out of her fascination with them and their writing created a new and sympathetic appreciation for these women after nearly two hundred years of scholarly neglect and even derision. The following article is meant to complement Myers's fascination with the eighteenth-century book landscape by sketching a fuller view of books printed for children in England, Scotland, and Ireland up to the year 1800.

THE PRESENT STATE OF THE BIBLIOGRAPHY OF EARLY BRITISH CHILDREN'S BOOKS

For decades, histories of printing and publishing have drawn principally on title page information to date a book's first and subsequent appearances.[1] And yet, a title page can intentionally mislead its readers. An enterprising publisher might call a first-time published book a second or third edition, and in so doing, falsely claim a prior and successful sales history that he hoped would recommend it to the buying public. "Newly corrected," another frequent title page phrase, was as much an eighteenth- and nineteenth-century trope as many of the book trade's other spurious assertions of newness.

Author's note: The material in this article was originally presented at a conference organized by Matthew O. Grenby, "The Child Reader 1740–1840," at de Montfort University in Leicester in 2002.

Library catalogs have a certain leeway in recording title page assertions. Research library entries usually correct false title page claims, providing recondite publishing data in the process. But even research libraries are sometimes hampered by the absence of a broad bibliography of books published for children in the years before 1800.

It is that painful lack that I've undertaken to remedy. The great bibliographer d'Alté Welch was hard at work on a bibliography of early English books for children when death cruelly and violently overtook him. His correspondence with book collectors such as Elizabeth Ball and Ruth Adomeit lists hundreds, if not thousands, of children's books he was in the process of documenting as he prepared a companion volume to his bibliography of early American children's books.[2]

In the nearly twenty years since Welch's death, book history has emerged as a powerfully transformative scholarly force. With histories of authorship, reading, and publishing has come a keen awareness of books as a bundle of intentions directed at defined readerships and consisting of material components. A bibliography at the beginning of the twenty-first century naturally incorporates more and different descriptors from those that Welch envisaged. Some are familiar, but not usually included in bibliographies; others are conceptually new and require explanation.

Readers will note my use of "British" in some places where "English" might be expected, and an explanation is in order. London was Britain's center of book printing in all genres, including children's books. Nonetheless, Scotland and Ireland both had lively print trades, as did many provincial English towns. Diffusion was largely from London outward, and much can be learned by studying the pace and intensity of that process of diffusion. Often co-publication occurred simultaneously in London and one or more provincial towns. Occasionally, important books moved from the British periphery or the English provinces to London. Hence, using the term "British" when referring to early children's books as a whole offers greater accuracy.

THE NEED FOR A BIBLIOGRAPHY OF EARLY ENGLISH CHILDREN'S BOOKS

Histories of children's *literature* have tended to marginalize the majority of instructional and didactic children's books in favor of those that fit into a later tradition of playful fictional fantasy. Similarly, past histories of childhood have tended to ignore the effects that class, confession, century, and gender had on early children's reading, with the result that an impossibly generalized figure, "the child," has marched anonymously across the pages of histories of children's literature.[3]

Books available to young buyers and readers crossed many different literary and social boundaries. Bible stories imparted religion, and books of manners and bilingual textbooks taught social graces, while instructional manuals taught artisanal skills. Riddle books and chapbook romances lightened leisure hours, and a broad array of other chapbooks ranged from piously instructional through practically instructional to bawdily amusing.[4]

We don't need a history of the printings of early children's books to tell us that Isaac Watts's *Divine Songs* was a bestseller; nonetheless, such a bibliography is a worthwhile undertaking because of what it reveals about other books for children. Mme Leprince de Beaumont's *Young Misses' Magazine*, for example, is with good reason a well-known title: it introduced the "Beauty and the Beast" story in the enduring form in which it has continued to be reprinted for two and a half centuries. It is, even more than Sarah Fielding's *The Governess*, a quintessential "girls' book." Yet, who knows of its companion "boys' book," François Fénelon's *Telemachus*, a dark star of the eighteenth century? Translated by Isaac Littlebury, *Telemachus* was first published in 1699 as *The Adventures of Telemachus. Pt 1.* by Awnsham and John Churchil, the London publishers who brought John Locke's *Some Thoughts Concerning Education* to the world. Littlebury's translation continued in print for years. In 1712 it was versified. In 1719 *Telemachus* was translated anew, together with the *Adventures of Aristonous* in two volumes; in 1719 A. Boyer also touched up Littlebury's translation.

The buying public was large enough to absorb yet another *Telemachus* edition, however, and by 1735 a Mr. Ozell had *his* translation on the market as well. Littlebury and Boyer's translation was evidently prospering, coming out with a syndicate of eighteen publishers the same year. By 1742 J. Kelly had joined the list of nominal translators of *Telemachus* with an illustrated edition published by J. Walthoe and T. Waller, which can be found in the Opie collection [C198 Myth] in the New Bodleian Library in Oxford. By no means does this listing include all documented editions. When the London firm Nourse & Vaillant brought out *Les Aventures de Télémaque* (1756; [Opie C203 Myth]) at mid century, it was used to teach both French and Latin. *Telemachus* had a 1764 presence in Ireland and, in the same year, was made into a Latin reader as *Telemachus Ulyssis filius seu exercitatio ethica moralis, ex lingua Gallica*. By 1765 *Telemachus* was in the north of England, published by L. Taylor in Berwick. By then it was time for another translator, W. H. Melmoth, to try his hand. Each of the "translations" subsequent to Littlebury's was in all likelihood more in the nature of a reworking of Littlebury's prose, but that is another question still to be investigated.

What's remarkable, given the prominence of *Telemachus* in the market for children's books, is that John Newbery did *not* put *Telemachus* onto *his* list of books for children. Although he ignored it, his stepson Thomas Carnan carried an abridged edition on his list, one copy of which can be found in the Cotsen collection at Princeton University. After Carnan's edition, printings are recorded every year or so until 1800, with the book's triumphal march continuing well into the nineteenth century.

Despite *Telemachus's* notable sales history, nothing about its remarkable commercial and cultural success appears in histories of children's literature except for a few sentences in Harvey Darton's *Children's Books in England*, where he dryly noted that Charles Lamb's 1808 *Adventures of Ulysses* "was a vast advance on the dismal morality of Fénelon's *Telemachus*, then still very rife in translations for juvenile readers" (192). If Fénelon's *Telemachus* has lurked unseen, uncounted, and unanalyzed among eighteenth-century books for children, what other unknown or little-known books await discovery?

CONTENT OF A BIBLIOGRAPHY OF EARLY ENGLISH CHILDREN'S BOOKS

Date of Publication

In a historical consideration of children's books, the first piece of relevant information is—for obvious reasons—the year of publication. That simple marker establishes a history for printings of an individual book; viewed over time, dated books provide a sense of diachronic shifts in composition, production, marketing, sales, consumption, gender issues, and confession.

Title: Short and Complete

For many early books, a title more reliably identifies a book than does the name of its author. The title on the title page was the title that buyers and readers saw, and it remains a book's title, however cumbersome it might seem to contemporary readers. That means that Sarah Trimmer's 1786 book usually listed by its familiar short title, *Prints of Scripture History*, appears as *A Description of A Set of Prints of Scripture History: Contained in a Set of Easy Lessons*. The verbiage of complete titles is wonderfully evocative of an atmosphere very different from that of the contemporary world. It also forms part of the history of changing designations for books that sold over a long time. There are limits, of course, and I have occasionally had to elide some of that verbiage.

Author

Dizzying changes can be rung on an author's name. The 1658 textbook *Arithmetick or The Ground of Arts*[5] was written by Robert Recorde, augmented by John Dee, and enlarged by John Mellis. At the other end of the spectrum is the seventeenth-century Richard Johnson, so seldom properly credited for his authorship of *The Seven Champions of Christendom* and *The Life and Death of Tom Thumb*. The Richard Johnson who wrote some 300 years ago did not personally leave evidence of his authorship, as did the eighteenth-century Richard Johnson, who left behind a daybook that recorded payments for the many little books that he wrote. Margaret Weedon documented those proofs of the eighteenth-century Richard Johnson's authorship, and yet his name rarely appears in square brackets next to the fictitious "Reverend Mr. Cooper" whom he—or his publisher—invented to beguile the credulous.

Other authors' identities hide behind initials. "T. W." was Thomas White, and "R. B." was Nathaniel Crouch, who also tried to disappear behind pseudonyms, such as "Richard Burton" and "Robert Burton." On the other hand, authorship by William Lily (or Lilly) was claimed long after his contribution to a book had been edited beyond recognition. Then there were comically ironizing authors' names, such as John Newbery's "Michael Angelo of the Vatican," author of Newbery's drawing book, and his "Tommy Trapwit," who wrote about being "Merry and Wise." As for "Aesop" as an author, that ancient Greek's name was a cover for a list of Britons that begins with Alexander Neckham, John

Henryson, and John Brinsley; continues with Roger L'Estrange, Nathaniel Crouch, Bernard Mandeville, Charles Hoole, and Samuel Croxall; and flowers in the eighteenth century with John Locke, Samuel Richardson, and Robert Dodsley. The last "Aesop" was Abraham Aesop, whichever of John Newbery's hack writers he might have been. That jokey Newbery pseudonym was akin to authorial monikers such as Nurse Truelove, Nurse Lovechild, Mrs. Teachwell, and Mrs. Teachum. This brief excursus points toward the desirability of organizing books by their titles, with authors' names appended as secondary information.

In the early publishing of books for English children, the extent to which publishers relied on dead authors, or at least on authors whose departure from this world made it impossible for them to claim royalties, is simply extraordinary. Good examples are William Camden and William Lilly, both of grammar fame; Isaac Watts; and Mme d'Aulnoy as Mother Bunch. The final reason to put authors' names in a secondary position is the fact that authors' names often seem to be invoked rather than recorded, as in *Thomas Wises Animadversions upon Lillies Grammar, or Lilly Scanned.*[6]

Place of Publication

Although most of the books printed before 1800 were London products, provincial presses made a far greater contribution than is generally recognized. Before 1800 children's books rolled off presses in Reading, Salisbury, Gainsborough, Berwick, Alnwick, Wrexham, and Wellington, as well as in centers of print such as Newcastle-upon-Tyne, York, Edinburgh, Glasgow, and Dublin. (This list is not complete.)

Printer and Publisher

Printers' names and often their addresses appear on title pages, particularly in the early years of print. The urban geography of book production, a subject of its own, emerges from the printers' and publishers' addresses. For instance, "T. B." printed *The Right, Pleasant, and Variable Trachical [sic] History of Fortunatus* for Hanna Sawbridge, who sold it "at the Sign of the Bible on Ludd-Gate-Hill near Fleet-bridge" in 1682.[7] Around 1721 "Tho. Norris" was printing and publishing his own books "at the Looking-glass on London-bridge." Soon after this, printers' names generally stop appearing on title pages, and it is publishers' names alone that document a slow drift westward. In 1725 Aaron Ward sold books "at the King's Arms in Little-Britain," for 150 years a bookselling center in the heart of the city of London. But the book trade was moving, and in 1729 we find R. Walker some distance to the west "at the White-Hart, adjoining to the Anodyne Necklace, without Temple-Bar," the same neighborhood ("at the Bible and Crown near Devereux Court without Temple-Bar") in which John Newbery could be found until 1745, after which he was "at the Bible and Sun in St. Paul's Church-Yard." Mary Cooper was just around the corner "in Pater-noster-row." Somewhat later, descriptors such as "opposite the Great Turnstile in Holborn" gave way to street addresses, for instance, T. Carnan in the 1770s at "65, in St. Paul's Church yard."

Each of the publishers named here is a single person, but many books, especially textbooks and books for instruction in one form or another, were published corporately. Take, for example, the following list of books published in London in the year 1729:

- The second edition of *The English instructor; or, The art of spelling improved by Henry Dixon*, printed for J. Hazard and J. Leake
- *Histories, or Tales of Past Times* written by Charles Perrault, translated by Robert Samber, and published by R. Montagu and J. Pote
- The first edition of *A New History of England, by question and answer* by John Jefferies, which N. Prevost and B. Motte published
- The eleventh edition of *Orbis Sensualium pictus* by Johan Amos Comenius, translated by Charles Hoole, and published by Aaron Ward
- The eleventh edition of *The Pantheon, Representing the Fabulous Histories of the Heathen Gods and Most Illustrious Heroes* by Andrew Tooke, the extended title of which made clear that it was meant for use in "Schools" and was published corporately by J. Walthoe, J. and B. Sprint, A. Bettesworth, and B. Motte
- François Fénelon's *Twenty Seven Moral Tales and Fables . . . French and English . . . Schools* published by J. Wilcox, W. Meadows, T. Worral, A. Vanderhoeck, and J. Jackson

Complete listings of publishers reveal publishing practices obscured from view by the customary practice of listing at most one or two of a consortium followed by " . . . " or "etc." Shifting distribution alliances hint at commercial canniness and marketing strategies that were part of everyday printing and publishing in the London world of books for children. Full publication data has the potential for uncovering booksellers' own assessments of the market they faced, an important aspect of the history of children's books and bookselling. For instance, in general, an examination of complete listing of publishers suggests that individual publishers aligned themselves with other suppliers in the case of an instructional book with an established sales record, but that when possible, they grabbed a corner of the market for themselves when they published a book of amusement.

Addressee

In the seventeenth century, the reader whom a book's author intended to reach generally formed part of its extended title. If a publisher counted young people among those who might read a particular book, then "young" was an all-purpose word to describe a variety of potential readers: young noblemen and mathematicians, young Latin scholars, young persons, young accountants, beginners, or communicants.

From the 1740s until about 1800, the broad array of young addressees listed above gave way to a socially limited grouping, "Young Gentlemen and Ladies," the usual addressee of amusing books for what we would now term late adolescence. As for young gentlemen's and ladies' younger siblings, seventeenth-century titles addressed them straightforwardly as "children" and "little children." But in the mid-eighteenth century they, too, became single-class "Little Masters and Misses."[8] In my estimation, "little masters and misses" were between the ages of five and about fifteen; the ages of "young gentlemen and ladies" overlapped slightly and could be as young as thirteen or fourteen or as old as young people at the age of their independent entry into society. It was only when the Kilners began to title their books with specific ages that this pattern changed.

Genre

If you aren't actually holding a book in your own hand, it's sometimes hard to tell precisely what it contains from its title alone. To characterize a book's genre, *Genre Terms*, a reference tool for rare book and special collections cataloguing, directs readers to use "Juvenile Literature" for "Books for children" and "Children's Books." Within these categories, *Genre Terms* offers narrow terms such as "Bible stories," "Fairy tales," "Nursery rhymes," and "Nursery stories." However, children's books, especially in the seventeenth and eighteenth centuries, included vastly more genres than this, and *Genre Terms* lists them separately from "Abecedaria" to "Verse." (See "Genre" in "Typical Entry Examples" at the conclusion of this article.) A further, hierarchical list classifies genre terms by seven "broad functions,"[9] of which "content of work," "illustrated works," and "literary form" (67–73) relate closely to the project of briefly characterizing books for children. The natural overlap and repetition evident in the listings is a reminder that books and literature for children are as polymorphic as their authors and readers.

Illustration

A book's illustrations are that part of a book that makes the most difference to a child's often impetuous desire to own it. Illustrations in old books can be categorized and described in bibliophilic, or aesthetic, terms; in bibliographic terms as copperplates, engravings, or woodcuts; and in craftsmanly terms such as relief printing (as in some woodcuts) or intaglio (as in copper engravings or other kinds of woodcuts); or in terms of planographic processes, such as lithography. These bits of information can be easily garnered from any number of existing sources, such as library catalogues or from published catalogues such as Gumuchian's *Les livres de l'enfance*.

Illustrations in books for children can also be characterized in book production terms. Does an illustration appear on a separate sheet tipped in during the binding process? Are illustrations an integral part of the folded sheets that make up each gathering? Do they combine tipped in illustrations, such as a frontispiece, map, or charts with integral illustrations? If we wish to understand and characterize an illustrated book as part of past technological, commercial, and social processes (printing, publishing, marketing, purchasing, and reading), then it is in details about illustration production that we will find additional relevant information for a bibliography of books for children.

Binding

Binding became a relevant category within bookselling for children as a whole when John Newbery began to sell pre-bound books. Using bindings as a commercial lure ultimately affected the book market as a whole, whereas richly tooled Morocco or quarter-bound calf bindings on individual books continued to reflect the purse and the taste of individual purchasers who ordered those bindings. Binding descriptions of individual books are provided in the catalogues of libraries that house them, and I therefore generally omit them.

Price

Pricing information, on the other hand, is critical to the nexus between the book on the bookseller's shelf and the book in a child's hand. A known price is an invaluable component in the project of delineating the range of potential first-time buyers in socioeconomic terms. Almost anyone could purchase a penny chapbook, but a one- or two-shilling book cost twelve to twenty-four times as much and was beyond the reach of humble first-time buyers. In the absence of other information, price alone can identify the economic class of intended initial buyers.

Size

Although it offers at best a very slowly changing set of parameters in the years up to 1800, size is important. It is a parlous category, because book size so often depends on the size to which a bookbinder was directed at some point in the past to cut a book. Nonetheless, book size remains a useful first approximation for a book. The following descriptors augment the value of a notation about book size.

Number of Pages and Format

One imagines that the number of pages is important from a child buyer's point of view. Is the book in question a promisingly fat book of riddles and jokes? Or is it a thin little catalog of London cries?

If paper consumption is uppermost in the researcher's mind, then notations about a book's format—$8°$, $12°$, $24°$, $32°$, or $64°$, or in-6 or in-8—together with the number of gatherings, make it possible to calculate more efficiently the amount of paper used in producing a book than does simple size and a tally of leaves and pages. And since paper long constituted a printer and publisher's greatest financial outlay in book production, knowing how many sheets of paper are in a book is surely significant.

Book Location

How often have researchers groaned in frustration, when they couldn't locate a volume referred to in a scholarly study? I, for example, spent years searching for an elusive book on women's medical complaints by a Nicolas Fontaine, whose dates of birth and death were identical to those of the author of a profoundly influential compilation of Bible stories. "My" Nicolas Fontaine had been a fuzzy-cheeked lad of fifteen when he joined the Messieurs de Port-Royal at their isolated community south of Paris and taught young boys the classics. Having spent most of his early life there, and with his later days well documented, a book on gynecological complaints seemed unlikely. Nonetheless, it was necessary to check the text in case he was more a man of parts, or a translator of greater range, than I had realized. No source library had been given; no one knew where the book could be found; numerous searches remained fruitless. It was only in the spring of 2002 that I found it in the Folger Shakespeare Library in Washington. Once I saw the book, I realized that it couldn't possibly be by "my" Nicolas Fontaine, and that its author's dates were therefore necessarily in error. If only the first citation had included the library that housed the book. Computerization has improved book searches dramatically, but it didn't locate this Fontaine for me because the holdings of many municipal and some research libraries haven't made their way onto Worldcat, OCLC, or the net. It's imperative to include the library location of every relatively rare book so that later researchers can revisit, re-evaluate, and perhaps, reinterpret prior observations and conclusions.

Fingerprint

A book's fingerprint is a randomly, and unintentionally, produced piece of information that is peculiar and specific to an individual print run, as shown in fig. 1.1. Once type had been set and locked into a form,

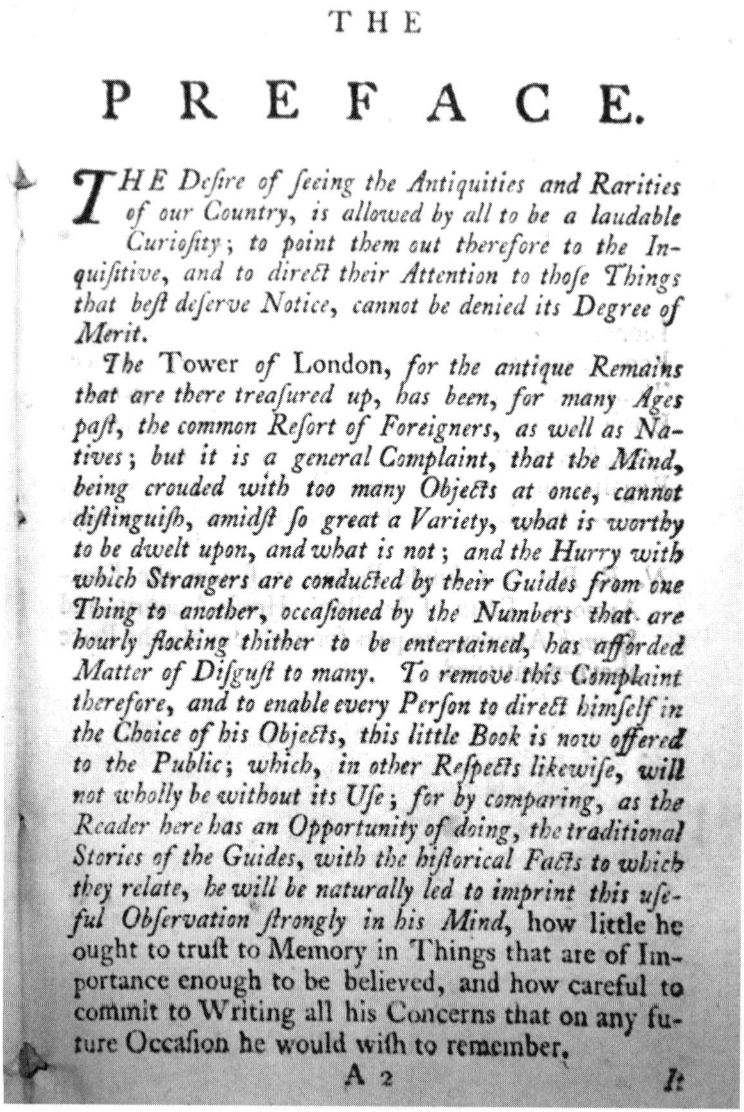

THE

PREFACE.

THE Desire of seeing the Antiquities and Rarities of our Country, is allowed by all to be a laudable Curiosity; to point them out therefore to the Inquisitive, and to direct their Attention to those Things that best deserve Notice, cannot be denied its Degree of Merit.

The Tower of London, for the antique Remains that are there treasured up, has been, for many Ages past, the common Resort of Foreigners, as well as Natives; but it is a general Complaint, that the Mind, being crouded with too many Objects at once, cannot distinguish, amidst so great a Variety, what is worthy to be dwelt upon, and what is not; and the Hurry with which Strangers are conducted by their Guides from one Thing to another, occasioned by the Numbers that are hourly flocking thither to be entertained, has afforded Matter of Disgust to many. To remove this Complaint therefore, and to enable every Person to direct himself in the Choice of his Objects, this little Book is now offered to the Public; which, in other Respects likewise, will not wholly be without its Use; for by comparing, as the Reader here has an Opportunity of doing, the traditional Stories of the Guides, with the historical Facts to which they relate, he will be naturally led to imprint this useful Observation strongly in his Mind, how little he ought to trust to Memory in Things that are of Importance enough to be believed, and how careful to commit to Writing all his Concerns that on any future Occasion he would wish to remember,

It

Figure 1.1. "The Preface." A2 from *An Historical Description of the Tower of London, and its Curiosities.* Printed by J. Newbery at the Bible and Sun in St. Paul's Church-Yard. Price Six-Pence. M DCC LXV. Private collection, reproduced with permission.

printshop workers inserted signatures to ensure that the printed sheet would be folded so that pages followed one another in the proper order in each gathering. Although signatures normally appear in the lower center to the lower right of the first several pages of a gathering, a signature's location was not precisely specified. It was, in short, random.

Signatures were placed randomly, and this randomness makes it possible to use them as an identifying tool. The letters, partial letters, spaces, and punctuation marks that appear in the space delineated by the first and last signatures of front matter, text, and back matter comprise a book's complete fingerprint (Vriesema 93–100).[10] Although some children's books consist of separately published components, most can be adequately identified with a single fingerprint, taken from A2, or if that is not possible, from A3, or the first following usable signature.

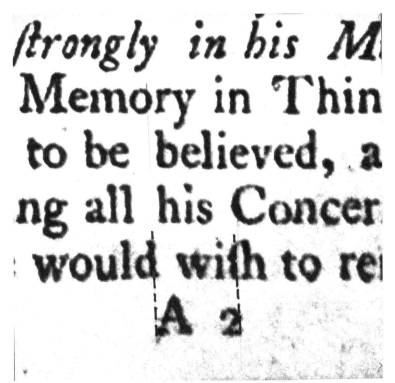

Figure 1.2. Enlargement of part of A2, from *An Historical Description of the Tower of London, and Its Curiosities.*

The fingerprint for this print run of *An Historical Description of the Tower of London* is (d)_wiſ. The defining fingerprint area includes the letters (partial or complete), spaces (partial or complete), and punctuation marks (partial or complete) that lie within two imaginary vertical lines (here shown as broken lines) that rise along the farthest outside point of the signature, here A2.

(d) parentheses around the letter "d" indicate that the letter "d" falls only partly within the fingerprint area.

_ indicates a space within the fingerprint area.

wi a space and the letters "w" and "i" fall wholly within the fingerprint area.

ſ indicates an eighteenth-century "s"

The A3 signature in this illustration identifies the following page of this printing of *An Historical Description of the Tower of London*. In this case

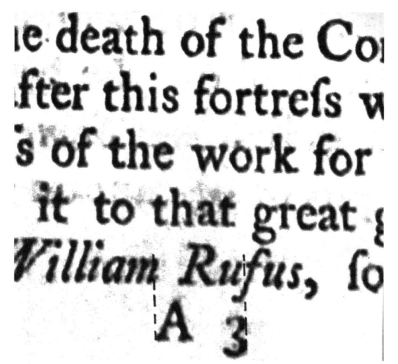

Figure 1.3.   Enlargement of part of A3, from *An Historical Description of the Tower of London, and Its Curiosities*.

the letters lying within the signature area are a partial "m," a space, an "R," a "u," and a partial "f." The letters are all in italics, and so the fingerprint is *(m)_Ru(f)*.

d'Alté Welch wrote that he was "now more than ever convinced that we know little about the vast horde of Newbery variants. Every book I pick up seems to be a variant. It is the exception to the rule that two Newbery items are identical if they are undated" (qtd. in Roscoe vii). Fingerprints are the tool that would have made it possible for Welch to tell one print run from another with ease.

Sidney Roscoe addressed the question of print runs obliquely, when he noted that among Elizabeth Newbery's undated publications, "printings were very frequent—almost annual, it may be—and from new settings of type" (vii). But the extent of his puzzlement emerges only from Diane Bauerle's "Checklist of Newbery Family Children's Books at the Lilly Library." There she shows how Roscoe had to rely on details of line height, word placement, and typographical error in his efforts to distinguish one undated Newbery family imprint of a book *Anecdotes of a Little Family* from another imprint of the same book (17–18). Roscoe's invaluable bibliography of Newbery family imprints is full of notations that exemplify the limitations he faced:

> In this edition Preface on A2^r is 5.6 cm long and is followed by a plane swelled rule 3.6 cm long. On p. [1] [the word] ANECDOTES is 4.9 cm long. On p. 156 [the word] FINIS is approx. 4.7 cm below last line of text. (46)

Bauerle's discussion of an Elizabeth Newbery imprint of *Little Robin Redbreast, A Collection of Pretty Songs* offers another example of the bibliographic difficulties presented by variant editions. She notes that of three recorded copies, one lacks a title page, the second has 32 textual woodcuts, and the third has 34 textual woodcuts. Her discussion of photocopy comparisons, of woodcut quality and quantity, and of different typesettings makes it clear how problematic it is to assess the sameness and differentness of imprints that cannot be directly compared with one another because they are housed in libraries hundreds or thousands of miles distant from each another.

Until the late 1970s, no generally applicable standard existed by which one imprint could be measured against another, and consequently, Roscoe and other bibliographers were unable to reach consensus about how many times a book bearing the same title was typeset and printed.

Using fingerprints to determine the number of actual print runs for a book that—according to its title page—was often reprinted would illuminate the true size and activity of the early market for children's books.

Librarians, bibliographers, and bibliophiles have examined books with an eye to establishing distinctions unique to a book's print run. These details remain an intensely local and, therefore, relatively inaccessible form of information. Written on the finding cards of library catalogs and occasionally on their updated electronic counterparts, they are all too seldom utilized in histories of children's books. Fingerprints, however, offer a broadly accessible way of identifying differently title-paged books that are the product of a single print run.

The fact that many early books printed for children are undated presents another, and significant, problem. Rough dating can often be worked out for a book from dates of acquisition penned in by their owners. (See below for further information on the relationship between dates of acquisition and dates of publication.) When acquisition dates are collated for a known print run that has been identified by its fingerprint, then metatextual information from individual books can serve as a means of dating (even if only approximately) a given title's given print run.

Fingerprints are also an effective lie detector that shows when a title page's claim is false. Here are a few examples. The first comes from the *Piacevoli Notti* of Giovan Francesco Straparola, a sixteenth-century Venetian who invented the "Puss in Boots" story with its novel plot—from rags, through magic and marriage, to riches—and published it for the first time in 1553.

Initially it seemed that Straparola's *Piacevoli Notti*, a longseller both in Italy and in France, was snapped up when it first appeared, with recorded imprints in three successive years: 1555, 1556, and 1557. That fact suggests a phenomenal rate of sale. It has been noted that the "three" print runs actually represented new releases in 1556 and 1557 of the 1555 edition (Pirovano 64), and a check of the fingerprint of copies dated 1555, 1556, and 1557 demonstrates incontrovertibly that a sole and single print run existed. There is every likelihood that the 1555 print run consisted of 1,000 copies, the more or less standard number, and that partway, probably one third of the way, through the print run, the printer changed the date on the title page to 1556. Another third of the way, he changed the date again, now to 1557. Therefore, instead of having sold 3,000 copies, that is, a thousand copies a year in each of three years, the far greater likelihood is that Straparola's publisher sold a total of 1,000 copies over three or more years.

A second example comes from the publishing history of Fontaine's *Histoire du vieux et du nouveau testament* in Dutch for Jansenist families in exile. The 1695 and the 1715 *De Historien des Ouden en nieuwen Testaments* have the same fingerprint, which betrays a commercial secret that the new title page tried to obscure: unsold sheets from the 1695 printing were repackaged by the publisher as his own twenty years later.

A third example, directly relevant to early English children's literature, concerns "two" English editions of Perrault's fairy tales. Textbooks of the history of Anglophone children's literature accord Perrault's fairy tales a preeminent role in the development of English children's literature, basing their purported popularity on the number of times Perrault's tales were published. In simple English translation, Perrault's tales sold poorly, and most subsequent reprintings were dual-language French textbooks, which also sold poorly.

Nonetheless, J. Melvil of London and Exeter brought out a dual-language edition of Perrault's *Histories* in 1764. The book did not do well, which we know because his sheets (identifiable by their fingerprint) appeared the following year with Van Os, a publisher with offices in London and The Hague. Van Os substituted cheap copies of Melvil's fine illustrations and a new title—*Mother Goose's Tales*—on a new title page. The 1764–1765 edition of Perrault's *Tales* provides the final piece of evidence for the decelerating pace of sales of Perrault's tales in England from their first appearance in 1729 to the 1760s.[11]

Witnessing Sydney Roscoe grappling with descriptions of letter size and line separation in a vain effort to separate one imprint from another, and considering the publishing frauds perpetrated by the Italian, Dutch, and English publishers of merry tales and Bible stories, confirms the utility of fingerprints. They offer a remarkably simple and accessible tool for historians of early children's books; it goes without saying that fingerprints can be equally useful to librarians or booksellers who wish to describe or identify a book that is missing its title page.

Remarks

Individual books often contain information useful for a history of the booktrade as a whole. Some append invaluable book catalogues that relay titles of books that in some cases are no longer extant. Ownership marks in undated imprints, if a new owner has written in the date of acquisition, provide a rough guide for dating an otherwise undated book, namely, a date *after* which the book could not have been printed and before which it had to have been printed.

Shelf Life

More often than not, child owners inked their names onto a book's flyleaf or title page. Linking a title page date of publication with a child's dated declaration of ownership tells us with fair reliability how long that particular book lay on a bookseller's shelf before it got into a child's hand. The 1804 copy of *Aesop's Fables* that Edward Odlin Spaulding acquired on July 5,1824 waited twenty years to be purchased. J. Cherry bought his 1835 copy of *The Flower of English Fable* in 1853, and Augustus Frederick's mother gave him some *Fables* in 1835 that had been published in 1805! One breathes a sigh of relief for the booktrade when one finds books being bought in their year of publication, such as William Freeman Helton's purchase of *Tales and Fables* in 1785, and Louisa Mastriter's of Sarah Trimmer's *Ladder of Learning* in 1832.[12]

Overall, the average shelf life for books I've seen with ownership marks is seven to nine years. That simple observation spawns a host of questions. Did shelf life change over time? If so, then *how* did it change? What kinds of books sold fast? (Probably school textbooks.) Which ones sold slowly? (Improving books more favored by hopeful parents than by their unwilling offspring.) What did English children *have* to buy? (School textbooks, again.) And what can we conclude about what English children *wanted* to buy?

Shelf life translates into another much-used and often misused word, "popularity." Contemporary historians of books for children often refer to a book's popularity without having definitively identified a print run, without having reliably determined how frequently a book was republished, and without having estimated as carefully as possible how long unsold sheets lay on a bookseller's shelf. These are three basic indices that make it possible to assess the popularity enjoyed by any book, and they should all be taken into consideration by anyone who is tempted to use the word "popular" about an early book for children.

Translation

Even a cursory glance at a list of early English children's books reveals how large a presence translation is. The beloved Bevis and most of the courtly romance figures who dominated chapbooks came from abroad— Italy or France—and conquered London when Caxton and Wynkyn de Worde printed them in heavy Gothic black letters for English readers. In the seventeenth and eighteenth centuries first Nicolas Fontaine's French children's Bible in 1691, and then Campe's German Robinson, Mme de Genlis's French plays, Mme Leprince de Beaumont's French conversational pedagogy, and the Abbé Fénelon's French *Telemachus* entered England unhindered by their alien origins.

With the development of a native pool of children's literature, a tide of English-language books washed onto Continental shores. Mrs. Pilchard's *Blind Girl* became *La Jeune Aveugle ou la Famille anglaise. Histoire intéressante destinée à l'instruction de la Jeunesse* (Paris: Bargeas, 1823 [Gumuchian 990]). After Campe's Robinson entered England, he himself brought *Sandford and Merton*'s three volumes to Germany (Braunschweig: Schulbuchhandlung, 1788–1800–1808 [Gumuchian 2069]). Richardson's *Young Grandison* represents a striking example: it first journeyed to France with Arnaud Berquin, and then returned home to English soil in Mary Wollstonecraft's English, twice-translated and somewhat altered.

PRELIMINARY RESULTS FROM THE BIBLIOGRAPHY

The bibliography I've been working on so far has produced a few general observations about developments in the history of books for children. For instance, gender as a meaningful category emerged after 1800 when separate books for boys and for girls first begin to appear, as the following book titles suggest: *The Boys Own Book* 1836;[13] *Boys Games, or Holiday Recreations* (1815);[14] *Juvenile Dialogues, or Recreations for School Boys, during their leisure hours at Boarding-School by Billy Merrythought* (1815).[15]

"Old" forms part of the title of many nineteenth- (but not eighteenth-) century children's books: *Old Daddy Longlegs, Old Dame Trot; Old Gingerbread; Old King Cole; The Old Man, His Son and His Ass; Old Mother Hubbard and Her Dog; The Remarkable Adventures of an Old Woman and Her Pig; Old Woman and Her Silver Penny; The Old Woman and Her Three Sons;*

The Account of the Old Woman (Gumuchian 4319–4338). One ponders the significance of this change in titling practice.

"Little" as the principal word in a title takes a different place after 1800. Before 1800 there were "little books" for "little children," along with the famous *Little Goody Two-Shoes*. But after 1800, book titles including the word "little" abounded: *Little Bantam Blue* (c.1835); *Little Bo-Peep* (c.1850); *Little Boy's Book* (c.1840); *The Little Curricle* (1803); *The Story of Little Dick* (1823); *The Adventures of Little Dog Trim* (c.1810); *The History and Adventures of Little Eliza*; *Little Goody Goosecap*; *Little Jack Horner*; *Little Lucy. The invalid or Nursery Dialogues* (1835); *The Little Maid and the Gentleman* (c.1820); *Little Meg's Children* (c.1880); *The Little Reader* (1835); *The Little Warbler* (1816, Gumuchian 3805–3833); *The Little Visitors* [Gumuchian 4029]; *The Little Foundling* (Gumuchian 4243); and *The Little Sister* [Gumuchian 4244].

Once the diminutive style with its many uses of "little" took hold, diminution appeared in other guises. "Peeping" became a modish form of observation: *Nursery Calculations, or A Peep into Numbers;*[16] *A Peep at the Esquimaux, or Scenes on the Ice;*[17] or *Peeps into Natural History.*[18]

A puzzling shift in familial relationships within titling practices occurred after 1800 when, in family terms, extended family relationships began to appear in quantity: *The Gift of an Uncle* (1829);[19] *Grandmama's Book of Rhymes for the Nursery* (1835);[20] *Grandmamma Easy's Merry Multiplication* (c.1850);[21] *The Grandmother* (1808);[22] *Harry and William, or The Two Cousins* (1821);[23] *Hartlepool and Seaton, written for the amusement of the Author's Nephews* (1817);[24] *Northern Regions, or A Relation of Uncle Richard's Voyages for the Discovery of a NorthWest Passage* (1825);[25] and *Aunt Carry's Ballads for Children* (1847).[26]

It is well known that animal tales flourished toward the end of the eighteenth and the beginning of the nineteenth centuries. New after 1800, however, were titles that recorded a four-legged social life of masquerades, balls, and levees in their own voices,[27] a genre at which the indefatigable Catherine Ann Dorset excelled. Dogs didn't just dance, however. Bob the Spotted Terrier, a "Dog of Knowledge," produced his memoirs,[28] while a hare related her own dangerously adventurous life.[29] Remarkably, inanimate objects—pennies, Bibles, and peg tops—also undertook accounts of their lives.

Also new after 1800 was an acquaintance with and sentimentalization of the English countryside and its inhabitants.[30] This was fostered by board games like the *Geography of England and Wales, Accurately Delin-*

eated on 52 Cards, including the Boundaries, Extent, Products, Manufactures, etc. of each County.[31] In addition, there were numberless accounts of shepherds, rural toils, and agricultural produce (for example, by Jefferys Taylor[32]), as well as of holidays in the country.

Englishness was far overshadowed, however, by the entry of the world beyond England into the English child's universe after 1800: Priscilla Wakefield set her *Juvenile Travellers* on their way in 1801.[33] The mode continued with a board game tour through Scotland,[34] and expanded with books about the kinds of clothing worn by foreign people[35] and their appearance.[36] Such eye- and mind-opening books and games reached their apogee in *Wallis's Complete Voyage round the World. A new geographical pastime.*[37] No one was more energetic in producing such books than Isaac Taylor, who chronicled *Scenes in America, Scenes in Europe* and *Scenes in Asia*, before turning his gaze homeward with *Scenes of British Wealth, in Produce, Manufactures, and Commerce for the Amusement and Instruction of Little Tarry-at-Home Travellers.*[38] Geography books like these clearly shows us a developing British self-awareness of differentness from other nations to be communicated to the young.

Early English books for children differed profoundly from those in other national traditions. Religion and morality are far less represented in English nineteenth-century books for children than in France, which undoubtedly reflects unspoken tensions in a multiconfessional English nation vs. the relatively monolithic religious identity in a country like France. Textbooks of elocution and rhetoric were far less prominent on English booksellers' lists than they were for American schoolchildren in the same period.

England's urban and provincial printers and publishers in the early modern period offer another point of comparison. It has long been axiomatic that cultural change develops in urban centers and emanates outward to the surrounding provinces. Nonetheless, in the printing and publishing of books for children in the eighteenth and early nineteenth centuries, there is repeated evidence that many innovations entered the London publishing world from the provinces. One minor example is the fact that the first mention of Valentine celebrations in a children's book occurs not in a London imprint, but in a Mozley book from Gainsborough around 1790.[39]

One would like to know what contemporaneous readers thought of the books produced for them. We have some idea of what their elders thought from Sarah Trimmer's *Guardian of Education*, newly edited by

Matthew O. Grenby, with its reviews catalogued by Andrea Immel, and from reviews of Barbara Hoflund's books.[40]

Each reader of this article potentially has something to contribute to a bibliography of early British books for children. Sydney Roscoe couldn't locate a 4th edition of John Newbery's *Holy Bible Abridged for the Use of Children*—"fourth edition not found" he noted (14)—but he wrote before the Opie Collection had become publicly accessible, and there it is, as L28. Other new titles and editions will be found in small and out of the way libraries. There are scores of pre-1800 books for children printed and published in England, Scotland, Wales, and Ireland that have never been recorded. An attention-worthy fact in this regard is Margaret Clark's observation that "by 1800 some 600 books for children were being published annually . . ." (473). Those were books on the bookseller's shelf, most or all of which eventually made their way into children's hands.

Scholars of early books for children are at the beginning of a systematic examination. The formation of collections of children's books has placed rare old books in accessible libraries and in some cases, such as the Hockliffe Project at De Montfort University, in electronically accessible form. Constructing a bibliography of early English books for children—and thereby reconstructing the early British landscape of books for children—will provide an overview of first and subsequent imprints of longsellers and bestsellers and will lay before our eyes the broad world of children's books in the British Isles up to 1800 and will contain much of interest and importance for both historians and historical sociologists.

NOTES

1. There have been some few exceptions, such as a history of the print run of the Seville Polyglot Bible, in the course of whose printing a few pieces of type cracked, which allows distinctions to be made between pre-crack and post-crack imprints. In the realm of fairy tales, one can distinguish between the first printing of Charles Perrault's *Contes* and the second, corrected printing. See Barchilon III.

2. It is housed in the Rare Book and Manuscript collection of the University of California at Los Angeles.

3. This is even the case in an otherwise excellent article by J. H. Plumb, "The New World of Children in Eighteenth-Century England."

4. The best available study of chapbooks is Gilles Duval, *Littérature de colportage et imaginire collectif en Angleterre à l'époque des Dicey (1720–v.1800).*

5. London: Joseph Cranford 12° [Gumuchian 526]. Bibliographical information for early children's books is included in the endnotes; secondary sources are listed in the Works Cited. "Gumuchian" followed by a numeral indicates the reference number assigned to books in *Les livres de l'enfance,* published by Gumuchian in 1930.

6. 1625 Thomas Wise. Printed by W. Stansby for Richard Hawkins. Grammar. No illus. No price. 9 cm × 15 cm. 8° Fingerprint of copy in the Lilly Library at the University of Indiana from the Ball collection: A3=peak K2=*des_*. Another copy is in the British Library.

7. The full title and publishing information follows: *The Right, Pleasant, and Variable Trachical (sic) History of Fortunatus Whereby a Young Man may Learn how to Behave Himself in all Worldly Affairs and Casual Chances. First Penned in the Dutch Tongue There-hence Abstracted, and now First or all Published in English, by T. C.* Printed by T. B. for Hanna Sawbridge at the Sign of the Bible on Ludd-Gate-Hill near Fleet-bridge. Chapbook. integral illus. no price. 8.5 × 16 cm 8° 159 p. Ball A2=(o)ints K4=_tha (black letter).

8. It was only in the last years of the eighteenth century that "little" began to be applied not to a book's readers but to its subject matter: Vernor and Hood, for example, published an "elegant collection of delightful little pieces for the instruction and amusement of young persons" [Gumuchian 1726] and another London publisher brought out *The History of Young Edwin and Little Jessy.* See O'Malley 40.

9. These seven "broad functions" include: 1. authorship, 2. conditions of publication, 3. content of work, 4. illustrated works, 5. literary forms, 6. musical works, 7. purpose of work (*Genre Terms* 65–78)

10. An earlier discussion of fingerprints appears in Roger Laufer, *Introduction à la textologie.*

11. For more on the early publishing history of Perrault's tales in England, see Bottigheimer, "Misperceived Perceptions: Perrault's Fairy Tales and English Children's Literature."

12. These examples come from books in the Opie Collection in the New Bodley, Oxford.

13. London: Vizetelly, 1836 [Gumuchian 897].

14. London: Hodgson and Co, ca. 1815 [Gumuchian 896].

15. Chelmsford: I. Marsden, ca. 1815. 15 woodcuts. 2d. [Gumuchian 1627].

16. London: W. Belch c.1815 [Gumuchian 4303].

17. London: H. R. Thomas, 1825 [Gumuchian 4399].

18. J. Fairburn c.1845 12° [Gumuchian 4400]

19. London: William Joy, 1829 [Gumuchian 2732].

20. John Harris 1835 8° [Gumuchian 2793].

21. London c.1850. 17 wcuts [Gumuchian 2794].

22. E. Hemsted for the Proprietor, 1808 6 engravings 16° [Gumuchian 2795].

23. Harvey and Darton, 1821 16° [Gumuchian 2958].

24. Darlington: 1817. 11 etchings 16° [Gumuchian 2960].

25. London: J. Harris, 1825 [Gumuchian 4286].

26. London: Joseph Cundall, 1847. 4° [Gumuchian 4287] See also Gumuchian 5683–89 which record Uncles Buncle, Charles, George, Philip, and Timothy.

27. The following books contain descriptors from the Gumuchian catalog (which may be accurate in terms of the folds they describe, but which I have found often designate size). Gumuchian attributes them to "Mrs. Dorset"; Marjorie Moon, however, lists them as "anonymous." *The Eagle's Ball* (London c.1800 12° [Gumuchian 2238]); *The Lion's Masquerade, A sequel to the Peacock at Home. By a Lady* (London: J. Harris, 1807 16° [Gumuchian 2239]); *The Peacock at Home* (J. Harris, 1807 [Gumuchian 2244]). See other such titles such as *Butterfly's Ball, The Peacock and the Parrot, The Horse's Levee* (J. Harris, [1]1808 16° [Gumuchian 3079]).

28. *The Dog of Knowledge, or the Memoirs of Bob the Spotted Terrier. Supposed to be written by himself. By the Author of Dick the Little Pony.* (J. Harris [1]1801; Tabart, 1809 12° [Gumuchian 2234–5]).

29. *The Escapes, Wanderings, and Preservation of a Hare. Related by Herself* (J. & C. Evans [1]c.1820 3 engravings [Gumuchian 2938]).

30. *The Cottage Girl. A poem comprising her several avocations during the year* (London: K. Longman [1]1810 8° [Gumuchian 2906]); The Rev. Legh, *The Dairyman's Daughter: an Authentic and Interesting Narrative* (Penrith: Joseph Allison, 1821 [Gumuchian 4755]).

31. London: J. Wallis, 1799. 4 × 2 1/2" in case [Gumuchian 3273].

32. Jefferys Taylor, *The Farm, A New Account of Rural Toils and Produce* (London: John Harris, [1]1832 [Gumuchian 5549]).

33. Priscilla Wakefield, *The Juvenile Travellers; containing the Remarks of a Family during A Tour through the principal States and Kingdoms of Europe: with an account of their Inhabitants, Natural Productions and Curiosities* (London: Darton and Harvey, 1801. 12° [Gumuchian 5777]).

34. *Geographical* Tour Through *[my emphasis] Scotland. An Instructive Pastime* (London: Walker for Wm. Darton jn 1812 8° hand-coloured map of Scotland with numbers on principal places [Gumuchian 3272]).

35. *Costume, Manners and Peculiarities of Different Inhabitants of the Globe* (London: John Harris, 1821, 1831; Grant and Griffith c.1832; Edinburgh: William

Darling [Gumuchian 1881-84]); *Costume of the Lower Orders in Paris* (c.1805 28 engravings 12° [=*Cries of Paris*] [Gumuchian 1950]).

36. *People of all Nations. A Useful Toy, for Girl or Boy* (London: Darton and Harvey, 1806 [Gumuchian 4404]).

37. London: John Wallis, 1802. [Gumuchian 3429].

38. London: Harris and Son, 1823. 12°

39. *Cupid's Present, or Valentine's Choice; being a brief and compendious History of the Most Favourite Heathen Gods and Goddesses* (Gainsborough: H. & G. Mozley, c.1790, 19 woodcuts 16° [Gumuchian 1972]).

40. Denis Butts discussed Hoflund at the 2002 conference, The Child Reader 1740–1840 (de Montfort University 2002).

WORKS CITED

Barchilon, Jacques, ed. *Contes de Perrault. Fac-similé de l'édition originale de 1695–1697.* Geneva: Slatkine Reprints, 1980.

Bauerle, Diane. "A Checklist of Newbery Family Children's Books at the Lilly Library." *Phaedrus* 13 (1988): 15–39.

Bottigheimer, Ruth B. "Misperceived Perceptions: Perrault's Fairy Tales and English Children's Literature." *Children's Literature* 30 (2002): 1–19.

Clark, Margaret. "Children's Book Publishing in Britain." *International Companion Encyclopedia of Children's Literature.* Ed. Peter Hunt. London: Routledge, 1996. 472–77.

Darton, F. J. Harvey. *Children's Books in England.* Rev. ed. Ed. Brian Alderson. 3rd ed. Cambridge: Cambridge UP, 1982.

Duval, Gilles. *Littérature de colportage et imaginire collectif en Angleterre à l'époque des Dicey (1720–v. 1800).* Talence: Presses Universitaires de Bordeaux, 1991.

Genre Terms: A Thesaurus for Use in Rare Book and Special Collections Cataloguing. 2nd ed. Chicago: Association of College and Research Libraries, 1991.

Grenby, M. O., ed. *The Guardian of Education: A Periodical Work.* By Sarah Trimmer. Bristol: Thoemmes, 2002.

Immel, Andrea. *Revolutionary Reviewing: Sarah Trimmer's* Guardian of Education *and the Cultural Politics of Juvenile Literature. An Index to the "Guardian."* Occasional Papers 4. Los Angeles: Dept. of Special Collections, U of California: Los Angeles, 1990.

Laufer, Roger. *Introduction à la textologie.* Paris: Larousse (Université-Series), 1972.

Les livres de l'enfance du XVe au XIXe siècle. Paris: Gumuchian. 1930.

O'Malley, Andrew. "The Coach and Six: Chapbook Residue in Late Eighteenth-Century Children's Literature." *Lion and the Unicorn* 24 (2000): 18–44.

Pirovano, Donato. "Per l'edizione de *Le Piacevoli Notti* de Giovan Francesco Straparola." *Filologia Critica* 26.1 (2001): 60–93.

Plumb, J. H. "The New World of Children in Eighteenth-Century England."
Past and Present 67 (1975): 64–95.

Roscoe, Sydney. *John Newbery and His Successors 1740-1814: A Bibliography.*
Wormesley, Hertfordshire: Five Owls, 1973.

Vriesema, P. C. A. "The STCN Fingerprint" *Studies in Bibliography* 39 (1986):
93–100.

Weedon, M. J. P. "Richard Johnson and the Successors to John Newbery." *The
Library*. London: Bibliographical Society, 1949.

• 2 •

Virtue in the Guise of Vice
The Making and Unmaking of Morality from Fairy Tale Fantasy

Karen E. Rowe

*M*adame Le Prince de Beaumont's adoption in her 1756 *Magasin des enfans* of "La Belle et la Bête" as a mode of inculcating virtuous morals existed within a context of debate in the eighteenth century about the fantastical and the useful, and whether fairy tales should be introduced at all to children, or only in the carefully controlled domestic and literary preserve of "maternal" and "moral" instruction. In her pioneering juvenile book review, *The Guardian of Education* (1802–1806), Sarah Trimmer often denounced the deleterious influences of fairy tales. Her 1803 review of *Histories and Tales of Past Times, Told by Mother Goose* is, for example, curiously nostalgic and dismissive:

> Though we well remember the interest with which, in our childish days, when books of amusement for children were scarce, we read, or listened to the history of *Little Red Riding Hood*, and *Blue Beard*, &c., we do not wish to have such sensations awakened in the hearts of our grandchildren, by the same means; for the terrific images, which tales of this nature present to the imagination, usually make deep impressions, and injure the tender minds of children, by exciting unreasonable and groundless fears. Neither do the generality of tales of this kind supply any moral instruction to level the infantine capacity. (2: 185–86)

Even more vitriolically, she condemns the allegedly gory prints that accompanied the tale of *Blue Beard* in Tabart's 1804 sixpence color-plate issue (4: 75). Similarly, Madame de Genlis castigates the delusions engendered by romantic fairy tales, advising mothers to refrain from giving them to daughters, because "love is the subject in them all; you find a princess persecuted on account of her beauty; a Prince, handsome as the day, dying for love of her, and a wicked ugly rival, consumed with envy and jealousy . . . all these ridiculous ideas given them only encourage false notions, [and] stop the course of their reasoning" (1: 62–63).

Beaumont was inspired by Sarah Fielding, author of *The Governess; or, Little Female Academy* (1749), one of the earliest of Mitzi Myers's Georgian authors of educational treatises. Beaumont's "domestication" of the fairy tale by embedding it within a governess manual (along with fables and biblical stories) mitigates its supposedly deleterious effects on the imaginations of youthful women, suggesting that fairy tale accounts of love pursuits by bestial suitors prepare young women to defend their virtue and recognize "sweet gentility" beneath ugly deformity. The earliest adoption of Beaumont's "Beauty and the Beast" was likely R. Baldwin's retelling in the miscellany *The Polite Academy* (1762), followed later by the (in)famous *Tabart's Collection of Popular Stories for the Nursery* (1804) and *Fairy Tales, or the Liliputian Library* (1817). How then, this essay asks, did the once "moral" fairy tale, first propagated by Charles Perrault in 1697 in his *Histoires ou Contes du temps passé. Avec des Moralitez*, metamorphose into Trimmer's condemned "fantastical"? Or, how did eighteenth-century sociocultural shifts, new publishing venues and audiences, and reimagined literary frameworks radically alter the primacy and even the definition of "morals"? Salutary entertainments in the capable hands of Fielding's Mrs. Teachum and Miss Jenny Peace or Beaumont's Mrs. Affable, the tales became suspect indoctrinators of Trimmer's castigated "false philosophy" and fearful terrors when illustrated for Tabart's juvenile library of nursery stories, which was only a forerunner of what became the staple of the nineteenth-century nursery—the popular fairy tale. One might also trace how the "moral" tale, once ensconced within the provenance/province of the rational dame, the maternal nursery, or polite academy, becomes fodder for such writers as Charles Lamb (possibly spurious attribution) in *Beauty and the Beast: or, A Rough Outside with A Gentle Heart. A Poetical Version of an Ancient Tale* (1813). Or, what happens when morality transforms into entertaining (even silly) spectacle in a melodramatic musical comedy by James Robinson Planché? This essay explores the complicated mingling of the usefully moral and the fantastical, so much so that children as well as adult audiences might take the imprint of deeply conflicted messages about the dangerous immorality of unleashed passions, violence, and terrors of the fairy tale, yet also the pleasures of the entertaining fabulous that stimulates the imagination with visions of romance, virtue rewarded, and vice punished.

Avec des Moralitez, Charles Perrault (1628–1703) claims, when titling his originary collection, *Histoires ou Contes du temps passé* (1697). With this delightful first recounting of the "contes de ma mère loye," as Clouzier's frontispiece placard reads, a preoccupation with the instructive utility of fairy tales takes root in the French and English literary tradition. Mademoiselle L'Héritier de Villandon, whose nouvelle, "The Discreet Princess," would accompany Perrault's volume in subsequent editions after 1721, speaks "of the excellent education which he [M. Perrault] gives his children, of their ingenuity, and finally of the *Contes naïfs* which one of his young pupils has lately written with so much charm" (*Bigarrures* 3; qtd. Lang xxv).[1]

Although sometimes attributed to Pierre, Perrault's own son "and young pupil," and supposedly recollected from childhood tales told by a nursemaid, such stories, replete with ironic touches and witty descriptions despite their seeming naiveté, reflect the deceptively elegant simplicity of a masterful storyteller, member of the French Academy, and writer, such as Perrault, *le père*. Praised at his death in 1703 more for his honorable position, publication of *Les Hommes illustres* (a portrait-laden biographical dictionary of modern luminaries), and civil services to society, Perrault would later be lauded by the renowned nineteenth-century fairy tale collector and publisher, Andrew Lang, as "a good man, a good father, a good Christian, and a good fellow," "astonishingly clever and versatile in little things, honest, courteous, and witty, and an undaunted amateur" (xvi).[2] But, Lang adds with unbounded respect for Perrault's talent, "the little thing in which he excelled most was telling fairy tales. Every generation listens in its turn to this old family friend of all the world. No nation owes him so much as we of England, who, south of the Scottish, and east of the Welsh marches, have scarce any popular tales of our own save Jack the Giant Killer, and who have given the full fairy citizenship to Perrault's *Petit Poucet* and *La Barbe Bleue*" (xvi). Thus, the venerable English tradition of fairy tales created for and told to children begins in Paris, with a loving, educated father as author and a fictionalized "Mother Goose" as the lower-class hearthside nursemaid cum *mère*, the ostensible oral transmitter of the fairy tale.

This family reconstellation, a blending of the real educative domain of a middle-class French household and a fictionalized nursery, constitutes the first "academy" for the instruction of young minds through the vehicle of entertaining fairy tales, "'une petite Académie des contes de fées'" calculated not only to allure the young but also to inculcate *des Moralitez* (Rouger ed. xvi). The fictional conceit of the wise woman taleteller proves more enduring than any factual determination of a presumed child's authorship and paternal transmission (Rowe). That the appellation, Mother Goose tales, would come to dominate the titles of numerous French and English reprintings, new editions, verse adaptations, and bowdlerizations of Perrault's first-told versions points to the increasing eighteenth-century fascination with maternal education and popular instructional books for children.

In his dedicatory epistle for the 1697 edition, to the twenty-year-old Mademoiselle Elisabeth Charlotte d'Orléans (1676–1744), the niece of Louis XIV and grandmother of Marie Antoinette, the author defends the literate morality of these seemingly frivolous bagatelles. Elisabeth Charlotte, Perrault admits, is likely more accustomed to the fashionably embroidered romances that were commonplace courtly entertainments. But he hopes she will not dismiss his "Contes" in all the "simplicité de ces Récits," because they "give an image of that which takes place in lower-class families, where the laudable eagerness to instruct young children causes them to imagine stories destitute of reason, in order to adapt them for these same children who have none as yet" (my translation, Lang 5; see also Zarucchi 122–23). What these tales lack in ornamented language or stylish *préciosité* and in enlightenment by strict appeals to reason, they make up by containing "tous une Morale trés-sensée," the wise morals that Perrault foregrounds in his subtitle.

This dedication makes clear that the tales are designed to be morally instructive for children, while also delightfully entertaining the upper-crust ladies of the court. Even more particularly for those who are destined to oversee and lead "les Peuples," to find in these instructive tales the common-folk lives and moral virtues displayed becomes an essential educational tool, even for a princess of the blood royal whose cultivated intelligence Perrault shamelessly flatters. Had they been used, as custom and first-hand testimony seems to suggest, within the domestic academy of Perrault's own household, as an exercise in writing and in moral instruction, Perrault's determination to publish them launches the "old wives tale" from the private nursery into the public marketplace and creates a new lineage of children's stories distinct from the elegantly retold salon tales of his contemporaries.

Until the publication of Perrault's *Histoires ou Contes du temps passé*, the staple French and English fare for children would have been treatises of theology, history, and manners and La Fontaine's *Fables Choisies, mises en vers* (1668) and his Aesop, though not explicitly or even primarily geared for the youthful audience (Hearn v). By emulating in his own tales the qualities he so admired in Fontaine, the "incomparable Beauty, wherein there concurs an ingenious Simplicity, a sprightly Honesty, and an original Pleasantry," Perrault legitimated his own enterprise, since La Fontaine had also "join'd to the good sense of Esop, the Ornaments of his own invention, so suitable, so judicious, and so diverting . . . that it is difficult to read any thing more useful and more agreeable all together" (*Characters* 188). More agreeable and "useful" still, Perrault had argued earlier in his "Préface" to his *Contes en vers* (1695) were tutorials in vice and virtue told *en famille*: "Is it not praiseworthy that mothers and fathers, when their children are not yet capable of tasting solid truths devoid of all sweetening, make them love these truths, and as it were, swallow them, by wrapping them in agreeable tales proportioned to the weakness of their young age" (my translation, Lang 80; see also Zarucchi 120–22). Children find their "innocent souls," in which "nothing has yet corrupted the natural rectitude," drawn to "these hidden lessons," so much so that it instills both empathetic "sadness and despondency" over the misfortunes of the hero or heroine and exuberant "joy when the time of their happiness arrives" (Lang 80–81). Such sentimental excess would later draw the ire of the rational dames and moral mothers, whose inculcation of virtue privileged a less emotive responsiveness. Nonetheless, the making of the "morality" of fairy tales took root in their very literary inception, drawing forth from Perrault an academician's as well as a parent's counsel in how to instruct the young. As he claims for his *Contes en vers*, so too for the 1697 fairy tales, "these bagatelles were not mere bagatelles" because "they incorporated a useful moral," and the "sprightly story in which they were wrapped (or disguised) was chosen only to enable the morals to enter with more pleasurable charm into the mind, and in a manner which would instruct and divert altogether" (Lang 77).

Through Robert Samber's 1729 translation of Perrault's originary collection, titled *Histories, or Tales of Past Times . . . With Morals*, the now famous fairy tales entered English children's literature, including in order (altered from the 1697 French): "The Little Red Riding-Hood," "The Fairy," "The Blue Beard," "The Sleeping Beauty in the Wood," "The Master Cat, or Puss in Boots," "*Cinderilla*, or the Little Glass Slipper," "*Riquet a la Houpe*," and "Little *Poucet*, and his Brothers." Perrault and Samber thus brought to maternal nurseries and little academies what had hitherto been oral traditions passed down by nursemaids, old wives, or women of the countryside hearth, like the Mother Goose of Perrault's placard whose visual presence lent an aura of authenticity to offset the literary retellings of the paternal academician. Supplanting the complimentary, yet patently obsequious (and politically astute) epistle of Perrault's volume, Samber's more expansive dedication addresses a slightly less aristocratic patroness and decidedly older English matron, "The Right Honourable, the Countess of Granville," who has already proven her "Maternal Care" as the "Head of a numerous and noble Offspring" by educating Lord Carteret to maturity (A2r, A2v). Like a "Roman Lady," the Countess is to be commended for providing a "virtuous Education," one designed to cultivate her offspring as "serviceable and ornamental" contributors to their "Country," who, through her "Care and Influence, will shine in their several Spheres, with equal Radiancy and Splendor" (A2r, A2v).

Samber quickly hastens over the obligatory modesty of his "little and trifling" offering, which "has notwithstanding no little Merit" (A2v). He lauds first the salutary "Excellency of Instruction by Fable," so esteemed by the "Divine Plato" that he "desires Children might suck in those Fables with their Milk, and recommends it to Nurses to teach them to 'em, since we cannot accustom our selves too soon to Wisdom and Virtue" (A2v, A3r). Even fables, however, pale before the artful tutelage of fairy tales, since "however instructive the Stories of Animals may be, it is certain they do not make such strong Impressions on the Mind, nor move the Affections so much as those related of human Kind" (A3v). Samber deliberately heightens his rhetoric to underscore the palpably vivid appeal of tales to the sensibilities of "Children" who "have been known to weep at the Distress of the two Children in the Wood, who would not be any wise affected with the Adventures of Cocks and Bulls, &c." (A3v). Dismayed at the "Venting [of] some poor insipid trifling Tale in a little tinkling Jingle, adding some petty Witticisms, or insignificant useless Reflection, which they call a Moral," which he decries as the mode of latter-day "Fabulists," Samber comes down squarely in praise of the "admirable Design and Execution" of Perrault's *contes de fées* (A4v, A3v). "Very low and childish," they may seem to some, but Samber defends Perrault's stories "designed for Children" as so "ingeniously and masterly contrived . . . that they insensibly grow up, gradually one after another, in Strength and Beauty, both as to their Narration and Moral, and are told with such . . . innocent Simplicity, that not only Children, but those of Maturity, will also find in them uncommon Pleasure and Delight" (A4v, A4r). Samber creates for the English the image of Perrault not as the French modernist who dabbles in charmingly instructive divertissements for children, but as the deliberate moralist, who "made himself their Morals, as knowing they tended to the Encouragement of Virtue, and the Depressing of Vice: the former of which is ever rewarded in them, and the latter ever punished, the true End and Design of Fable" (A4r).

Lacking neither in "Pleasure and Delight," nor in "Morals," the fairy tale, translated from Perrault, enters thus into the domain of children's literature in England. Throughout the eighteenth century, reprints and new editions of Perrault and Samber would multiply, including a 1764 sixth edition in which the tales appear side-by-side on facing pages, an ingenious vehicle for teaching French to young ladies still enchanted with childhood tales. In their simplicity and supposed naiveté, Perrault's tales were designed primarily as divertissements, and the defense of their moral utility hangs not only on the slender prefatory epistle, but also on the verse "moralités" attached to each of Perrault's stories. Constructed in the manner almost of an emblem book, each story is preceded by an engraved woodcut that appears above the title and concludes with a poetic "Moralité." Read as tutorials for *les enfans* (a child considered to be such till the age of fourteen), the tales seem to extol the childhood charity of "Le Petit Chaperon Rouge," delineate dichotomous qualities of haughty scorn and benevolent kindness exhibited by *deux jeunes filles* in "Les Fées," caution young girls to beware malicious stepmothers and wicked fairies in "Cendrillon ou la Petite Pantoufle de Verre" and "La Belle au Bois Dormant," and warn against a wife's near fatal curiosity in "La Barbe Bleuë."

But the bare outline of moral abstractions ill serves to capture the witty ironies and cultural commentaries embedded in rather more mature counsels than one might imagine suitable for unworldly toddlers, suggesting instead an audience of precociously bright *élèves* approaching adolescence or young women the age of one's entrance into a society fraught with the dangers of romantic seduction or, perhaps worse, an arranged, loveless marriage. While easily read as charming amusements that Perrault intended for young children, these benign *récits* also covertly convey to the adult and perceptive reader latent (and some blatant) warnings about erotic desire. Presenting at one level a caution directed toward "what conduct all young people ought to learn" (6), so obvious it goes unstated, that little girls shouldn't talk to strangers, animal or human, or stray from the path to grandmother's house, Samber's ornamented variant of Perrault's versified "Moral" for "The Little Red Riding-Hood" pointedly addresses "above all, the growing ladies fair, / Whose orient rosy Blooms begin t'appear" (6). Too easily, Samber suggests, these "Beauties in the fragrant spring of age" hearken "ill" to "tongues" that "enchant and lure like Syrens songs," till "over-powr'd" and by the "Wolfe devour'd" (6, 7). Had he stopped there, Perrault's moral might have been merely a gentle admonition to naïve girls, but Samber's graphic dissection of hypocritical deceivers, those seeming "tame" and "full of complaisance," who turn to "ogle and leer, languish, cajole and glance" rise up to haunt the urban streets of Paris or London (7). These "Wolves" are all too human sexual predators who "follow young ladies as they walk the street, / Ev'n to their very houses and bedside"(7–8), an apt translation of Perrault's archly witty "Jusque dans les maisons, jusque dans les ruelles" (Lang 22). Visually reinforcing the moral, the engraving showing a wolf lunging from beneath the bed curtains to devour a supine "lady fair" speaks also to erotic dangers that await heedless young women deceived by wolves "of every sort, and every character" and beguiled by honied tongues (7). Whether couched with sly French subtlety or embroidered English alarm, Perrault's moral is a tutorial in "how to read the Wolf," much less how to interpret the fairy tale, and—should we bring into play the "old wife" as taleteller—it anticipates the later maternal guidance of wise governesses.

That Samber's abstractions lack some of Perrault's elegant witticism is self-evident, but for the English tradition of fairy tale the *dulce* is amply accompanied by the *utile* in the verse morals—often in more than one. To conclude "The Blue Beard," Perrault moralizes on the obvious dangers of an uncontrollable "Curiosity, thou mortal bane!" (30). But, he also takes pains in "Another" moral to exculpate husbands and mitigate the terrors potentially induced by the violent threatenings of an abusive tyrant, since "this a. story is of time long past, / No husbands now such panick terrors cast; / Nor weakly, with a vain despotick hand, / Imperious, what's impossible, command" (31). Yet, he cannot resist a wry domestic observation on marital power struggles, since men with beards "of whatever hue," whether "black, or blue, / Grizzled, or russet, it is hard to say / Which of the two, the man or wife, bears sway" (31). None too sure that his cautionary message to young women will be heeded in a pell-mell rush to "get a husband rich, genteel and gay, / Of humour sweet" (57), Perrault in "Sleeping Beauty" counsels a patiently sweet romantic approach to "Hymen's blisses," yet he's loathe to dampen fond exuberant affections, lacking the "will" to "preach this moral to 'em" (58). For young women or mothers, whether an Elisabeth Charlotte or maternal Countess of Granville who must raise daughters to virtuous duty, the lessons, as in "Cinderilla," often point directly at a recurrent dichotomy between external beauty and internal grace, most desirable when combined in one figure, but only truly beneficent when civility, wisdom, and gracious kindness illuminate the being, not just the face. Hence, Perrault opines that "Beauty's to the sex a treasure, / We still admire it without measure," but "that thing, which we call good grace, / Exceeds by far a handsome face" (89).

It's notable that the most often addressed figures in the morals themselves are the "fair ladies," the "Beauties in the fragrant spring of age," "all the sex," and "the hearts of the fair," and the lessons are often those of beauty perceived through character rather than complexion, of love triumphing over lowly circumstances, lost shoes, and one hundred years of dream-drenched sleep, or of virtue tested and rescued from near fatal enchantments, disobediences, or undisciplined desires (curiosity). Equally powerful are the contravening warnings to those who, lacking "civil behaviour" and "complaisance," treat old women in rags dishonorably ("The Fairy"), sisters whose haughty self-indulgence dooms their sister to the scullery ("Cinderilla"), and those princesses who value only appearances or covet wealth rather than judge by good deeds, words, and character ("Riquet a la Houpe," a variant of the deformed or beastly lover tale type). The moral that Madame de Beaumont will later draw forth for "ses élèves de la première distinction" from her "Beauty and the Beast," Perrault anticipates in his tale of the "ugly Marmot" ("Riquet a la Houpe"): "In whom we love appear rare gifts of mind / And body too: wit, judgment, beauty, youth" (93, 109). Even those objects in which "nature's band" draws out "beautiful traces" of "complexion," with all their fits "have not so much command / On hearts, as hath one secret charm alone / Love there finds out, to all besides unknown" (110). Perrault and Samber take account of a gendered, social reality that meant that a young woman's destiny would be determined by her marital estate, with or without her consent, love and companionate affection, or the assurance of fidelity, generosity, or solicitude—and with no guarantees against disease and deformity, much less emotional and physical abuse. Albeit veiled with a seeming antique charm, the fairy tale world is not innocent of truths and harsh realities.

Despite the brevity of his "Epistle," Perrault's self-assumed position as both a defender of his deceptively simple *contes de vieilles* and an advocate for moral interpretation resurfaces within the morals themselves, as if he mediates between the lower-class Mother Goose who talks the tale and the more elevated, literate readership, comprising (as contemporary witnesses testify) in part courtly ladies, some themselves the authoresses of tales, romances, and nouvelles. "From this short story easy we discern" (6), he claims, or "yet this Fable seems to let us know" (58), or again, "We draw our moral from this Tale" (90)—so Perrault speaks to the collective readership through the voice of the ethical arbiter. He forestalls casual dismissals of the "imaginary" tale as too fabulous a history to warrant serious attention when at the end of "Riquet a la Houpe," he declares, "What in this little tale we find / Is less a fable than the real truth" (109). The *Moralitez* foregrounded in Perrault's title and Samber's plainer declaration of *With Morals* are conveyed as well through a repetitive tripartite constellation: an engraving heads each tale in Perrault's and Samber's editions, the narrated story itself is designed for both reading and oral recounting, and the versified moral acts as a capstone preachment. Thus, Perrault constitutes the *recueil des contes de fées* as an instructive collection rather than as piecemeal *jeu d'esprit*. Yet, the absence of a continuously directing consciousness, or authoritative speaker perpetually intervening, except in the form of appended morals, leaves open to the reader's or listener's imagination any visual, aural, or emotional response. Whether the tale elicits Perrault's "sadness and despondency" or exuberant cries of "joy" from children isn't mediated or dictated by an intrusive commentator. That the tales might be heard and/or read absent a reciting of the morals, or even as singular stories repeated over and over again, opens the space for both the child's and the parent's interpretive freedom, as would the tales' later publication, often without morals, in small chapbooks hawked by colporteurs or as sixpence items from Tabart's Juvenile and School Library. It's an opportunity to cultivate—or miscultivate—the imaginations of young children, which the reactionary Sarah Trimmer will later find horrifyingly lacking in discipline, reason, and moral rectitude.

Attached to the publication of Perrault's *Histoires ou Contes du temps passé* as early as 1721 is a "fabulous story," called a "novel" (*nouvelle*) by its authoress, Mademoiselle Marie-Jeanne L'Héritier (1664–1734), a niece of Charles Perrault, and among those courtly ladies who had a passion for elaborated romances. Samber then incorporates "The Discreet Princess; or the Adventures of *Finetta*" into his English translation, suggesting that it represents the most "grown-up" of the tales, if we take his proclamation about a progressive design seriously to include this lengthier fairy tale, listed as number IX on the title page's catalogue of the volume's contents. Its importance for our consideration, however, is the French authorship by a mademoiselle, the forerunner of those French governesses who would come to England, bringing with them a tradition of instruction using tales from the original to the self-created, ones modeled in part on the French courtly entertainments that brought Madame d'Aulnoy (1650/51–1705), Madame de Villeneuve (1695–1755) and Marie Le Prince de Beaumont (1711–80) into the history of fairy tale. Dedicated in the English edition to a noted aristocratic bluestocking, "Lady Mary Montagu" and previously in French to the "Countess of Murat," "The Discreet Princess" appeals to "persons of polite and refined tastes, of rare and elevated qualities of soul," who "have, in all ages, taken singular delight in such productions of the mind" (140). Samber points back to this earlier tradition of fairy tales as "intirely fabulous," but with the addendum that "they wrap up and infold most excellent morality, which is the very end and ultimate scope and design of Fable" (140).

Without the cover of a governess or coverture of a wife or mother to give her credibility, Mlle. L'Héritier calls upon "forefathers" who "knew to insinuate into young minds" the virtuous morals that her story likewise espouses: "That *Idleness is the mother of all vice*," and "That *Distrust is the mother of security*" (Samber 140–41). In her recounting of this tale of three sisters, the eldest Drone-illa, the mistress of indolence, and second, Babillarde, the loquacious mistress of gossip so ill-advised and readily spoken that "her mouth never was quiet," L'Héritier illustrates her first maxim, setting forth the negative example of sisters who never employ themselves in "thinking, reflecting or reading" (148, 149). By contrast, their shrewd, well-educated younger sister, Princess Finetta, commands all of the accomplishments of music, dance, oration, and handiwork, but she is also constantly employed, "had a great deal of judgment, and such a wonderful presence of mind, that she immediately found the means of extricating herself out of the greatest difficulties," often through a shrewd "penetration and fine genius" (150–51). In this cautionary tale, Finetta will outwit the seductive deceiver, a caddishly vengeful Prince Riche-cautelle, whether he's disguised as an old woman or simply himself, and happily wed his younger brother, the gracefully handsome, perceptively princely Bel-a-Voir, whom she (in a reverse of most tales) rescues from an ill-made oath of sibling fidelity. In the eighteenth-century world of "blooming Beauties," the "sage advice" that "on a just Distrust, and right address / Security depends, and future joy and peace," proves all too true, and a young, well-educated woman's reward for the artful employment of discerning reason is a virtuous marriage (141, 145).

The author writes not merely a form of prologue and epilogue with poetic morals fore and aft of the history, but she also strategically interjects authorial voicings throughout the tale, a self-conscious narrative intrusiveness frequent among later novelists and maternal pedagogues. L'Héritier traces the genesis of this "history" of Finetta to "very great antiquity, which assures us, that the Troubadours, or Storiographers of Provence invented Finetta a long while before Abelard, or the celebrated Count Thibaud of Champagne" (201). In her own childhood, she claims, "A Hundred times and more to me of old, / Instead of fables made of beasts and fowl / . . . / The morals of this tale, my nurse has told," identifying her story with the *contes de vieilles* (202). Consequently, she claims a lineage (fictionalized or not) of romantic tales as the province of children's literature: "It is certain, that these kinds of fables contain a great deal of good morality, and for that reason ought to be told to little children in their very infancy, to inspire them betimes with Virtue" (201–2). Her defense of her own embellished "fairy tale" (for indeed there is a benevolent fairy, "very able and expert," who enchants three "distaffs") anticipates language used by Robert Samber (in his translation redacted to suit an English readership) to justify moral instruction in the guise of delightful story (153).

Whether L'Héritier might be considered among Samber's suspect "romantic fabulists" is open to question, but his willingness to incorporate her tale as an extension of Perrault's genre of *contes naïfs* signals otherwise, as did L'Héritier's own ardent defense of Perrault's *jeu d'esprit* in writing his tales in all their simplicity for the education of his children. In the poetic postscript that closes her "Historiette," L'Héritier positions her "delightful tale" among morally reputable writings and addresses the utility of the genre she variously defines as fairy tale, *nouvelle* or short story, and adventuresome history, for the "Vicious punish'd, so we likewise see / Virtue triumphant, and prevail" (204). Even more extensively than L'Héritier, who praises the fairy tale's superiority over fables "du Singe & du Loup" (of the monkey and wolf), Samber extends his own critique to denounce scornfully a whole passel of silly modern-day animal "Fabulists":

> In fact, these Tales strike deeper on the mind,
> Afford diversion and instruction more
> Than those invented heretofore,
> Or in the modern mint of fable coin'd,
> Of beasts and birds, of gnats and flies. (205)

To replace these animal fables so relegated to a category of disreputably excessive inventions "retail'd in pretty sterile chiming Cant," Samber expands upon L'Héritier's subtler suggestion by calling on "young people" to privilege rather the "Reading, or hearing of these kinds of Tales," such as "Finetta," since "So much their sweet Simplicity prevails" (206), a reference back to Perrault's tradition as much as to L'Héritier's own creation. Like the appeals in prefaces that accompany Perrault's volume, Samber's translation, and her own dedication, L'Héritier's final pleading, recouched in Samber's English variation, is that "more diffusive would their [these tales] beauties rise / Of more extent their moral Virtues prove / Did noble Ladies in their Families / Admit them Audience, and their Lecture love" (206). Whether Samber was sufficiently steeped in late seventeenth-century French courtly romances and collections to know L'Héritier's authorship and her frequent apologia for *les contes* in *Bigarrures ingénieuses* (1696) is unclear. But, by translating the 1721 Desbordes edition (or its 1729 reprint) of *Histoires ou Contes du tems passé*, an "édition augmentée d'une nouvelle, à la fin,"

Samber contributed to a literary *trompe-l'oeil* by which "L'Adroite Princesse" joined the English pantheon of fairy tales, neither clearly by Perrault, nor definitively attributed to its true authoress. However, peers among female intellectuals (Madame de Genlis, la Comtesse de Murat, Madame d'Aulnoy) and transplanted governesses, such as Madame de Beaumont, who would take up the mode of storytelling rooted in the French culture of courtly entertainments and *contes de vieilles*, would surely have known this tale's origin. Though she wouldn't live to see the rise of the English governess manual as a genre within which fairy tales, such as she herself created, would take their honored and useful place, L'Héritier articulated the virtues of the moralized fairy tale and set a pattern of interpretive commentary designed to forestall the transgressive reader who might mistake as the true aim delight rather than virtue.

Albeit in poetry encircling the prose in the manner of Perrault, it is L'Héritier's framing of her tale that most clearly foreshadows the construction of the mid-century governess manual cum novel (and vice versa), among which we can identify both Sarah Fielding's *The Governess* (1749) as an English originator and Madame de Beaumont's *Magasin des enfans, ou Dialogues entre une sage gouvernante et plusieurs de ses élèves* (1756), as a Franco-English successor noteworthy for the introduction of "Beauty and the Beast" into the canon of English fairy tales. Both of these texts resituate the "moralité" of fairy tale storytelling from the appended "Moral" in Perrault's volume and Samber's translation, in which they are attached as a poetic afterword to exalt the virtues and decry the vices so movingly expressed in the tale itself. The appended *moralité* is designed to imprint on the mind of a listening child or adult reader the governing *raison d'être*, which is the employable caution to be abstracted from the tale-told experiences so sensibly impressed upon the youthful imagination. As we have seen, contrary to the rhetoric of childhood that surrounds the justification of fairy tales as instructive, Perrault's actual morals take aim at an older, often adolescent, female on the verge of emergence into womanhood, when her destiny is fraught with the temptations of sexual seduction, marital duplicity, hypocritical lovers, spousal violence, and alluring vices—just as often as the tales seek to promote healthy skepticism, rational discourses, wise choices of the good, and charitable benevolence as characteristics becoming the young woman of a truly excellent nature. What is appended in early tales as the "Moral" becomes in Fielding (1710–68) and Beaumont (1711–80) the imbricatory frame narrative, within which fairy tales, whether translated and redacted from earlier versions or self-created, function as tutorial exempla, mingled as often with animal fables Aesop or La Fontaine might approve and, increasingly, with scriptural preachments or biblical stories in order to instruct children in Christian virtues and behaviors.

What already existed in the literary world of fairy tales, a female circle of tale-tellers (real and fictive) and a primarily female audience, finds mid-eighteenth-century representation in the novels and governess manuals addressed to young girls and their mothers. Long proclaimed the first novel in English for children, Fielding's *The Governess: or, Little Female Academy* reconstitutes the cultural milieu and purposes of female storytelling, once associated with late-seventeenth-century French salons, by leaving behind the world of sophisticated aristocrats in favor of the upper- and middle-class domestic household. This *ménage des femmes* is descended more nearly from Perrault's, Samber's, or L'Héritier's visions of an instructional nursery, presided over by a wise woman, the ubiquitous Mother Goose with children gathered round a hearthside, or by the "noble Ladies" and maternal educators of the dedicatory epistles. Nothing points so clearly to a shift in audience than Fielding's epistle "To the Honourable Mrs. Poyntz," whom she flatters as the "living Pattern of every Lesson I would teach them," a "Lady, who, tho' bred in a Court, where she was the Object of Universal Admiration, no sooner became a Wife, than she turned her Thoughts to all the Domestic Duties that Situation requires, and made the maternal Care of her Family her first and chief Study" (xi). As Arlene Wilner argues, Fielding thus participates in a broader ideological shift that saw the mid-century rise of a bourgeois culture, the realignment of roles for women to position them securely in the domestic realm, and yet the new entrusting to women of the social and moral development of young children and fledgling adolescent girls. The rise of childhood is signaled by this early emergence of a children's literature that dates back to Perrault but accelerates markedly, at least for young women, with the publication of this first "pioneering . . . school story for girls" (Cadogan, *Governess* vii).

Her "Design," Fielding enunciates, is "to cultivate an early Inclination to Benevolence, and a Love of Virtue, in the Minds of young Women," primarily by taking natural endowments and "improving those amiable Dispositions into Habits" and by "keeping down all rough and boistrous Passions," so that such well-cultivated young women may themselves "arrive at true Happiness, in any of the Stations of Life allot-ted to the *Female Character*" (xi). Unlike Perrault and L'Héritier, Fielding never explicitly anticipates the perils of romantic seduction or erotic de-sire, nor does she feature prominently the most likely future for all women—that of wife; instead, her whole intent focuses on laying down principles and pedagogies for the proper socialization of young "daugh-ters" to become part of a harmonious community of sisters, willingly submissive to duty rather than individual ambitions and always obedient listeners to maternal counsels. Her conservative ideology inscribes the cult of the domesticated woman, even during an age that would see the rise of women as writers (herself included as author of nine works of fic-tion) and advocates on behalf of the (still circumscribed) empowerment of women as educators. In the era of Enlightenment and not yet revolu-tion or Romanticism, Fielding nonetheless carved out a system of tute-lage that fostered the natural process of "discovered" virtue which un-dergirded a rising middle-class emphasis on female self-effacement, a tempered restraint of passions, prudent wisdom, and Christian fortitude in contrast to aristocratic excess, ornamentation, ostentation, self-exalta-tion, or unwholesome indulgence.

To communicate these lessons Fielding's text relies almost dizzy-ingly on multiplying maternal voices, a veritable multilayered imbrica-tion of female instructresses. Herself the self-conscious novelist and au-thority whose epistle and preface set the "Design" for respectively mothers and "my little Readers," Fielding then installs Mrs. Teachum, "a Gentlewoman who undertook the Education of young Ladies," as the ever-vigilant "governess" of this academy (xv, 1). Mrs. Teachum in turn authorizes fourteen-year-old Miss Jenny Peace to recount approvable stories in order to teach younger tutees how to interpret lessons in social virtues, which they offer up through their own self-created confessional autobiographies. What would become a familiar trope of the governess as both mentor and "friend" becomes split in Fielding's history between Mrs. Teachum and Jenny, the latter serving as an amicable confidante. Mrs. Teachum, the sage advisor, hovers (often on the margins of the gar-den arbor) with a watchful "Eye," periodically intervening to counte-nance or correct Jenny's selection of fit materials and instructional strate-gies. Knowledgeably qualified by having been a clergyman's wife, well-tutored and "improved" by "his Instructions," her own prudent motherhood, and Christian fortitude upon the death of both husband

and children, Mrs. Teachum (at age 40) brings to her "Academy" all the requisite skills—"a lively and commanding Eye," "Dignity and Authority by her steady Behaviour," a "perfectly kind and tender" manner, and a disciplined approach to quelling rebellious or impassioned individuality (1, 2). Her curriculum seems short on subjects, long on "Reading, Writing, Working, and all proper Forms of Behaviour," since her "principal Aim was to improve their Minds in all useful Knowledge; to render them obedient to their Superiors, and gentle, kind, and affectionate to each other," yet "did she not omit teaching them an exact Neatness in their Persons and Dress, and a perfect Gentility in their whole Carriage" (1). The social and secular, a doctrine of appearances and cultivated inner virtue, and the affectionate bonding of friendship take precedence here over religious prescriptions, worldly knowledge, or substantive instruction in literary classics, such as might be expected from an author known for having translated Xenophon's *Memorabilia* and *Apologia* (1762). Raised herself by a maternal grandmother and educated at a boarding school, the learned Sarah Fielding turns to the popular domestic genres of stories, novels, fables, and fairy tales as instruments of maternal instruction, not yet so decried by evangelical reformers that they forfeit their social and moral reputability.

Fielding intentionally constitutes her female community of nine young women (ages seven to fourteen) in order to promulgate a pedagogy of "reading" and "tale-telling," and her polite academy (as well as her own discourse) becomes a perpetual tutorial in the "art of reading the text" with dutiful applications to one's own life (Suzuki). Fielding sets up the heuristic in her Preface, for she begs the reader to consider how if they accept "that the true Use of Books is to make you wiser and better, you will then have both Profit and Pleasure from what you read" (xiii). But, she also warns that books cannot be randomly consumed, for "a Head, like a House . . . crammed too full" by running "through Numbers of Books" has "no regular Order" and cannot take "Advantage of the Knowledge got thereby" (xiv). Consequently, it becomes the schoolmistress's fundamental mission to select wisely materials to be read, stories to be narrated, and critical methodologies to render "Knowledge" fittingly applicatory to one's life. Having heeded her mentor's lesson in pedagogy and told the first of her fairy tales to the younger charges, Jenny echoes her maternal guide, for "in order therefore to make what you read of any Use to you, you must not only think of it thus in general, but make the Application to yourselves" (37). That this method of "Application" of a prescribed text sounds like a sermon, in which Scripture once "opened" by the preacher gives rise to various applications or "uses" directed at the individual parishioner, is to be noted, if only to highlight Fielding's profound social secularism. In her lexicon for inculcating refined virtues, to make "Use" requires a perpetual tutorial in critical reading and interpretation, taught as Mrs. Teachum proclaims "by those Methods of Fable and Moral, which have been recommended by the wisest Writers, as the most effectual means of conveying useful Instruction" (xi).

The plethora of stories that accumulate (eighteen by one count), often with embedded narratives that create a palimpsestic text, vary from newly created fairy tales to nine schoolgirl histories in the mode of spiritual relations of vices admitted and amended, a romantic novella, a play synopsis, two aviary fables, not to mention tutorial dialogues, epistles read aloud, and conversations (Wilner 309). What's remarkable is the degree to which fairy tales partner with self-confessed autobiographies, the realm of the fantastical imaginary existing side-by-side with the "real" of personal experience. Fielding excels, as do her ventriloquists Mrs. Teachum and Jenny Peace, in bridging between the world of fairy tale and moral applications—and in setting by example a method of entertainment and instruction that mothers can emulate. Fairy tales, embedded and contextualized, become exemplary pedagogical instruments to be, however, carefully mediated and meditated so that these amusements never exist as ends unto themselves. Take for example, Jenny's telling of "*The Story of the cruel Giant* Barbarico, *the good Giant* Benefico, *and the pretty little Dwarf Mignon*," in which Mignon abets lovers parted by the abduction of the "Shepherd *Fidus*" by outwitting his master, Barbarico, and is rewarded by being reunited with his long-lost sister, the shepherdess Amata. Cruelty receives its just punishment when Beneficio "lifted on high the mighty Sword, and, with one Blow, severed his [Barbarico's] odious Head from his enormous Body," then held "in his Hand the Monster's yet grinning Head," while he exclaims, "See, here, my Friends, the proper Conclusion of a rapacious cruel Life" (31). What Trimmer makes of this graphic violence, so like what she decries in *Blue Beard*, isn't known, no doubt because Mrs. Teachum countenances Jenny's telling of the story, while cautioning against an extravagant indulgence in the fantastic and magical elements:

> I have no Objection, Miss *Jenny*, to your reading any Stories to amuse
> you, provided you read them with the proper Disposition of Mind
> not to be hurt by them. A very good Moral may indeed be drawn
> from the Whole, and likewise from almost every Part of it; and as you
> had this Story from your Mamma, I doubt not but you are very well
> qualified to make the proper Remarks yourself upon the Moral of it
> to your Companions. But here let me observe to you . . . that Gi-
> ants, Magic, Fairies, and all Sorts of supernatural Assistances in a
> Story, are only introduced to amuse and divert: For a Giant is called
> so only to express a Man of great Power; and the magic Fillet round
> the Statue was intended only to shew you, that by Patience you will
> overcome all Difficulties. Therefore, by no means let the Notion of
> Giants or Magic dwell upon your Minds. (34)

Fielding leaves little to be misunderstood, despite our ironic recognition
that the fairy tale Mrs. Teachum critiques is Fielding's own invention. She
plainly admits the instructional benefits of amusing stories, as long as the
obligatory morals are abstracted and supernatural magic is translated into
humanly applicable behaviors. She excuses also the "different Stile" when
properly deployed to convey Barbarico's "raging Cruelty" and righteous
condemnations of "his wicked Mind" (34). Taken apart from their moral
interpretation, however, fairy tales may become replete with "high-
sounding Language" and "supernatural Contrivances" antithetical to the
"Simplicity of Taste and Manners," so Mrs. Teachum's dissection of the
fairy tale's "utile" balances morality conveyed by entertaining storytelling
against extravagant excess unmediated by maternal guidance (34, 35).
Miss Jenny makes all too sure the next day that she repeats verbatim these
elucidations to her companions, while she also puts them through their
paces by requiring them to "consider the Moral of the Story, and what
Use they might make of it" (37). Warned once, Jenny never fails there-
after to request "Permission" to read another "Fairy-Tale, which was also
given her by her Mamma," an inherent validation of a transmittal of *contes de vieilles* through the matrilineal tradition (62). By extension, we pre-
sume, Fielding's text itself acts to validate and permit the use of fairy tales
in the nursery as well as the polite academy, or, in other words, only
within the imaginatively fertile "grove" yet disciplined mental maternity
ward where young daughters receive their educations.

Fielding condemns as senseless "Affectation" a too rarified denunciation of all things that might prove "entertaining" through Jenny's

account of her Mamma's rebuke when she refuses an "Amusement" at a
"Raree-Show" in favor of reading. When her mother laughs at this pre-
cocious "Pretence of being wise," this gentle remonstrance "cured me of
the Folly of thinking myself above any innocent Amusement" (63). With
maternal permission, backed by the governess's pedagogic tutelage in
"how to read," Jenny comfortably settles in to relate "The Princess Hebe:
A Fairy Tale," only in this case Mrs. Teachum, who has "so good an
Opinion of Miss *Jenny* . . . that she would read nothing to them but what
was proper" determines to "stay and hear this Fairy Tale" (64). Recounting "Princess Hebe" becomes a salutary occasion for Mrs. Teachum
to expound on the efficacy of innocent "Amusement," when the design
is to "draw such Morals . . . as may influence your future Practice," and
to reemphasize that "if the Story is well written, the common Course of
Things would produce the same Incidents, without the Help of Fairies"
(91, 92). The morals drawn from "Princess Hebe" promote social doctrines espoused by Fielding's own text, such as "Obedience" to "the
Commands of those who know better what is for your Good," notably
mothers and governesses (92). Any magic brought about by "Fairies"
must also translate into the real world, where giving sway to "the raging
of our Passions" leads to misery, "the *natural* [my emphasis] consequence
of Disobedience," while "the *natural* Consequence" of a "Return to her
Duty" brings Hebe "Content and Happiness for the rest of her Life" (92,
93). Mrs. Teachum leaves no doubt that her intention is to "imprint" the
morals, not the magic, "on their Memory for the rest of their Lives" (93).

Reasoned deduction, tutored self-discipline, lessons in reading for
the moral become the *modus operandi* for inculcating virtue, and in this
school, all manner of texts must be moralized. The regulation of passions,
a dutiful conformity to rules, improvement of the mind, and respectful fidelity to "a fond and indulgent Mother," so Jenny Peace calls Mrs.
Teachum, all act to ensure that young women will be safely, prudently,
wisely confirmed in their domesticated households, where harmony and
peace will reign (127). In this "female academy" fairy tales receive sanction as a respectable vehicle of literary improvement. By teaching the art
of abstracting the moral from the fantastic and the serious from the amusing, Fielding's text sets forth a model of instructional utility for "impeccable governesses, rational dames, and moral mothers" (Myers).

A novelist and essayist who emigrated to England in 1748 as an
"impeccable" French governess, Jeanne-Marie Le Prince de Beaumont

took up the cause of women's education in her *Nouveau magasin français, ou Bibliothèque instructive* (1750–52, 1758), becoming the "mother of the modern women's magazines," as Patricia Clancy proclaims (199). Beaumont joined English advocates (including Lady Mary Wortley Montagu, Samber's patron) in seeking to promote women's self-discipline, self-esteem, and self-knowledge through intellectual as well as social and spiritual instruction. Twenty years a teacher before becoming a governess for the English aristocracy, among others for the children of the Prince of Wales, Beaumont turned practical experience into instructional manuals that promoted the development of moral judgment, right reason, social responsibility, and religious belief among young girls and women to offset the exclusive focus of early century education on decorative female accomplishments. Derived as much from her French predecessors as from Fielding's model of tale-telling in a polite academy, Beaumont's *Magasin des enfans* (1756–57 French; 1759 English) likewise transformed French romances and *nouvelles* into fairy tales, usefully moralized to instill self-reflexive lessons in virtuous behaviors and domestic duties for her own gathering of six young women taught by Lady Affable. Her pedagogy, signaled by the subtitle, *Dialogues entre une sage gouvernante et plusieurs de ses élèves de la première distinction*, encouraged a mode of questions and answers as well as debate and gentle persuasion that enabled her *étudiantes*, ages five to thirteen, to develop independent minds as capable of deciphering moral lessons in fairy tale fantasy as they were of absorbing Scripture commentary or lessons in history or geography.

Most renowned, of course, is Beaumont's redaction of Madame de Villeneuve's *conte de salon précieux*, "La Belle et la Bête," first recounted by a fictional chambermaid (a variant of Mother Goose) to an affianced young woman, in *La Jeune Amériquaine et les contes marins* (1740–41), in order to "enchanter son Coeur, & charmer son esprit" (1: 38). Like Perrault and Fielding before her, Beaumont transforms the embellished *conte merveilleux* into a still enchanting story, but with a decidedly moral intent, for she comments in the extended subtitle for her 1759 English edition that "the Useful is blended throughout with the Agreeable, the Whole being interspersed with proper Reflections and Moral Tales." Stripped of excesses to become what today we accept as the definitive "Beauty and the Beast," Beaumont's variant makes Beauty the middle-class epitome of "humility and industry," a young woman (like Finetta) who spends "the greatest part of her time" in "reading good books," to be praised as much for her dutiful sacrifice to save her father as for her ability to discern true "virtue, sweetness of temper, and complaisance" beneath the monstrous features of a Beast, for whom she temporizes, "I have the highest gratitude, esteem, and friendship" (43, 41, 56). Cognizant of the potentially pernicious effects of sensationalized fictions, romanticized fairy tale, and even of Perrault's nursery tales, Beaumont in her advertisement to the 1757 (Volume 2) *Magasin des enfans*, defends their telling, when stylistically and interpretively adapted: "I have found the tales of my Mother Goose, however childish they may be, more useful for children than those that have been written in a loftier style. . . . The little bit of moral that is narrated therein is drowned beneath a marvelous absurdity, because it is not necessarily combined with the aim (end) that one ought to offer to children: the acquisition of virtues, the correction of vices" (my translation; qtd. Remy 13–14). Like Fielding, Beaumont embeds retellings of fairy tales in her "textual academy," as part of her primer for maternal instruction via moral dialogues, positioning tales filled with disguises, fairies, magical trials and tests alongside sober lessons drawn from the Bible, Greek myths, geography, ancient history, natural philosophy, and experimental science. Often reprinted (53 editions) into the nineteenth century, the *Magasin des enfans* established Beaumont, Patricia Clancy claims, as "the first to write entertaining, educational material especially for children," a feat Sarah Trimmer would applaud a half-century later (203). We might argue that Madame de Beaumont also becomes the French "mère" to Perrault's "père" by transmitting not only some of his verse tales ("Tale of the Three Wishes" and "Aurora," a variant of "The Fairy") and her own famous "Beauty and the Beast," but also tales, such as "Prince Fatal, and Prince Fortunatus," that would become popularized favorites in Benjamin Tabart's juvenile library.

What's at stake in this mid-century period of making morality from fairy tale fantasy is nothing less than the female claim, rooted in the matriarchal heritage of nursery and Mother Goose tales, to control the potentially transgressive reader and (female) subject. Orality, in the earliest traditions, allowed, one assumes, for the give and take of a curious child who queries the nursemaid or weeps, as Samber tells us, to hear stories that etch such impressions in the mind. But the "academy novel" and governess manual, such as those by Fielding and Beaumont, take on a far more difficult task in the midst of a transitional social climate in which women make strides in literacy at the same time as they experience personal freedoms, revolutionary upheaval, aristocratic excesses, and a mistrust of the passions and imagination devoid of rational enlightenment. Education, as Locke's treatises set forth, becomes serious business, and the female pedagogues fill in where Locke and others leave off, with the need not simply to educate men but also women, whose transgressions of sentiment and sexuality, engendered by romantic illusions as much as by realistic dangers, require regulatory control. Through the guise of a Mrs. Teachum or Madame Beaumont's Mrs. Affable, *une sage gouvernante*, young women are taught how to read "les moralités," like the maxims Perrault himself felt obliged to append. Only in these mid-eighteenth-century female-authored texts, the nursemaid *cum la sage femme*, once relegated to the placard on a frontispiece, emerges as the controlling creator, teller, interpreter of fairy tale. What remained latent in Perrault's, L'Héritier's, and Samber's making of morals was precisely what becomes more articulated in narratives of vigilant oversight of reading and interpretive application. The governess, as Judith Burdan argues with respect to Fielding's Mrs. Teachum, becomes an embodiment of the "panoptical gaze," always alert to the dangerously wandering imagination of a pupil, always ready with the obligatory tale of moral virtue, however diverting, to reign in an unbounded fantasizer, heedlessly disobedient miss (like Princess Hebe), or arrogantly presumptuous "know-it-all." Thus, fairy tales increasingly enable, as they had earlier but without a mediating voice, the teller and the reader to read behavioral signs and signifiers, specifically the dangers of unleashed desire, chastity threatened by bestial lovers, hypocritical seducers, intemperate desires for wealth, over-attention to visual appearances, or simply curiosity gone amok. If well managed in their telling and interpretation, fairy tales *can* tutor the percipient heart in its duteous pursuit of moral virtue.

By the late eighteenth century, the rationalists and "Sunday school" moralists find the fairy tale itself to be a dangerous transgression—or an alluring temptation. Their "unmaking of morality" through a repressive rejection of once and still popular nursery tales reflects an inversion of the equation that earlier validated their acceptability. Fairy tales originally taught lessons *by virtue* of their entertaining divertissements, engaging the untutored youthful mind with vividly rendered impressions designed to delight and amuse, while appended morals imprinted the cautionary observations. In mid-century, Fielding and Beaumont strike a balance that privileges abstracted and domesticated morals, yet without denying the innocent amusement of fairy tale narration as a vehicle for tutoring young girls' minds. But by 1803, in the midst of a culture of radical romanticism she deplores (her antipathy for Rousseau and William Godwin is well documented by Donelle Ruwe), Sarah Trimmer can only remember with fond nostalgia her own bygone childhood pleasure not only in hearing fairy tales, but also in reading *The Governess* and Madame de Beaumont's *Magasin des enfans*, while she clearly moves to supplant fairy tale with moral tales, illustrated Scripture histories, animal family fables, and the Bible as the predominant modes of juvenile instruction (Bottigheimer). Linking no longer *dulce* with *utile* but rather cultivating a "taste for truth and utility," domestic realism supplants fantasy in this maternal "remaking of morality," or as Myers argues, this later age saw the rise of "the Georgian woman educator's 'taste for truth and realities'" (121, 118).

In her splendid essay, "Impeccable Governesses, Rational Dames, and Moral Mothers: Mary Wollstonecraft and the Female Tradition in Georgian Children's Books," Myers documents the increased authority of mothers and their surrogates, who as writers dominated the genre of didactic children's books in England during the late eighteenth century, having created a "matrilineage of nursery novels" (33). Directed toward mothers and governesses who would offer moral instruction in domestic arts, accomplishments, and duties, the Georgian writers emphasized rational (though not necessarily dull) stories of "real life." These "mother–pedagogues" included the widely published Sarah Fielding, Madame de Genlis, Sarah Trimmer, Hannah More, and Maria Edgeworth, in addition to Mary Wollstonecraft and, I would add, the earlier figure of Marie Le Prince de Beaumont (35, 36). What became a "Georgian version of bibliotherapy," as Myers further delineates in "'A Taste for Truth and Realities': Early Advice to Mothers and Books for Girls," derived from the post-1780 explosion of educational literature— guides, treatises, essays, as well as novels and tales—that made female culture formation and reformation synonymous with textual reading (118). Insistently focused on "realistic adolescent socialization," these moral textualists offered their maternal advice through manuals and exemplary tales of female maturation that attacked the vogue of "sensibility," meaning not just empathetic feeling but, rather, "indulgent attitudes *about* romantic emotion as an irresistible force," imbibed too freely from sentimental narratives and the imaginative excesses of fairy tales and novels (Myers, "'A Taste'" 120). Although Georgian writers cultivated a "taste for truth and realities," it was not purely didacticism devoid of enjoyment or fictional discourse. Nevertheless, in a century of proliferating books and circulating libraries that overwhelmed the oral tradition of storytelling and in the political atmosphere of the French Revolution and Napoleonic wars, maternal advice on reading became more necessary than ever. The mother–pedagogues took up this moral mission by critiquing romances, novels, and fairy tales, all of which foreground love as a passionate obsession and privilege the nonsensical, irrational, and fabulous over common sense, domestic experience, and realistic truths ("'A Taste'" 119).

Myers takes her cue from Maria Edgeworth's comments about her recurrent heroine Rosamond, who must be taught to master her own emotionally susceptible temperament and a taste for self-indulgent fantasy, because Rosamond "was rather too fond of imaginary things, such as fairy tales and stories of giants and enchanters; and it would be advantageous to give her a taste for truth and realities" (11: 215). In her *Letters on Education* Madame de Genlis had also sounded the alarm about "ridiculous" romantic illusions engendered by hearing and reading fairy tales, presumably Perrault's oft retold Cinderella or Sleeping Beauty among them, that might encourage "false notions, [and] stop the course of . . . reasoning" (1: 63), detracting thereby from a young woman's devotion to a "more positive ideal of womanhood grounded in a more active model of reading response," compatible with "a new domestic heroinism and domestic realism" ("'A Taste'" 120). Having successfully avoided the suggestion that romantic love constitutes the be-all and end-all of a young girl's life, even Sarah Fielding fell prey to this evangelical maternal reformism. In a bowdlerized 1820 edition of *The Governess*, as Suzuki shows, Mary Sherwood substitutes preachments on Christian doctrine and human depravity for Jenny Peace's "fanciful productions" (iv), for "fairy-tales," Sherwood fears, "are in general an improper medium of instruction, because it would be absurd in such tales to introduce Christian principles as motives of action" and "all stories . . . without this [divine] help have a most exceedingly evil tendency" (iv, 88; qtd. in Suzuki 333). Sherwood throws into stark relief the dismissal of the fabulous, having transformed tales that Perrault and Fielding conceived of as tutorials in triumphant virtue into a poisonous evil themselves. Sherwood's censure may seem extreme, but it sets the capstone on four decades during which maternal educators battled a rising tide of popular productions, literary and theatrical, that kidnapped the fairy tale from its domestic province of the nursery into a public marketplace, from the girl's academy to the Covent-Garden stage, from governess manuals to proliferating illustrated chapbooks and collections.

In this milieu of a new print and revolutionary public culture, Sarah Trimmer levels her sallies in a holy war against *"false philosophy"* in order to propagate an educational agenda for middle-class parents, the hallmarks of which were religious instruction for children, moral guidance exercised by mothers and surrogate educators, and an unstinting parental surveillance—most particularly over the growing literature of "children's books" (1: 64, 63). Trimmer's periodical, aptly titled *The Guardian of Education* (1802–1806), established the first catalogue of children's literature to direct parents toward the wisest choices for picture-book toddlers to blushing adolescents. In volume one, she draws forth "Observations on the Changes Which Have Taken Place in Books for Children and Young Persons," tracing the gradual devolution which has "taken place since the Reformation, from a method *entirely* Christian, to one in which there is too frequently a *mixture* of *false philosophy*" (1: 61). Despite a reservation that much is not "said expressly in Mr. Locke's book [*Treatise of Education*] upon the subject of Religion," she countenances his "forming of the minds of children to *virtue* by checking the growth of unruly passions, and teaching them to govern their appetites . . . as it is conformable to *Christian principles*," and endorses him for recommending strongly "teaching children the Creed, the Lord's Prayer, and the Ten Commandments at an early age" (1: 9). Among instigators of a false philosophy, metaphysical fumes, and deleterious education reforms, she excoriates Voltaire, Frederick II of Prussia, D'Alembert (Perrault's employer and sponsor for the French Academy), Diderot, and the French Encyclopedists (1751–80) who advocated deism and scientific rationalism, thus "propagating throughout Europe their abominable principles, which they contrived to mix with the doctrines of truth in such a manner that they were frequently insinuated into the mind of the unsuspecting reader, without his being aware of the corruption" (1: 10). Little wonder that she attacks Jean-Jacques Rousseau, whose "system, given to the world in the history of *Emilius*, an imaginary pupil, educated upon an entirely new principle; which proposed to banish Christianity from the nursery and the school" (1: 10). To counteract this looming "*conspiracy against* Christianity *and all* Social Order," promulgated by an insidious "endeavour to infect the minds of the rising generation, through the medium of *Books of* Education and *Children's Books*," Trimmer lays down the bedrock of her instructional ideology: "the foundation of a good education should be laid in *the* Nursery" and the "commencement of a Christian Education from the very *cradle*" (1: 2–3). Childhood, for Trimmer, lasts from the cradle to age fourteen, and young persons are susceptible consumers of juvenile literature till age twenty-one (1: 66). Thus, Trimmer seeks to institute her own system of education in Christian religion, one that rescues deceived mothers and young children from the thralls of misguided philosophy, corrupting immorality—and, in most cases, all things French, German, or simply foreign.

Through *The Guardian of Education* Trimmer becomes the public voice of the archetypal maternal pedagogue whose "surveillant Eye" reviews a veritable library of texts and oversees the act of reading texts— and the education of children. She maps out her own literary domain, within which even governesses and rational dames fall under the panoptic gaze, subject to socio-religious principles of proper moral instruction. Fearful that a 1765 edition of Fielding's *The Governess* has "lain for years upon the shelf," Trimmer "cannot but wish that this little volume, which had for its author one of the best female scholars England has produced, may be estimated according to its real merit" (1: 137, 138). It's an ominous "sign" when "such Works as this cease to be admired and approved . . . that good morals and simplicity of manners, are banished from the system of English Education, to make room for *false Philosophy* and *artificial refinement*" (1: 138). Fielding's maternal tutorials in moral uses control potentially aberrant readings of fairy tales, against which, in this strictly regulated context of an educational novel, Trimmer levels no criticism. By contrast, she disparages the tutelage of imported French masters and governesses, who were "adventurers" and "*papists* by profession," catered to a decadent infatuation with all things French, and established "*French academies* and *French boarding schools*" which privileged polite accomplishments over religious training (1: 6, 7). Yet, a footnote absolves "Madame le Prince de Beaumont, [who] contributed greatly by her teaching and writings towards forming the minds and manners of many of our nobility who have adorned their high stations" (1: 7). Elsewhere, Trimmer recommends "some valuable *French books* for children and young persons likewise . . . namely, '*La Magazine des 'Enfans,'* and '*La Magazine d' Adolescence,'* by *Madame le Prince de Beaumont,*" which "were afterwards translated into English" (1: 63). Trimmer embraces Fielding and Beaumont as vigilant maternal instructresses, whose moral applications of fairy tale and fable, interlaced with female confessions, socializing lectures, and biblical teachings, prove praiseworthy in contrast to the circulating libraries, penny volumes, and colporteur blue books. Her philosophy of reading and parental education echoes in some respects Mrs. Teachum's lessons and those of Beaumont's "wise governess," although Trimmer's own chosen literary genres—moral tales, illustrated Scripture stories, animal fables, Bible editions—for instilling high-church Anglicanism and "*revealed religion*" will supersede Fielding's and Beaumont's social secularism and eclectic blending of amusing tales with useful truths.

It's precisely the absence of matronly mediation and vigilant observation that provokes Sarah Trimmer to unleash a righteous fury against juvenile libraries that traffic in amusing tales, romances, and fables, including those famous Perrault nursery tales that Samber took pains to praise as charming stories for Elisabeth Charlotte d'Orléans or for the Countess of Granville to use when instructing her children. Even Trimmer admits that "we well remember, as the delight of our childish days . . . *Mother Goose's Fairy Tales*; *Esop and Gay's Fables*; *The Governess, or Little Female Academy,*" all of which she historicizes as "books written in what may be called *the first period of Infantine and Juvenile Literature* in this country" (1: 62). Esteemed as treasured memories or reliquaries, these volumes no longer carry alone the burden of childhood education, nor do they carry the same weight when popularization refashions them into purely delightful diversions in fantasy, lacking their moral standing because denuded of the prefaces, dedicatory epistles, and verse morals that Perrault, L'Héritier, and Samber appended. Quoting an extract from "an Address to the Public from the Society for the Suppression of Vice," Trimmer finds in it sanction for her own mission with respect to vetting "*Children's books,*" which have become a

> most successful channel for the conveyance of infidel and licentious
> tenets. It is indeed no longer safe to trust to the titles of books: the
> terms *virtue* and *vice* have no longer the same signification as formerly.
> . . . Even the fairy tales and little histories, which under the garb of

fiction, have long taught the tender mind to distinguish vice from virtue, and to admire the one, and abhor the other, have been either deprived of their most useful parts, or made the receptacles of new matter, which though the outline of the story be still preserved, corrupt the fancy, and lead the mind to false conclusions. (3: 148–49)

Where earlier authors found virtue hidden beneath the guise of delight in tales that don't gloss over vice (after all, monstrous giants are beheaded and ogrish mothers-in-law die), latter-day rationalists and religious educators found only vice in the guise of virtue—and in the unmediated reading of fairy tales, fables, and fictions. Trimmer comes so to mistrust the representation of prefaces and advertisements of juvenile libraries and publishers that she envisions a near conspiracy to defraud and deceive the reader.

What are the bases upon which Trimmer comes to distrust not only the "plausibility of Prefaces," but the plausible rationales for the reading of fairy tales at all (4: 94)? As we have seen in tracing out the claims for moral utility laid down by Perrault, Samber, and L'Héritier, as well as their successors Fielding and Beaumont, amusing diversions and delightful histories elicit from children affective responses that impress on the infantine consciousness the love of virtue and the abhorrence of vice through identification with the heroines and heroes, their trials and triumphs. A system of rewards and punishments is limned out in explicit terms (the wolf "eat[sic] her up," for instance) or morals are drawn to specify the desired lesson. The parent is invited expressly to read tales that give "a true relish for virtue, and a distaste for vice" (4: 95).

Nothing amiss, a mother or father might assume, unless you take into account Sarah Trimmer's deconstruction of the romantic fairy tale, when it excites an unregulated sensibility and tempts the mind to roam freely into pure fantasy. In reviewing an 1801 edition of *The Palace of Enchantment; or, Entertaining and Instructive Fairy Tales*, Trimmer mocks the "*promise* of the Preface" and tales in which "the *virtue* so highly extolled" signifies "an extravagant devotion of the hero's heart" that leads to "dangerous enterprises" that "risk the malice of . . . malignant Fairies and Magicians," merely to gratify "capricious wishes of his Fair-one . . . founded upon vanity and ambition" (4: 95). Romance with no domestic counterbalance, superficial virtue with no moral basis, affections so undisciplined—all fall outside the bounds of moralized tale-telling and maternal instruction. Although she acknowledges that "a good moral . . . may sometimes be traced in Tales of this kind" and attached to some, "for the most part, they answer no better end than to amuse the fancy; and not unfrequently at the hazard of inflaming the imagination and the passions of youth" (4: 95). Inflamed passion is antithetical to the stolid spirituality Trimmer espouses, nor does it tutor young women in the disciplined control of sexual desire or promote truth and reality; hence, the tales collected, unmediated, and romantically extravagant translate fairy tale virtues into artificial delights that "ignite" and promote vice—the vice of immoral reading. In Trimmer's religious pedagogy, imagination, that which transports us into another world in order to excite felt perceptions (the hallmark also of literary romanticism), has no place in the nursery. One must eschew fairy tale delights of "wonderful and supernatural events, brought about by the agency of imaginary beings," and seek instead mimetic exemplars in moral tales that tutor young minds to make discerning judgments of right and wrong, virtue and vice (2: 185).

Trimmer's critiques fall as heavily on the haphazard compilation, (false) advertisement, and illustrations as on the suspect content of fairy tales themselves. Tabart's collections, as well as individual sixpence volumes, put forth a mélange of tales drawn from multiple sources, thereby depriving the reader of the contextual matter that might judiciously guide the mother/ reader and her nursery brood. Trimmer reserves her harshest disdain for illustrated versions of fairy tales that Tabart published for his Juvenile and School Library, a total of 26 single issues, usually with three copper-plates, or gathered into the three-volume *Tabart's Collection of Popular Stories for the Nursery: From the French, Italian, and Old English Writers, Newly Translated and Revised* (1804) and a fourth volume (1809) to include the Sinbad, Aladdin, and Ali Baba stories. Tabart's collection redacted all of Perrault's tales, Beaumont's "Beauty and the Beast," and a few by Madame d'Aulnoy, but not until 1817 in *Fairy Tales, or the Liliputian Library* did he include L'Héritier's "Discreet Princess." In *The Guardian of Education*, Trimmer reviews only sixpence issues of "*Cinderella, Blue Beard, and Little Red Riding Hood*" (4: 74).[3] She bristles with horrified indignation at misrepresentations of these "*new translations*," since they are "the identical *Mother Goose's Tales*, with all their *vulgarities of expression*, which were in circulation when those who are now grandmothers, were themselves children" (4: 74).

Reading she can control, or at least Trimmer advocates that parents, guided by her reviews, exercise wise choices in selecting and narrating stories. But it's the visual theatrics of "embellishments, consisting of coloured prints, in which the most striking incidents in the stories are placed before the eyes of the little readers in glaring colours, representations we believe of the play-house scenes, (for the figures are in theatrical dresses)" that so egregiously violate Trimmer's sense of fit instructional matter for the young (4: 74). "In Blue Beard," she writes,

> the second plate represents the opening of the *forbidden closet*, in which appears, not what the story describes, (which surely is *terrific enough!*) "*a floor clotted with blood, in which the bodies of several women were lying (the wives whom Blue Beard had married and murdered,")* but, *the flames of Hell* with *Devils* in frightful shapes, threatening the unhappy lady who had given way to her curiosity! The concluding print is, *Blue Beard* holding his terrified wife by the hair, and lifting up his sabre to cut off her head. (4: 74–75)

No hell flames or devils appear in the sixpence 1804 issue, in which light illuminates a woman who sadly cradles another woman's body in her lap, a small pool of blood signifying the former wives' tragic fate [see fig. 2.1].

The forbidden Closet.

London Publish'd by Tabart & C.º Sep. 18. 1804.

Figure 2.1.   Illustration from *Blue Beard; or, Female Curiosity: and Little Red Riding-Hood: Tales for the Nursery. From the French of C. Perrault.* With copperplates. 7th ed. London: Tabart, 1804. Courtesy of the Department of Special Collections, Charles E. Young Research Library, UCLA.

Blue Beard about to cut his Wifes head off.

London Publish'd by Tabart & C.º Sep. 15. 1804

Figure 2.2.   Another illustration from *Blue Beard; or, Female Curiosity: and Little Red Riding-Hood: Tales for the Nursery.* **Courtesy of the Department of Special Collections, Charles E. Young Research Library, UCLA.**

In black and white engravings from Perrault and Samber forward, editions repeatedly display Blue Beard with a drawn sword, his all-too-curious wife fending off the impending stroke, but just as often the two heroic brothers, as in Tabart, burst through the door to rescue their sister from her brutal husband [see fig. 2.2]. Representational fidelity aside, Trimmer warns that visual fantasy threatens to ignite the malleable imaginations of "little children, whose minds are susceptible of every impression; and who from the liveliness of their imaginations are apt to convert into realities whatever forcibly strikes their fancy" (4: 75). Impressionable minds, so intentionally directed by Perrault, Samber, L'Héritier, Fielding, and Beaumont to the contemplation of moral consequences, are for Trimmer reservoirs of sensations too uncensored, too undisciplined to be trusted—not with the reading, nor with the visualizations of the fairy tale.

What, might we ask, becomes of Perrault's *moralités*, and does Sarah Trimmer have a point about the dissociation of imaginative fictions from their moral functioning as tutorials for young minds? Does a volume such as Tabart's in which copper-plates are hand-colored to enhance the visual effect, awaken feelings of fear and horror? But are they any less graphic in depicting violent or erotic acts than those black-and-white engravings that headed each story in Perrault's and Samber's originals? When visual interpretation must be controlled, how successful will the governess or reviewer be in separating the narrative proper from its colorful representation? For Trimmer, visualized fantasy and its theatricalization joined with the fairy tale genre itself to exile these old *contes de vieilles* from the new "matrilineage of the nursery," and her own moral tales, Scripture prints, and animal fables (as in *Fabulous Histories*) became the fare with which she challenged the immorality and seeming cultural hegemony of the fairy tale.

Sarah Trimmer tried valiantly to create the bounded female bibliothèque—or English academy—of true learning that would re-privatize instruction of the young within the nursery hearthside environs that Perrault's placard portrayed with its "contes de ma mère loye." And she was not wrong in suspecting that what had gone before her by way of making morality from fairy tale fantasy had unraveled as surely as Mother Goose's thread on a distaff. In Benjamin Tabart's volumes morals have evaporated, prefaces and epistles to noble ladies replaced with a publisher's self-promotions for juvenile circulating libraries. The culture of the private world of female life, impeccable governesses, moral mothers, and rational dames was also being challenged by the masculine reappropriation of fairy tale for public theater. Once the unmaking of morality was done, the remaking of fairy tale into extravagant entertainment had begun. Could Trimmer, one wonders, have known—and deplored—the production of *Blue-Beard; or, Female Curiosity! A Dramatick Romance; First Represented at the Theatre Royal Drury-Lane, on Tuesday January 16, 1798* (Kelly and Colman)? With what horror would she have greeted the later farces, melodramas, and extravaganzas, such as Henry Byron's *Blue Beard, or, Female Curiosity and Male Atrocity* (1860) or E. H. Keating's *Blue Beard! From a New Point of Hue: A Burlesque Extravaganza* (1860), wherein fairy tales become a nineteenth-century version of adult entertainment. Trimmer intuited the latency in fairy tales of sexual desires, romantic illusion, the magical, and the supernatural, which once engendered through transgressive reading and visualization could not be eradicated from children's impressionable minds and would subject children to temptations and vice, that is, to the consequences of "plaisir" and "désir." Dislocated from the secure control of the family or polite academy, from moral tutelage and maternal instruction, *contes de fées* were no longer the innocent entertainments Perrault intended them to be. Once the inspiration for visions of virtue triumphant and vice thwarted, fairy tales became a purveyor of vice in the guise of virtue.

The very medium of the melodramatic stage spectacle suggests how cut loose from morality the fairy tales could become, even as nineteenth-century authors and publishers would accelerate the publication of volumes for the nursery and for children. Perrault's *dulce* and *utile* and the impeccable governess's taste for rational truths and realities as portrayed in fairy tales no longer might serve to instruct children and young ladies in the self-control of their natural instincts, imaginative excesses, and irrational fears. Lacking the formatted regulation of the text, whether through prefaces, epistles, appended or abstracted morals, or framed and mediated tutorials, and let loose from the matrilineage of the nursery, family, and polite academy, female control over textuality, reading, and the child's response are let loose as well—and the unmaking of morality in fairy tale fantasy that finds virtue even in the guise of vice has begun.

NOTE ON THE TEXT

My work has been assisted by ready access to the Children's Book Collection, UCLA; by Renoir in Interlibrary Loans; and by the superb staff, notably Suzanne Shellaby and Octavio Olvera, the latter who remembers with admiration Mitzi Myers's labors of love and joys of discovery in our Special Collections reading room. This research, assisted by Ph.D. candidate Anne Sheehan, and the photographic reproductions have been supported by annual research grants from the UCLA Academic Senate. All illustrations are published by permission of UCLA's Special Collections, Charles E. Young University Research Library.

Translations from the French are my own and based on archival review (and transcriptions) of the original texts. I've included citations also to readily available modern editions and facsimile reprints, or when available, other translations of hard-to-obtain prefaces and epistles, as in the case of Zarucchi's translations of Perrault's. L'Héritier's *Bigarrures ingénieuses* is only available through microfilm, and comparisons with Samber's translation of "L'Adroite Princesse" reveal the lineage of dedications and Samber's deviations and embellishments from the original poetic prologues and afterword.

To capture the authenticity of the original texts, when quoting, I preserve the typographic use of italics for maxims, character names, titles of works, and emphasis, but romanize dedicatory epistles and poetic morals. For bibliographic citations of French sources, I adhere to recent MLA guidelines, except for cases in which research custom dictates otherwise, as is the case with Perrault's *Histoires ou Contes du temps passé. Avec des Moralitez*.

NOTES

1. L'Héritier's dedication to "Marmoisan, ou l'Innocente tromperie. Nouvelle héroïque et satirique" is addressed to Perrault's daughter, "A Mademoiselle Perrault." The collection, *Oeuvres mêlées contenant l'Innocente tromperie . . . nouvelles et autres ouvrages en vers et en prose de mlle. L'H**** (Paris, 1695) was retitled *Bigarrures ingénieuses* (1696).

2. Lang's *Perrault's Popular Tales* republishes Perrault's collections, *Histoires ou Contes du temps passé. Avec des Moralitez* (Barbin, 1697) and the *Contes en vers* (1694 and 1695), collated with tales published in Moetjens's *Recueil de pièces curieuses et nouvelles, tant en prose qu'en vers*.

3. Trimmer's review (4: 74–75) refers collectively to these tales as "*Nursery Tales. Cinderella, Blue Beard, and Little Red Riding Hood*; with coloured plates. Price 6d. each. Tabart. 1804." Often published with a subtitle designating them *A Tale for the Nursery*, each sold singly for a sixpence, although a few Tabart issues feature two tales together. See *Beauty and the Beast* (1806); *Blue Beard; or, Female Curiosity: and Little Red Riding-Hood: Tales for the Nursery. From the French of C. Perrault* (1804); *Cinderella, or, The Little Glass Slipper; A Tale for the Nursery. From the French of C. Perrault* (1806).

WORKS CITED

Baldwin, R. "Beauty and the Beast." *The Polite Academy; or, School of Behaviour for Young Gentlemen and Ladies*. London, 1762. 56–84.

Barchilon, Jacques, and Henry Pettit, eds. *The Authentic Mother Goose Fairy Tales and Nursery Rhymes*. Facsim. ed. of *Histories, or Tales of Past Times . . . With Morals*. By M. Perrault. Trans. [Robert Samber.] London, 1729; and *Mother Goose's Melody: or, Sonnets for the Cradle*. London, 1791. Denver: Swallow, 1960.

Beaumont, Jeanne-Marie Le Prince de. *Magasin des Enfans: or, the Young Misses Magazine, Containing Dialogues between a Governess and Several Young Ladies of Quality Her Scholars*. 2 vols. in 1. London, 1759.

———. *Magasin des enfans, ou Dialogues entre une sage gouvernante et plusieurs de ses élèves de la première distinction*. 4 vols. in 2. Londres, 1756–57.

———. *Nouveau magasin français, ou Bibliothèque instructive*. 1750–52, 1758. *Oeuvres mêlées de mme Le Prince de Beaumont*. Ed. J. Eidous. Maestricht, 1775.

Bottigheimer, Ruth B. *The Bible for Children: From the Age of Gutenberg to the Present*. New Haven: Yale UP, 1996.

Burdan, Judith. "Girls *Must* Be Seen *and* Heard: Domestic Surveillance in Sarah Fielding's *The Governess*." *Children's Literature Association Quarterly* 19.1 (1994): 1–14.

Byron, Henry J. *Blue Beard! From a New Point of Hue: A Burlesque Extravaganza*. London, 1860.

Clancy, Patricia A. "A French Writer and Educator in England: Mme Le Prince de Beaumont." *Studies on Voltaire and the Eighteenth Century* 201 (1982): 195–208.

Edgeworth, Maria. *Rosamond. Works of Maria Edgeworth*. Vol. 11. Boston, 1825. 146–392. 13 vols.

Fielding, Sarah. *The Governess; or, Little Female Academy . . . Calculated for the Entertainment and Instruction of Young Ladies in Their Education*. London, 1749. Rpt. ed. Ed. Mary Cadogan. London: Pandora, 1987.

Genlis, Stéphanie-Félicité, Comtesse de. *Adelaide and Theodore: or, Letters on Education*. 1782. London, 1783. Trans. "some ladies." 3rd ed. 3 vols. London, 1788.

Hearn, Michael Patrick. Preface. *Histories, or Tales of Past Times*. By Charles Perrault. Trans. Robert Samber, 1729. Facsim. ed. New York: Garland, 1977.

L'Héritier de Villandon, Marie-Jeanne. "L'Adroite Princesse, ou les Avantures de Finette. Nouvelle." *Bigar[r]ures ingénieuses, ou Recüeil de diverses pièces galantes en prose et en vers*. [Netherlands] Suivant la copie de Paris. Jean Guignard, 1696. 169–228.

———. "L'Adroite Princesse, ou les Avantures de Finette. Nouvelle." *Histoires ou Contes du tems passé, Avec des Moralitez*. Par Mr. Perrault. Nouvelle édition augmentée d'une nouvelle, à la fin. Suivant la copie de Paris. Amsterdam: La Veuve de Jaq. Desbordes, 1721. 126–84.

———. "The Discreet Princess; or the Ad[v]entures of *Finetta*. A Novel." *Histories, or Tales of Past Times . . . With Morals*. By M. Perrault. Trans. [and Ed. Robert Samber.] London, 1729. 137–206.

Keating, E. H. *Blue Beard, or, Female Curiosity and Male Atrocity: An Extravaganza in Two Acts*. London, 1860.

Kelly, Michael, and George Colman. *Blue-Beard; or, Female Curiosity! A Dramatick Romance*. London, 1798.

La Fontaine, Jean de. *Fables Choisies, mises en vers par m. de la Fontaine*. Paris, 1668.

[Lamb, Charles]. *Beauty and the Beast: or, A Rough Outside with a Gentle Heart. A Poetical Version of an Ancient Tale.* London, 1813.

Lang, Andrew, ed. Introduction. *Perrault's Popular Tales.* Oxford, 1888. Rpt. ed. New York: Arno, 1977.

Myers, Mitzi. "Impeccable Governesses, Rational Dames, and Moral Mothers: Mary Wollstonecraft and the Female Tradition in Georgian Children's Books." *Children's Literature* 14 (1986): 31–59.

———. "'A Taste for Truth and Realities': Early Advice to Mothers on Books for Girls." *Children's Literature Association Quarterly* 12.3 (1987): 118–24.

Perrault, Charles. *Charles Perrault: Memoirs of My Life.* Ed. and trans. Jeanne Morgan Zarucchi. Columbia: U of Missouri P, 1989.

———. *Contes.* Ed. and Intro. Gilbert Rouger. Paris: Èditions Garnier Frères, 1967.

———. *Contes du tems passé de ma Mere L'Oye. Avec des Morales. Par M. Perrault. Augmentée d'une nouvelle, viz. L'Adroite Princesse.* 6th ed. Avec des joli estampes, and *Tales of Passed Times by Mother Goose. With Morals. Written in French by M. Perrault, and Englished by R. S. Gent. To Which Is Added a New One, viz. The Discreet Princess.* 6th ed. corrected. London: For S. van den Berg, 1764.

———. [Epitre]. "A Mademoiselle." *Histoires ou Contes du temps passé. Avec des Moralitez. Perrault's Popular Tales.* Ed. Andrew Lang. Oxford, 1888. Rpt. New York: Arno, 1977. 5–6.

———. *Histoires ou Contes du temps passé: Avec des Moralitez.* Paris: Claude Barbin, 1697.

———. *Histoires ou Contes du temps passé. Avec des Moralitez.* Par le Fils de Monsieur Perreault [sic] de l'Academie Françoise. Suivant la copie, à Paris. [Amsterdam: Jaques Desbordes], 1698.

———. *Histoires ou Contes du tems passé, Avec des Moralitez.* Par Mr. Perrault. Nouvelle édition augmentée d'une nouvelle, à la fin. Suivant la copie de Paris. Amsterdam: La Veuve de Jaq. Desbordes, 1721.

———. *Les Hommes illustres qui ont paru en France pendant ce siècle, avec leurs portraits au naturel.* 2 vols. Paris, 1696 and 1700. English trans. *Characters Historical and Panegyrical of the Greatest Men That Have Appeared in France during the Last Century.* Trans. J. Ozell. London, 1704.

Planché, James Robinson. *Songs, Duets, Chorusses, &c. in the New and Original Grand Comic, Romantic, Operatic, Melodramatic, Fairy Extravaganza, in Two Acts, Founded on the Nursery Tale, and Entitled, Beauty and the Beast.* London, 1841. 1–16.

Remy, Paul. "Une version méconnue de 'La Belle et la Bête.'" *Revue Belge de Philologie et d'Histoire* 35 (1957): 5–18.

Rowe, Karen E. "To Spin a Yarn: The Female Voice in Folklore and Fairy Tale." *Fairy Tales and Society: Illusion, Allusion, and Paradigm.* Ed. Ruth B. Bottigheimer. Philadelphia: U of Pennsylvania P, 1986. 53–74.

Ruwe, Donelle. "Guarding the British Bible from Rousseau: Sarah Trimmer, William Godwin, and the Pedagogical Periodical." *Children's Literature* 29 (2001): 1–17.

Samber, Robert, trans. and ed. *Histories, or Tales of Past Times . . . With Morals.* By Charles Perrault. London, 1729. Rpt. ed. Ed. Michael Patrick Hearn. New York: Garland, 1977.

Sherwood, Mrs. [Mary Martha]. *The Governess: or, the Little Female Academy.* Wellington, Salop: Houlston, 1820.

Suzuki, Mika. "The Little Female Academy and *The Governess.*" *Women's Writing* 1 (1994): 325–39.

Tabart, Benjamin, comp. *Fairy Tales, or the Liliputian Library, Containing Twenty-Six Choice Pieces of Fancy and Fiction.* London: Tabart, 1817.

———. *Tabart's Collection of Popular Stories for the Nursery: From the French, Italian, and Old English Writers, Newly Translated and Revised.* [Ed. William Godwin.]. 3 vols. London: Tabart, 1804.

———. *Tabart's Collection of Popular Stories for the Nursery.* Ed William Godwin. 4 vols. London, 1809.

Trimmer, Sarah. *The Guardian of Education.* 5 vols. London, 1802–6.

Villeneuve, Gabrielle-Suzanne Barbot de. *La Jeune Ameriquaine et les contes marins.* 5 vols. Haye, 1740–41.

Wilner, Arlene Fish. "Education and Ideology in Sarah Fielding's *The Governess.*" *Studies in Eighteenth-Century Culture* 24 (1995): 307–27.

Zarucchi, Jeanne Morgan, ed. and trans. *Charles Perrault: Memoirs of My Life.* Columbia: U of Missouri P, 1989.

• *3* •

"Delightful Task!"
Women, Children, and Reading in the Mid-Eighteenth Century

Julia Briggs

$\mathcal{T}$his essay takes as its starting point three general and familiar observations in order to explore their connections and illustrate their impact on a selection of texts chosen mainly from the mid-eighteenth century. First (and most obviously), this was the century when children began to be recognized as distinct and separate creatures, with particular needs and tastes, and as consumers of reading matter, commercially speaking. Second, children's education, in bourgeois circles traditionally entrusted to male schoolmasters and tutors, now began to be domesticized and feminized, so that women increasingly contributed, whether as mothers, schoolmistresses, or governesses. Finally, as women began to establish themselves on the literary scene, they contributed to a particular ethos of moral sensibility, of fine distinctions and discriminations that defined itself in the novel as the study of character, motives, and morals. All three developments might be seen, in part at least, as long-term effects of the Protestant revolution, with its emphasis on the need for everyone—including women and children—to be able to read the Bible and undertake some form of personal moral education. At the same time, a growing emphasis on the value of family life encouraged a more domestic interest in education, while moral education came to be regarded as the responsibility of the family rather than of the community at large.

John Locke's *Some Thoughts Concerning Education* (1693) contemplated its subject from a masculine, upper middle-class perspective, aiming to turn out a confident, rational, worldly man-about-town. Locke's assumptions were challenged by Pamela, Richardson's teenage nonconformist maid servant, who had so narrowly escaped seduction by Locke's thoughtless educational end-product, Mr. B. For Pamela, as for Marjorie Meanwell (heroine of *The Renowned History of Little Goody Two-Shoes*), reading does not merely give access to social mobility—it is a means to personal salvation. In this new popular mythology, it was no longer courage and daring, or even good looks or hard labor, that opened the doors of opportunity. Instead, it was intelligence and study, and this change was particularly significant for young women for whom, for a variety of reasons, Dick Whittington had never been a possible role model (though Goody Two-Shoes' appeal was not limited to young women). Goody Two-Shoes is, of course, the spiritual grandmother of all those women who use their skills of reading, writing, and interpretation to earn a living.

Yet, while both *Pamela* (1740–1) and *Goody Two-Shoes* (1755) have a distinctly feminine, and even a feminist aspect, we should not overlook the fact that *Pamela* was undoubtedly authored by a man, and *Goody Two-Shoes*, according to tradition, was the work of Oliver Goldsmith. While I read these texts as voicing gendered aspirations, it may be that what they voiced for their authors were class aspirations—that need for the underprivileged to make their way within a conservative social system, which constituted a key pressure point of the century, ultimately exploding into the French and American revolutions. My final example, therefore, is a text by a woman, Sarah Fielding's *The Governess* (1749), itself another repudiation of the Lockean model of education, since instead of governor and pupil, we here encounter a class of little girls who through judicious advice learn to teach themselves, thus replacing a masculine and hierarchic model of education with a feminine and democratic one. This feminine model, instead of assuming that the child is a *tabula rasa*—in Locke's words, "white Paper, or Wax, to be moulded and fashioned as one pleases" (265)—assumes that children have "selves" that can participate in the learning process: once they have learned how to look, they can find within themselves answers to at least some of the questions under investigation. In Sarah Fielding's view, children learn from a complex blend of experience, traditional narrative, and wise advisers—hers was a comprehensive vision, which was one source of her appeal for later readers and writers.

The domesticizing of education, in the form of fresh ways of thinking and feeling about the bourgeois family and the nature of childhood, were already apparent earlier in the century, when they were cel-

ebrated by James Thomson in "Spring," the third of his four poems on
The Seasons, published in May 1728:

> Delightful task! to rear the tender thought,
> To teach the young idea how to shoot,
> To pour the fresh instruction o'er the mind,
> To breathe the enlivening spirit, and to fix
> The generous purpose in the glowing breast. (34)

His sentiments register new attitudes to education, as they came into being, and his image of the child as plant anticipates the engravings of
William Blake, at the end of the century, where flowers cradle children
in the illustrations to his poems "Infant Joy" and "The Blossom," and after Blake, Wordsworth—and today, a world of advertising schmaltz.

As an image of process and organic growth, that of the child as
plant placed a new emphasis on the importance of environment, reject-
ing earlier images of innate sin or neo-Platonic angel-infancy. In *Some
Thoughts Concerning Education*, Locke helped to popularize this analogy
by representing education in terms of cultivation: the child becomes a
little garden, often requiring the weeding out of bad or the planting of
good habits, or the prevention of the seeds of vice from taking root.
Vigilance and regular care were now as necessary for the guardian as for
the gardener.

In the third and fourth volumes of Richardson's novel *Pamela*
(1741), his young heroine negotiates married life and child rearing, and
offers an extended critique of *Some Thoughts Concerning Education*, which
Mr. B. had given her on the birth of her first son. Reading Locke,
Pamela anticipates the moment when "the little Buds of their Minds will
begin to open, and their watchful Mamma will be imploy'd, like a skil-
ful Gardener, in assisting and encouraging the charming Flower thro' its
several hopeful Stages to Perfection, when it shall become one of the
principal Ornaments of that delicate Garden, your honour'd Family" (4:
304). "Pardon me, Sir," she hastily adds, "if . . . I am too figurative."

The image of the child or of the child's mind (both Thomson and
Richardson are inclined to elide the two) as a sensitive plant allows for
a complex blend of environmental influences and acknowledges individuality, an important point for Locke also. The eighteenth century
was an age of gardeners as well as of educators. It was now recognized

that careful cultivation and informed intervention might radically improve the production of flowers and fruit. The goal of the nursery was to optimize good growth. Thomson's phrase "delightful task" thus expresses the pleasures of cultivation, whether of children or of plants—perhaps even of feelings.

But while the image of the child as plant allowed for the representation of process, it scarcely affected that of agency: only the gardener possesses agency, so that though this image generally set the power relations between adult and child in a more benevolent mode, the distribution of power remained unchanged. The silence or disappearance of the child from the educational text is tellingly revealed in a later eighteenth-century novel that, in its own eccentric way, offers an exemplar of the role of education in the bourgeois household. Sterne's *Tristram Shandy* is the autobiography of the child as *tabula rasa*. It is preoccupied with John Locke and his theories, both of mental association and education. In the course of the novel, Mr. Shandy sets out to write a "Tristrapaedia" or system of education for his son Tristram, the narrator. Inspired by the example of Xenophon (though the subject was a fashionable one), this was to be a book of instruction for the government of Tristram's childhood and adolescence:

> at which . . . he was three years and something more, indefatigably at work, and at last, had scarce compleated, by his own reckoning, one half of his undertaking: the misfortune was, that I was all that time totally neglected and abandoned to my mother; and what was almost as bad, by the very delay, the first part of the work, upon which my father had spent the most of his pains, was rendered entirely useless,— every day a page or two became of no consequence. (300)

Mr. Shandy approaches his son's education, as he approaches all subjects, from a theoretical rather than a practical angle, with the result that he never actually catches up sufficiently to put his theories into practice. Meanwhile his failure transfers power from the male to the female educator, from the father to the mother; apart from his role as narrator, Tristram himself is nowhere to be seen.

Thomson's lines had set education in a domestic context, seeing it as an aspect of the parents' pleasure in rearing their offspring. Such education had a strong social dimension, since its primary function was to promote "the generous purpose," that love of one's fellow creatures which the age valued so highly. In doing so, his lines reflect a series of crucial shifts in middle-class mores which would help to determine attitudes to the bourgeois family, to women and to children in the next two centuries. The first half of the eighteenth century constituted a point of transition, when the picture of family life suddenly required the child's presence to complete it. One immediate and practical consequence was a renewed interest in the processes of early learning, evident both in educational debate and in the commercial provision of first reading books. Attention to the child within the family was accompanied by a recognition of the importance of the mother's role, not only in early learning but also in the earlier stages of breast-feeding and nurturing. Greater emphasis on the importance of moral and social education further acknowledged women's expertise in these areas, while new educational texts set out to fulfill Thomson's notion of the "delightful task" by making themselves delightful to young readers and their parents. This middle-class domestication of education revealed and began to revalue the previously hidden contributions of women as mothers, teachers, and governesses.

Some of Locke's particular solutions to traditional problems in *Some Thoughts Concerning Education* may unintentionally have contributed to this process of domestication. Locke was anxious to avoid the use of fear to promote discipline. He believed that education was potentially pleasurable and that children's high level of activity, their desire "to be busie," only needed redirecting (190; sec. 129). He saw that the child's division of its activities into work which it didn't enjoy, and play which it did, was essentially arbitrary, especially if you took into account how much of child's play involved imitating adult activities. Problems arising from this distinction might therefore be treated as some kind of "category mistake," which only required redefinition: "I have always had a Fancy, that Learning might be made a Play and Recreation to Children" (208; sec. 148). They might thus be tricked or cheated into enjoying it, since "it is in their Governour's choice, whether Scotch-hoppers shall reward their Dancing, or Dancing their Scotch-hoppers; whether Peg-top, or Reading; playing at Trap or studying the Globes shall be more acceptable and pleasing to them" (190; sec. 129).

This insight inspired Locke's proposal to disguise early lessons by turning them into dice games, with letters replacing the spots, or using a multisided ivory ball such as was used for lottery prizes. The throwing and identifying of particular letters could then be rewarded with apples or cherries. Pamela, with her dissenting background, saw this as " a very pretty Method to cheat Children, as it were, into Learning" (4: 355), and could not approve: "For what may not be apprehended from so early allowing, or rather inculcating, the Use of Dice and Gaming upon the Minds of Children?" (4: 355) she enquired. As Jill Shefrin has shown in her essay "'Make It a Pleasure and Not a Task,'" publishers were nevertheless quick to see the possibilities that Locke's recommendations opened up, and dice were soon replaced with "A totum, or teetotum . . . a spinning top" (255). John Newbery's *Little Pretty Pocket Book* (1744) ("instruction with delight") was sold with a ball or a pincushion, now that learning had legitimately become a game. Mary Collins's *The Child's New Play-Thing* of a year or two earlier came with a folded sheet of alphabet cards such as Locke had recommended, while J. G.'s *"A Play-Book for Children* to allure them to read as soon as they can speak plain" set out to "decoy children into reading." This book, published in 1694, either represents a particularly prompt response to Locke's proposals, or else indicates that the subject was already a topical one in the early 1690s. Twenty years earlier (1675), William Winstanley had issued a pack of geographical cards in which each of the suits was represented by a different continent, so the idea of bringing learning and play together was not entirely new.

J. G.'s *Play-Book* exists in a unique copy in the Bodleian—the more popular such books were, the more likely they were to be loved to death. This one was "composed of small pages not to tire children," anticipating the many miniature books that followed, often on a scale with dolls' tea sets. Thomas Boreman's series of *Gigantic Histories* from the 1740s are miniaturized accounts of London sights—St. Pauls, the Tower, Westminster—complete with appropriate woodcuts and tiny lists of child subscribers in the back, in imitation of the adult books of the day. Though miniature books were scaled down to little hands, books for children were often intended to be enjoyed by mother and child together, if we are to judge by the engraved frontispiece of Newbery's *Little Pretty Pocket Book*, where a fashionably dressed mother reads to her daughter and son in front of the domestic hearth. But how widely available were such children's books? Newbery's were sold at the famous sign of the Bible and Sun in St. Pauls Churchyard, and Boreman's *Gigantic Histories* from the Guildhall, but were similar books for children beginning to be available to mothers living in the provinces?

One mother of the 1740s, Jane Johnson, bringing up a family at Olney in Buckinghamshire, herself prepared a series of early learning aids for her four children. She began with alphabet cards, progressing to individual syllables, words, and then short verses, lessons, prayers, and story cards. Each card is carefully lettered by hand as if printed, and decorated with patterns cut out of Dutch floral paper; many of them incorporate cutout engravings of animals, figures, or scenes. The cards have holes so they can be strung together to make words or sequences of words, and they fit into a series of handmade boxes. The names of the Johnson children—Barbara, George, Robert, and Charles—are worked into the word lists and rhymes. A picture of a dove illustrates the lines:

> O had I wings, I would
> Fly like a dove
> To visit Miss Wrighte
> Who so dearly I love. George Johnson.

Jane Johnson also wrote a fairy tale in which she related the magic adventures of her two elder children, Barbara and George.[1] Here was a mother who clearly found the teaching of her children a delightful task, devoting many hours and much thought to it. The cards and games that Jane Johnson devised are now in the Lilly Library at Indiana; they anticipate the later commercial production of learning cards and manuals, such as those of Ellenor Fenn.[2] But the odds against a collection of this kind—so many little pieces of paper—surviving are enormous. We do not know how many other mute inglorious mothers employed a comparable energy and ingenuity, but one fictional mother, Pamela, was also in the habit of telling stories carefully adapted to her small listeners.

Pamela's role as the teacher of her children confers on her an element of *gravitas*—"delightful task" it may be, but it is also a responsible one. The importance that Locke attributed to early education indirectly enlarged the role of mothers; it also encouraged this particular young mother to embark upon an extended critique of Locke in an area—that of the nursery—where her experience and knowledge presumably exceeded his. Pamela disagrees with several of Locke's propositions on practical grounds, dismissing, for example, his suggestion that children should be encouraged to make their own toys: "whatever be the Good . . . it cannot be equal to the Mischief Children may do themselves in making these Playthings" (4: 351). The kind of tools required to do so were precisely the sort to be kept away from young children. She goes on to suggest that, rather than allowing the child one toy to play with at a time, as Locke had recommended, he should have a cupboard of his own and be encouraged to put his own toys away in it (4: 352).

On the age's great question as to whether children should be whipped, she agrees with Locke, that it must only be used in the last resort, but she rejects his suggestion that punishment is better deferred until the parent has had time to calm down, pointing out that a parent who cannot master his or her own feelings is in any case unfit to punish a child for a comparable lack of control (4: 343). The misbehavior of parents also becomes part of an argument as to whether children should be educated at home by a tutor (as Locke had recommended), or should be sent away to boarding school (the number of boarding schools grew rapidly in the early eighteenth century): "were we to speak of the Generality of Parents, it is to be fear'd, [their conduct] would be an almost insuperable Objection to a Home Education" (4: 337).

The significance of Pamela's critique of Locke is by no means limited to matters of nursery practice: their disagreements act out the central ideological battle of the age—that between the old property-owning classes and the rising bourgeoisie, a struggle as fierce and unremitting (though much more metaphysical) as that between Pamela herself and Mr. B., which had occupied much of the first two volumes of the book. Pamela picks up Locke's argument that giving children small rewards for tasks performed only panders to their love of pleasure, and she counters with the point that even God himself employs a system of rewards. More tellingly, she remarks that a great deal of human life depends on our willingness to undertake unattractive tasks for reward: "he is not the less a good Servant, or a virtuous Man, if he own the Conditions painful, and the Reward necessary to his low State in the World, and that otherwise he would not undergo any Service at all" (4: 308).

Pamela begins to expose Locke's silent class-assumptions in earnest when she reaches the description of the ideal governor or tutor for children: this paragon must have such a host of virtuous qualities that, as she observes, "such a one is hardly possible to be met with, for this *humble* and *slavish* Imployment" (4: 312). She defines it as such on the grounds that domestic tutors "are frequently put upon a Foot with the uppermost Servants" (4: 312), a situation of which she had first-hand experience.

She stumbles painfully over Locke's throwaway phrase, "Besides being well-bred, the Tutor should know the World well" (4: 314), and repudiates his strictures on the bad influence of servants on young children, and his recommendation that a proper distance be observed between children and servants. She points out that to maintain such a distance is to fill children's minds with contempt for those below them (4: 331, 333), and that this is inconsistent with the more humane point Locke had made elsewhere, that children should not be allowed to treat servants rudely, "as if they were of another Race or Species beneath them" (4: 332, 333), and she repeats this phrase in order to endorse the point. Moreover, as she observes, the risks to children from servants might with greater justice be laid at their parents' door: "Give me Leave to add, That it is then of no Avail to wish for discreet Servants, if the Conduct of the Parents is faulty. . . . That Master and Mistress, who would exact from their Servants a Behaviour which they themselves don't practise, will be but ill observ'd" (4: 338).

The underlying point of Pamela's critique of Locke lies in its educational outcome, the eighteenth-century gentleman. She seizes upon Locke's snobbish condemnation of "sheepish Bashfulness" (4: 354) as a form of ill-breeding, in order to point out that "a harden'd Mind, that never doubts itself, must be a Stranger to its own Infirmities; and, suspecting none, is impetuous, over-bearing, incorrigible; and if rich, a Tyrant; if not, possibly an Invader of other Mens Properties" (4: 354–55). The ultimate failure of Locke's educational method is thus Mr. B. himself, who required to be re-educated by Pamela in crucial matters of respect for other people's property, to put it delicately. In thus reassessing self-doubt and the mind that recognizes its own infirmities, Pamela speaks for all the subservient, for servants as well as young women, and perhaps even for children, too. Their position of inferiority may give them special human insights hidden from their masters. Yet at the same time, Pamela can criticize the tendency to dismiss unexpected achievement: "when a poor Girl, in spite of her narrow Education, breaks into Notice, her Genius is immediately tamed by trifling Imployments, lest, perhaps, she should become the Envy of one Sex, and the Equal of the other" (4: 320).

The fourth volume of *Pamela* ends with a letter to Lady G. in which Pamela relates two very simple stories she had made up for her own children, stories of the pleasures that await the four good children who

"Loved the Poor: Spoke kindly to the Servants: Did every thing they were bid to do; . . . there was a happy Family . . . the Masters at their Books; the Misses at their Books too, or their Needles"; and when they grew up, "they marry'd, and made good Papas and Mammas" (4: 439, 440). On the other hand, miseries, suffering, and even death await the four naughty children. The simplicity of the narratives suggests that these listeners were very young—in contrast to the quite different tale Pamela makes up for her illegitimate stepdaughter, Miss Goodwin. Here, her focus on the sexual temptations surrounding young girls recalls the sad fate of Miss Goodwin's mother, Sally Godfrey, as well as Pamela's own story (so different in outcome). As Pamela explains to Lady G., in the tales of the ill-fated Coquetilla, Prudiana, and Profusiana, she had given "the Characters of Persons I have known in one Part or other of my Life, in feigned Names, whose Conduct may serve for Imitation or Warning to my dear attentive Miss" (4: 437). As Pamela finishes the contrasting tale of Prudentia, Miss Goodwin, "smothering [Pamela] with her rapturous Kisses," exclaims "'Prudentia is YOU! Is YOU, indeed!—It *can* be nobody else! . . . I shall be a SECOND PRUDENTIA, indeed I shall!" (4: 452). Yet Prudentia's story is virtually a blank, and thus substantially different from Pamela's own (as the reader, at least, must recognize). The contrast between the stories made up for her own children and the moral tale for Miss Goodwin reflects the power and limitations of maternal education. Billy and Jemmy can be taught by their mother only while they are little; at a later stage, the professionals will be called in, whereas young women, destined for life in the home, can acquire their whole education there.

With a complex mixture of humility and pride that must ultimately be attributed to her author, Pamela rewrites Locke's educational program, anticipating women's increasing involvement in education, both in the home and out of it. This new project aimed at producing "affectionate wives and rational mothers," and began with the teaching of reading and writing, the process that took the child on its first steps towards subjectivity. For to be able to write is to be able to save yourself, as Pamela had saved herself from the exploitation and degradation that threatened her. But if that process began with teaching the child to read, it did not end there. The sixteen-year-old Pamela had taught Mr. B. to acknowledge the existence of other human beings and the validity of their feelings, something that John Locke and his superior education had overlooked. From this point on, the importance of moral teaching began to be recognized, and it soon became the chief aim of writing for children. Eighteenth-century children's books are regularly despised and rejected on the grounds that they are too didactic. Their subsequent neglect suggests our own intolerance of moral earnestness, as well as our failure to identify the comparable, if more covert lessons, present in writing for children today.

Narrow though it was, Pamela's education and her powers of persuasion were her cultural capital, acquisitions that enabled her to save herself and change her situation. While Richardson expressed these acquisitions in the form of a subtle and moving critique of some of his society's favorite assumptions, such an outlook was easily simplified, and vulgarized for consumption by child readers: in 1755 John Newbery ("Trade and plumb cake for ever. Huzza!") published *The Renowned History of Little Goody Two-Shoes*, a book that simultaneously taught reading and acted as an exemplar of the power that reading can give. The text was designed to instruct the young reader, offering her alphabet games to play: "Now, pray little Reader, take this Bodkin, and see if you can point out the Letters from these mixed Alphabets, and tell how they should be placed as well as little Boy Billy" (31). The text gradually introduces the child to the alphabet, syllables, and short words, and then proceeds to give examples of simple sentences, prayers, and lessons, as the method then was. Yet, these lessons are contained within an unforgettable fable of self-help, the story of a female Dick Whittington, a little girl left entirely alone in the world, and who nevertheless climbs out of total destitution by borrowing books from other schoolchildren (she is too poor to afford the minimal fees necessary to attend the village school), teaching herself to read, and then reusing her skills to teach other children. She rises first to become mistress of the dame school, then to marry into the gentry and, finally, as Lady Jones, to spend her last years as a rich and philanthropic widow.

Her first promotion, to teaching the dame school, can be contextualized within society's growing awareness of women's roles in such institutions—from Shenstone's poem *The School-Mistress* (1737–42) to Wordsworth's celebration of his "dame" in the early books of *The Prelude*. Teaching was increasingly a resort of poor but literate women who earned a few pence from it while retaining a degree of respect (even though such schools tended to remain unofficial and unregistered). Goody Two-Shoes combines her teaching with various other adventures—exposing a ghost, preventing a robbery, being ducked for a witch. She also demonstrates in its purest form the ability to pull oneself up socially by one's own boot straps—and entirely without supernatural aid, since part of her purpose is to offer rational explanations of apparently supernatural effects. The book not only tells her story, but, used as an early reader, it also provides all the knowledge necessary for following in Marjorie Meanwell's footsteps. We may go and do likewise.

Goody Two-Shoes is thus an important feminist fable and in some respects markedly ahead of its time in celebrating the pleasures of the independent single woman (in contrast to so much Victorian fiction). Nothing makes Goody happier than becoming dame of the school, while her marriage is treated as a mere interlude, one that confers status rather than companionship (at a time when status was unavailable to women in other forms). Her husband conveniently dies after six years so that she can get on with the serious business of making herself socially useful. Although the story seems to have appealed as much to boys as to girls (or so Charles Lamb's enthusiasm suggests), it is heavily gendered in the sense that working-class lads expected to earn their living by using their physical labor. Books, therefore, served only to distract. As a teacher, Goody can win and retain respect on the basis of her knowledge and intelligence, without having to exploit either her looks or her labor. For boys, education was always class-controlled and end-directed: scholarship and learning, or hunting and war lay open to gentlemen, and a profession or training in a trade or skill to the middle classes, but for a girl, the goal aimed at was marriage, and for that, learning was not always an advantage. Education was thus seen as highly gendered, and it had very different significances for boys and girls.

Because women's resources were so limited, educational books for girls came to lay special emphasis upon the necessity of a moral education. In a society that valued most forms of generosity except female sexual generosity, women had little that they could call their own to give. Yet the very materiality of the world of men might limit their possibilities of spiritual development: what, after all, does it cost Pope's Man of Ross to sustain the poor and needy when he already has a private unearned income? Women, who seldom had any rights to actual property or capital, could find in education a source of spiritual sustenance that was also practically useful, a skill that was more than menial, that could be converted into a living, exchanged, given to others, and recirculated so as to create new readers as well as new recipients for the later stages of moral education, in which women increasingly came to be recognized as expert.

Located halfway between Richardson's *Pamela* and Newbery's *Goody Two-Shoes*, Sarah Fielding's *The Governess, or, Little Female Academy* of 1749 takes moral education for girls as its primary concern. Written by a woman, it has strong claims to be the first fiction specifically addressed to children, the first school story, and the first story to depict children naturalistically. For the rest of the century and well into the next, it was regularly reprinted and widely adapted and adopted as a model by later writers for children—among them, Mme le Prince de Beaumont, Mary Wollstonecraft, Charles and Mary Lamb, and Mrs. Sherwood. Like *Goody Two-Shoes*, it describes a learning process that it sets out to teach, although the process here is far more sophisticated, for this is a book intended for much older readers, and it employs a correspondingly more complex form of interaction with the reader: that of a framing narrative with further inset stories.

Sarah Fielding endorses Pamela's opinion that a good boarding school may prove a more reliable source of moral education than an unsuitable home, but like Pamela, she also recognizes the value of maternal feeling in the education process. Mrs. Teachum opens her school, having lost her husband and two young daughters, and the school becomes an outlet for mothering instincts that would otherwise be frustrated. *The Governess* reflects just how rapidly views of education had changed in the half-century following *Some Thoughts Concerning Education*. Here we are offered a positively maternal vision of education, by women for women, as exclusively female and as closely focused on sensibility as Locke's had been exclusively male and focused upon (good) sense. Moreover, its central concerns point forward to later developments in fiction: *The Governess* was published within six weeks of her brother Henry 's novel *Tom Jones*, another novel about education, which broadly burlesqued both traditional and rational approaches through the pair of schoolmasters, Thwackum and Square, as well as through Blifil, their gruesome end-product, while Tom himself blithely learns from experience, as if anticipating Rousseau's *Émile*. But for Sarah Fielding, a moral education doesn't simply happen through happenstance; it is the outcome of thought and labor. Richardson told her that he considered her knowledge of the human heart superior to her brother's: "His was but as the knowledge of the outside of a clock-work machine, while your's was that of all the finer springs and movements of the inside" (*Letters* 7 Dec. 1756, 330). The value of a serious moral education for women would later be proclaimed by Mary Wollstonecraft, and exemplified by Jane Austen: the scenes of Fanny at Portsmouth in *Mansfield Park* are in a direct line of descent from the kind of moral lessons that Sarah Fielding's *Governess* proposes.

Mrs. Teachum runs a select boarding school for nine young ladies between the ages of eight and fourteen. After the tumultuous quarrel with which the book begins, the girls listen to each others' stories, and each comes to recognize and identify her own characteristic fault, describing how she came to acquire it. The structure formalizes and elicits educative meaning from female narrative, from conversations about people and how they behave. All stories increase our knowledge of the world, and here a series of different types of writing—fairy tale, Eastern tale, drama, allegory, fable—are read aloud and made to yield useful lessons. They alternate with the different and more valuable (because more hard-won) truths of personal experience. Though superficially quite different, *The Governess* has close connections with *Pamela* both in matters of detail and in its more general concerns: the initial idea of writing about a girls' boarding school probably came to Fielding from the scene in the second volume in which Mr. B. takes Pamela to visit just such a boarding school in order to meet his illegitimate daughter, Miss Goodwin. The school turns out to be a model of its kind, and its governess rewards her best pupils by allowing them a "dairy-house breakfast" (2: 330–1). Mrs. Teachum's pupils also visit a dairy for pleasure and exercise. More significantly, Sarah Fielding gives us some sense of what an education along Pamelian lines might actually involve, using something like Pamela's teaching by example through stories specially designed for their particular recipients and derived from personal experience. One crucial point of difference, however, is that where *Pamela* made use of the writing process itself as a way of defining consciousness, Sarah Fielding uses the voice, conversation, and spoken narration—a mode of communication, learning, and recording traditionally associated with (unlettered) women.

Despite being set in a boarding school, *The Governess*, too, subscribes to the view (still much in evidence in the media today) that the bourgeois family is the ultimate source of human happiness. The book ends with the departure from school of Jenny Peace, the eldest and wisest pupil, who had devised and governed the proceedings throughout. The girls' final excursion is a visit to a local stately home. Though its beauties impress the more thoughtless and giddy of the young ladies, when Jenny is invited to give her opinion of it, "she was afraid that poor Lord X—and his Lady were not so happy as might be wished" (226). "Grandeur and Happiness do not always go together," observes Mrs. Teachum sententiously: "all my Endeavours to make you good, are only intended to make you happy" (227). She then asks Jenny to read the fable of the Assembly of the Birds (like Johnson's *Rasselas*, a story of the search for happiness). The winner of the contest turns out to be the only bird that fails to attend the assembly at all, the dove, who is also Jenny Peace herself, as she will be when she is a wife and mother. The dove is found hovering around her nest, waiting for the return of her mate. At this point the fable gears itself up into verse, quoting from Henry Brooke's poem "The Sparrow and the Dove" (*Fables for the Female Sex*, 1747), which culminates in a picture of the dove's domestic joy, as her partner feeds their nestlings:

> While all, collected at the Sight,
> And silent, thro' supreme Delight,
> The Fair high Heav'n of Bliss beguiles,
> And on her Lord and Infants smiles. (236)

The joys of familial nurture are, of course, ironized by the boarding school setting, as well as by the several inset stories of unhappy family and marital experiences that culminate in the girls' visit to the house of Lord X—, and we are left with the sad paradox that the new education in moral feeling here envisaged was directly derived from an ideal of bourgeois marriage that in practice regularly failed to meet the hopes and expectations it occasioned. Ahead lay two very different cultural developments, both of which may be traced back to the shift in women's role within education here described: the nineteenth-century idealism of (middle-class) motherhood, in which women utilized their moral education for the benefit of their families, and its opposite and counter, the Woman's Movement, in which education promised, ultimately, to carry women out of the domestic sphere altogether.

NOTES

1. This story is described by Victor Watson in "Jane Johnson: A Very Pretty Story to Tell Children." The notebook containing her story was acquired by the Bodleian in 1996.

2. See Shefrin for a discussion of Ellenor Fenn's learning cards 263–64.

WORKS CITED

Anon. *The Renowned History of Little Goody Two-Shoes*. 1766. Facsim. ed. London: Griffith, 1881.

Brooks, Henry. "The Sparrow and the Dove." *Fables for the Female Sex*. Edward Moore and Henry Brooks. London, 1747.

Fielding, Sarah. *The Governess, or Little Female Academy*. 1749. Ed. Jill E. Grey. London: Oxford UP, 1968.

Locke, John. *Some Thoughts Concerning Education*. 1693. Ed. John W. and Jean S. Yolton. Oxford: Clarendon, 1989.

Richardson, Samuel. *Pamela*. 1740–41. 4 vols. Stratford-upon-Avon: Shakespeare Head, 1929.

———. *Selected Letters of Samuel Richardson*. Ed. John J. Carroll. Oxford: Clarendon, 1964.

Shefrin, Jill. "'Make It a Pleasure and Not a Task': Educational Games for Children in Georgian England." *Princeton University Library Chronicle* 60.2 (Winter 1999): 251–75.

Sterne, Laurence. *The Life and Opinions of Tristram Shandy, Gentleman*. Ed. Ian Campbell Ross. Oxford: Clarendon, 1983.

Thomson, James. *The Seasons* and *The Castle of Indolence*. Ed. James Sambrook. Oxford: Clarendon, 1972.

Watson, Victor. "Jane Johnson: A Very Pretty Story to Tell Children." *Opening the Nursery Door: Reading, Writing and Childhood 1600–1900*. Ed. Mary Hilton, Morag Styles, and Victor Watson. London: Routledge, 1997. 31–46.

Part 2

READING THE RATIONAL DAMES

Mother of All Discourses
Anna Barbauld's Lessons for Children

William McCarthy

For nearly a century after her death, Anna Letitia Barbauld was remembered chiefly as "Mrs. Barbauld," author of *Lessons for Children* and
Hymns in Prose for Children and creator of "Little Charles," the infant hero
of *Lessons*. *Lessons* and *Hymns* were immensely influential in their time;
they were reprinted throughout the nineteenth century in England and
the United States, and their effect on nineteenth- and early twentieth-
century middle-class people, who learned to read from them, is incalcu-
lable. *Hymns* has been credited with influencing Barbauld's younger contemporaries, Blake (Summerfield 215–19) and Wordsworth (Pickering;
Zall). Elizabeth Barrett Browning could still quote the opening lines of
Lessons for Children at age thirty-nine: "Oh! how I remember it, book &
all," she recalls in a letter (3: 87; 26 February 1845). Another woman,
this one nearly anonymous, remembered in 1869 how as a little girl she
used to take pleasure in reading *Hymns in Prose* "aloud, in a solemn voice,
page after page" (S. A. A.). In an 1881 essay on Barbauld, Anne Thackeray Ritchie, daughter of William Makepeace Thackeray and stepaunt to

Author's note: This essay was delivered as a paper at the Dedication Conference of the Cotsen Children's Library, Princeton University, 30 October 1997, and published in the *Princeton
University Library Chronicle*, 60 (1999): 196–219. The essay owes its existence to Mitzi Myers,
for it was she who urged the Cotsen's curator, Andrea Immel, to invite me to speak. My enormous intellectual debts to Mitzi are acknowledged, however inadequately, in the text. I am
happy to register once again my thanks to Andrea also, for her invitation and for much scholarly help. The text has been revised for the present volume.

Virginia Woolf, represents her own child as asking for *Lessons for Children* "every morning" (588).[1]

The way bits of these texts might get into a child's memory and stay there into sophisticated adulthood can perhaps be sensed by noticing verbal similarities between passages in Barbauld and lines in that formidable modernist poem, *The Waste Land*. The passages turn on the words "Come," "I will show you," and "shadow." From *Hymns in Prose*: "Come, and I will shew you what is beautiful" (20 [Hymn IV]); "Come, let us go into the thick shade" (43 [Hymn VII]); and from *Lessons for Children*: "Come, let us go home, it is evening. See . . . how tall my shadow is. It is like a great black giant stalking after me." There follows a sentence about how shadows differ at evening and at noon (1808 ed., 3: 42–43).[2] In *The Waste Land* Eliot writes:

> (Come in under the shadow of this red rock),
> And I will show you something different from either
> Your shadow at morning striding behind you
> Or your shadow at evening rising to meet you . . . (53–54)

Whether Eliot, as a boy in St. Louis, Missouri, circa 1891, learned to read from Mrs. Barbauld, I do not know, but I would not be surprised if he did. These four lines from *The Waste Land* are just the kind of conflation one would expect in fugitive memory-traces of impressive texts.

To her contemporaries, Barbauld was known originally as a poet and essayist, and subsequently as a political pamphleteer, a role in which she made conservatives nervous by showing rather too much approval of Enlightenment politics and the French Revolution. Later still she acted as an editor, a reviewer, the first biographer of Samuel Richardson, and the author of a substantial body of commentary on the English novel. She was also an eminent teacher, having managed, with her husband, a famous school for boys at Palgrave in Suffolk, where her children's books were written. She belonged to the first generation of really successful women of letters in England—a generation that included Maria Edgeworth and Hannah More, who also, of course, wrote for the young or the newly lettered. As Mitzi Myers observes, the women writers of that generation tended to perform as pedagogues ("Of Mice and Mothers" 256–58).

The fact that Barbauld performed as a pedagogue came eventually to count against her in literary history; the very books for which she was long most remembered came to be regarded as grounds for dismissing and even reviling her.[3] A reason for that eclipse may be found in the way the history of children's literature came to be imagined. At least to an outsider, the canonical story about the way children's literature developed appears almost Manichaean in its need to dichotomize, and then to extol or damn its dichotomized terms. Whether the binary terms are *instruction* and *delight*, *didacticism* and *imagination*, or—the title of one of the most fiercely Manichaean books on the subject—*Fantasy and Reason*, the canonical story consistently extols books in which it is pleased to find "imagination," "fantasy," and "delight," and as consistently deprecates, deplores, or denounces books it suspects of "didactic" intent or a "rationalist" agenda. F. J. Harvey Darton declared in 1932 that "children's books were always the scene of a battle between instruction and amusement, between restraint and freedom, between hesitant morality and spontaneous happiness" (v–vi), and in E. Nesbit's 1913 story, *Wet Magic*, there occurs a literal battle between the "Book People," who include Barbauld, and the child characters they seek to subjugate (188–89).[4] This dichotomizing reappears even in the most current forms of cultural critique. Thus Alan Richardson, in many ways an admirable historical researcher, nevertheless grounds an entire study of pedagogical texts published between 1780 and 1830 in a simple dualism between sinister forces making for an oppressive social hegemony and the "subaltern" groups— children, the poor, the colonized—whose willing submission to that hegemony the pedagogues were supposedly working to achieve. That the hegemonists in his version include Wordsworth, usually counted a hero on the side of child liberation, does nothing to change the Manichaean structure of his argument.

Mitzi Myers, to whom my understanding of issues in children's literature is enormously indebted, argued on more than one occasion that this dichotomizing should be understood as an ongoing reinscription of Wordsworth's myth of the "natural" boy, the Boy of Winander, tutored directly by wild Nature or at most by a "parent hen," and gloriously independent of formal instruction by socializing agents such as actual mothers ("Of Mice and Mothers" 265–67; "Little Girls Lost" 134–35).[5] His American descendant is, of course, Huckleberry Finn, always poised to "light out for the Territory" to escape some woman's tutelage. The ancestor of both boys, surely, is Rousseau's Émile, who is supposed to experience woman mainly in the form of the maternal breast, whose only instruction consists of interactions with the world mediated (when at all) by a father figure, and who must never hear of book learning before age fifteen. All these boys embody the deep hatred of culture itself that has been Rousseau's troublesome gift to modern ideology: "All our wisdom," he writes in *Émile*, "consists in servile prejudices. All our practices are only subjection, impediment, and constraint. Civil man is born, lives, and dies in slavery" (42).

Who, then, are those tyrannical "Book People" created by this dichotomizing? Myers argues that they are precisely the women who wrote for children. "Theorists," as she puts it in one place, "forget that in everyday life mothers mediate access to oral and written word alike; they are the bearers of language and literature—and historically women have authored the bulk of writing for children" ("Gender, Genres" 274). The maternal is associated with the transmission of culture, especially at a pre-rational level; culture, in Rousseau-inspired ideology, is a force for oppression; the maternal therefore corresponds to the oppressor. The male, on the other hand, is associated with a natural, wild freedom. One reason why we should distrust the canonical binaries of children's literature historiography is their pat coincidence with this other binary, gender. How curious that the historiography treats as Enemies of Childhood those women who publicized, who modelled in print, the role performed at home by countless middle-class mothers doing what middle-class mothers did for generations: reading with their children, teaching their children to read.

Barbauld published *Lessons for Children* in 1778–1779 in four volumes sized to fit a child's hand. In her preface to Volume I she lays claim to one innovation, the use of large type and wide margins to make the books reader-friendly. To appreciate her claim one need only compare pages from *Lessons* (see fig. 4.1) with pages from one of its predecessors, such as *The Child's New Play-Thing* (1763), as shown in fig. 4.2. Earlier publishers for children, such as Newbery, provided children with books of the right size for their hands, but they did not perceive that, while the *page* must be small, the *print* needs to be larger than ordinary in relation to it. They provided, instead, small pages with correspondingly crowded type. Barbauld may have been the originator, and was almost certainly the popularizer, of the modern practice of printing children's books in large type with wide margins.[6]

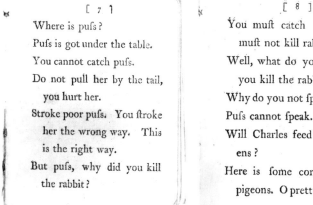

[7]

Where is pufs?

Pufs is got under the table.

You cannot catch pufs.

Do not pull her by the tail, you hurt her.

Stroke poor pufs. You ftroke her the wrong way. This is the right way.

But pufs, why did you kill the rabbit?

[8]

You muft catch mice, you muft not kill rabbits.

Well, what do you fay, did you kill the rabbit?

Why do you not fpeak, pufs? Pufs cannot fpeak.

Will Charles feed the chickens?

Here is fome corn for the pigeons. O pretty pigeons.

Figure 4.1. Pages from Anna Letitia Barbauld, *Lessons for Children from Two to Three Years Old*. Imperfect copy. London, 1782 (?). Private collection.

Barbauld's contemporaries, however, credited her with a much more important innovation: the method of "chit-chat," as one reviewer of *Lessons* called it (*Critical Review* 160), or informal dialogue between parent and child, a method which became for some decades a commonplace of books for children. It was she, Frances Burney noted, who began "the new Walk" in children's books (4: 187). Barbauld's imitator, Sarah Trimmer, accurately characterizes that "new Walk" as "a species of writing, in the style of *familiar conversation*, which is certainly much better suited to the capacities of young children than any that preceded it" (63–64).

To appreciate the sort of difference they had in mind, compare again the pages from *Lessons* (fig. 4.1) with those from *The Child's New Play-Thing* (fig. 4.2). The earlier primer is abstract and superficially analytical in its structure: abstract in that the lists of syllables and words are unconnected to or by any contextualizing narrative; analytical—but superficially so—in that they embody an "atomistic" concept of reading. In this pedagogy, first you learn sounds (such as "ska ske ski sko sku" [*Child's New Play-Thing* 20]), then you compose those sounds into words, and then you compose words into sentences. The analysis seems based more on ideas of permutation and combination than on the realities of English. (In English, how often does one encounter the combination *sko*?) It also

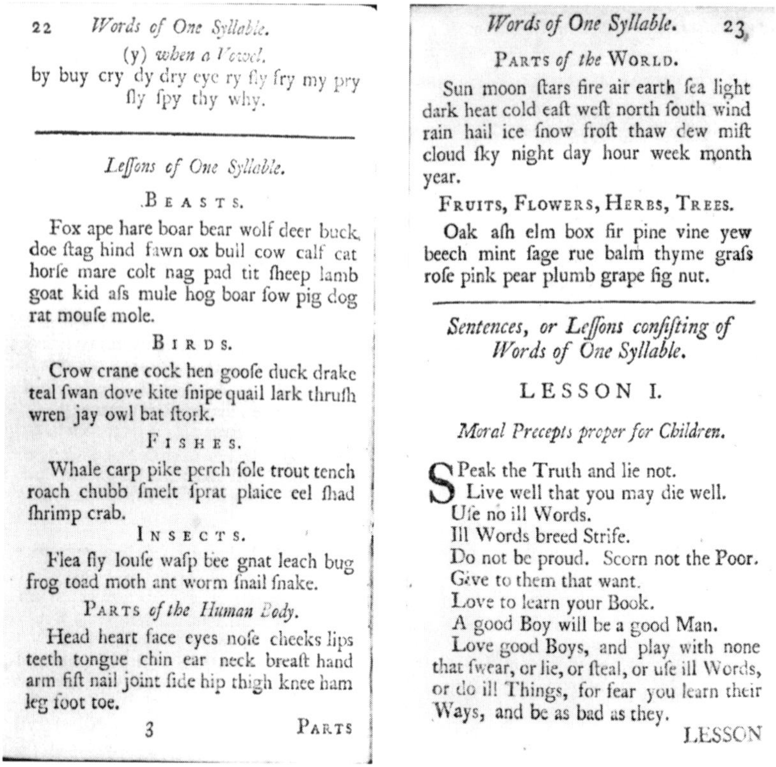

22   *Words of One Syllable.*
(y) *when a Vowel.*
by buy cry dy dry eye ry fly fry my pry
fly fpy thy why.

Leffons of One Syllable.

.B E A S T S.

Fox ape hare boar bear wolf deer buck,
doe ftag hind fawn ox bull cow calf cat
horfe mare colt nag pad tit fheep lamb
goat kid afs mule hog boar fow pig dog
rat moufe mole.

B I R D S.

Crow crane cock hen goofe duck drake
teal fwan dove kite fnipe quail lark thrufh
wren jay owl bat ftork.

F I S H E S.

Whale carp pike perch fole trout tench
roach chubb fmelt fprat plaice eel fhad
fhrimp crab.

I N S E C T S.

Flea fly loufe wafp bee gnat leach bug
frog toad moth ant worm fnail fnake.

P A R T S *of the Human Body.*

Head heart face eyes nofe cheeks lips
teeth tongue chin ear neck breaft hand
arm fift nail joint fide hip thigh knee ham
leg foot toe.

3   P A R T S

Words of One Syllable.   23,

P A R T S *of the* W O R L D.

Sun moon ftars fire air earth fea light
dark heat cold eaft weft north fouth wind
rain hail ice fnow froft thaw dew mift
cloud fky night day hour week month
year.

F R U I T S, F L O W E R S, H E R B S, T R E E S.

Oak afh elm box fir pine vine yew
beech mint fage rue balm thyme grafs
rofe pink pear plumb grape fig nut.

---

*Sentences, or Leffons confifting of
Words of One Syllable.*

L E S S O N   I.

Moral Precepts proper for Children.

S Peak the Truth and lie not.
Live well that you may die well.
Ufe no ill Words.
Ill Words breed Strife.
Do not be proud. Scorn not the Poor.
Give to them that want.
Love to learn your Book.
A good Boy will be a good Man.
Love good Boys, and play with none
that fwear, or lie, or fteal, or ufe ill Words,
or do ill Things, for fear you learn their
Ways, and be as bad as they.

L E S S O N

Figure 4.2. Pages from *The Child's New Play-Thing; Being a Spelling-Book Intended to make the Learning to Read a Diversion instead of a Task.* 8th ed. London, 1763. Courtesy of the Cotsen Children's Library, Rare Books and Special Collections, Princeton University Library.

produces a formidable page, uninviting in its remoteness from any child's
(or any language-learner's) ordinary linguistic experience. Because it cannot be connected to anything the child normally does, it can only be
learned by rote. It was of books such as these that a former pupil at Palgrave School, George Crabb (not the poet, but rather a general writer
best known for a work on English synonymy) must have been thinking
in an 1801 essay on *The Order and Method of Instructing Children*: education today, he writes, "is a mere system of mechanism. Children collect
a number of sounds to which no ideas are affixed. They learn sounds but
not things" (6).[7]

Ordinary linguistic experience is always contextual, always occurs in a time and place, in relation to some activity. A language, in the oft-quoted words of Ludwig Wittgenstein, is "a form of life" (11). Barbauld's *Lessons* anticipate Wittgenstein's understanding of language by being contextualized, by being forms of life. They consist of transactions between the boy, Charles, and a mother on whose lap he is young enough to sit. They take Charles through his day, from breakfast to bedtime. (Yes, *bedtime*. Volume I of *Lessons for Children* seems also to have been the first child's book to end with putting the child to bed.) In the course of that day the lessons notice people, objects, and animals from Charles's ordinary surroundings: Puss (the cat), Papa, garden insects, household wares, food and clothing, paraphernalia of rural daily life. Each lesson is a dialogue, a narrative, or a description situated in Charles's actual or potential experience, a "language game" in Wittgenstein's sense: a "form of life." Again, Crabb theorizes Barbauld's method:

> We ought to direct . . . [children's] attention to the objects as they occur in common life. Thus, whether we are eating, drinking, talking, walking, reading, or amusing ourselves, we shall find numberless things that deserve the attention of a child; by which at the same time the names of the several objects may be more strikingly fixed upon its mind. . . . Those objects ought to be as numerous as possible, in order to initiate the child into a general acquaintance with things and words; as the sun, moon, stars, animals, birds, beasts, trees, flowers, herbs, chairs, tables, and all the objects of art and nature which fall within the sphere of observation. (36–38)

Virtually every object Crabb here names is mentioned in *Lessons*, always represented as something experienced or observed by Charles.

In today's terminology, the reading pedagogy that *Lessons for Children* challenged would be called phonics, and the pedagogy of *Lessons* whole language. It is possible that Barbauld was the originator of whole-language reading pedagogy; at least, she appears to have been the first to publish it. To use these terms is, of course, to call up one of today's political hot potatoes. A few years ago Nicholas Lemann reported in *The Atlantic Monthly* on a battle in California between partisans of phonics and proponents of whole-language teaching. Whole-language pedagogy assumes that learning to read is like learning to speak in the first place, "a natural, unconscious process best fostered by unstructured immersion." In phonics, on the other hand, children must "learn the letters and letter combinations that convey the English language's forty-four sounds; they can then read whole words by decoding them from their component phonemes" (129).

The debate between these pedagogies is politicized because, as Lemann noted, phonics is "a longstanding cause of the political right," while whole language "is generally a cause of the left" (130). Were they so aligned in 1778? Not on the surface. Barbauld was indeed a political liberal; her aim as a teacher was to produce "intelligent citizens," citizens who could manage and criticize public affairs (McCarthy, "Celebrated Academy" 295). But Sarah Trimmer, who appreciated Barbauld's pedagogy in *Lessons*, was a social and political conservative. Still, Crabb's critique of phonics as a system of "mere mechanism" in which only sounds are learned does appear to imply a liberal Enlightenment preference for concepts, the materials of thinking, over memorized performance—the material, one is tempted to say, of unthinking submission.

The manuscript of *Lessons* is long lost, but the book's original form can be inferred from other, surviving manuscripts. These are little lessons written in print hand for Barbauld's great niece, probably around 1812, when the niece was four. In the lesson shown in fig. 4.3, "Anna" is the great niece and "Mrs Robley" is a neighbor in Stoke Newington, North London, where Barbauld was then living.[8] Another lesson for Anna refers to Queen Elizabeth's Walk in Stoke Newington, where Anna later remembered often walking with Barbauld in childhood (LeBreton 42). These details show that Barbauld's lessons were originally biographical: they probably arose from actual incidents and actual transactions. "Little Charles" was her adopted son, who came to live with her just short of his second birthday in the summer of 1777. Volume 1 of *Lessons* was printed by the end of the year and published in May 1778, and Volumes 2 and 3 in June. Volume 1 is for children between two and three years old, Charles's age at the time of publication. Volumes 2 and 3 are for children three years old, and Volume 4 (published in 1779) for children between three and four, again Charles's age. The lessons thus keep pace with the actual growth of the historic Charles. Since they presumably originated in real incidents of his and his mother's life together, they document Barbauld's performance as the mother of a small boy. They are materials for her biography as well as models of a pedagogy. They are

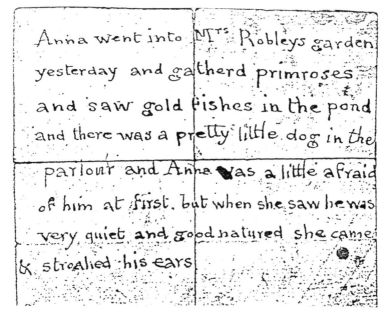

Anna went into Mrs Robleys garden yesterday and gatherd primroses and saw gold fishes in the pond and there was a pretty little dog in the parlour and Anna was a little afraid of him at first. but when she saw he was very quiet and good natured she came & stroaked his ears

Figure 4.3. Manuscript reading lesson by Anna Letitia Barbauld for her niece, ca. 1812. Reproduced with kind permission of Mrs. Alison Brodribb.

private, in some ways intimate, and at the same time public, even in some ways a manifesto. "This little publication," she writes in her preface, "was made for a particular child, but the public is welcome to the use of it" (1: [iii]).[9] That is an understated way of saying "Here is how I did it. Others can, too."

Did what? Taught my child to read; but also, more broadly, educated him. For *Lessons* is much more than a reading primer. While offering reading material suitably graded as to difficulty for children from ages two to four, it also initiates the child into the elements of society's symbol-systems and conceptual structures, inculcates an ethics, and encourages him to develop a certain kind of sensibility. All of this is accomplished narratively and dialogically by the voice of a "powerful mother who controls access to literacy and culture, naming the world and defining reality" (Myers, "Of Mice and Mothers" 269).[10] She is a mother who takes the preceptorial role assigned by Rousseau to the male, a mother whose understanding of the world is tacitly but deeply philosophical: an Enlightenment mother, *une philosophe*. But also she is a mother who does all this casually, and as it were by the way, in the midst of carrying on her daily chores; a mother who is an ordinary middle-class woman. Her voice represents the intellectual architecture of *Lessons* but never calls attention to it.

To do justice to the density of implication and breadth of reference in *Lessons*, one would have to go through it page by page, commenting on almost every line. This necessity is true especially of Volume 1, in which primal elements of conceptual systems seem to emerge out of the very blankness of the page. In the later volumes, as more formal structures are introduced, the texture of implication thins out a little. This thinning is a consequence of the graded, or developmental, order of *Lessons*, the aim of which is to secure the child's understanding of the concepts that ground other concepts. As Crabb puts it, "a child [ought never] to spell and pronounce what has not been previously presented to his understanding" (38). Barbauld's method, and Crabb's description of it, would appear to anticipate the development in modern cognitive science of what is called "schema theory."[11] A *schema* is the mental representation of an experience. Schema theory conceptualizes the mind as an organizing agent which works hierarchically, "embedding" one representation within another in an order ascending from simple to complex. Thus, for example, to understand the sentence, "The little girl heard the ice cream man and rushed upstairs to get her piggy bank," one needs not only to have a concept (or schema) of ice cream and of modes of selling ice cream, but also a schema (or set of schemata) for buying and selling; embedded in these would be subordinate schemata for money itself, for places where money is kept (piggy banks), and so on. It is on this kind of hierarchical, progressive structure that *Lessons for Children* is founded, in contrast to its predecessors.

For illustration, refer back to the pages from *The Child's New Play-Thing* (fig. 4.2). Like *Lessons*, previous primers had sought to inculcate an ethics, but they did it in the bluntest possible way, by sandbagging the child reader with lists of what Barbauld calls "grave remarks," sentences like "Speak the Truth and lie not" and "Live well that you may die well." Like the lists of syllables and words, these remarks are without context and abstracted from any reference to forms of life. In her preface to *Lessons*, Barbauld notes that "a grave remark, or a connected story . . . is above [the] capacity" of a child from two to three (1: [iii]); he cannot be expected to understand them, stripped as they are of any relation to his experience or previous learning. Hence, in *Lessons* she introduces its single specimen of a "grave remark" only after preparing a context for it:

> Now we must make hay. Where is your fork and rake? Spread the hay. Now make it up in cocks. Now tumble on the hay-cock. There[,] cover him up with hay. How sweet the hay smells! O, it is very hot! No matter; you must make hay while the sun shines. You must work well. (2: 20–21)

Here Mother is teaching Charles how to make hay, an operation which has to be performed during the heat of the day. It is therefore literally true that "you must make hay while the sun shines," and the literal truth of the remark underpins its figurative meaning—a meaning which she then states outright ("You must work well"). Charles is being introduced to the possibility of inferring from a specific experience to a general idea.

Likewise with "connected story," which Barbauld also thought to be above a small child's capacity. She departs from previous reading primers by introducing elements of story, or narrative, piecemeal before introducing her first story. Again, in terms of schema theory she can be said to be introducing the simpler schemata which, combined, constitute the complex schema, "story." Thus Charles is encouraged to think in terms of past-present-future (the schema of temporality) by being reminded that he *was* a baby, is *now* a little boy, and *will* (when older) have a horse to ride like Papa (1: 46, 36–37, 39). He is encouraged to think in terms of *sequentiality* by being led through the days of the week and the twelve months of the year (2: 5–8). Only after that does Mother tell him his first story.[12]

Barbauld does not, of course, expect a two-year-old reader to understand all the implications of what she is doing. It is a truism about children's books that they are written for two audiences at once, the child and the parent. They instruct and/or amuse each on different levels. In *Lessons for Children*, those levels are congruent and mutually supportive: the meaning available to the child's understanding enfolds philosophical and ethical possibilities which the adult will notice now and the child later, as he matures.[13]

This is already evident in the first lesson in the first volume, about Puss and the rabbit (1: 7–8 [see fig. 4.1]). Much food for thought is offered here. First, the fact of death: a rabbit has been killed. The structure of *Lessons* being, among other things, recursive, dead animals—and in particular, dead rabbits—are going to reappear throughout. Eventually the possibility that Charles himself could be injured or killed will be mooted (2: 20). Barbauld was never a euphemist in her view of life and did not encourage bowdlerizing experience for the young. (Some of the parents who bought *Lessons* felt differently: in the Yale copy of Volume 2, references to death have been vigorously inked out.[14])

But there is much more here than death to notice. The question put to Puss, "why did you kill the rabbit?" is both funny and profound. It is profound because it points toward ultimate issues: why are cats permitted to kill rabbits? Why is cruelty in the world? Or *is* it cruelty for one animal to kill another? Puss is supposed to catch mice, not kill rabbits— but "supposed" by whom? Is it part of the Divine Plan that cats are ordained to catch mice, or is it rather that human beings demand certain behaviors of them and condemn others? Is Puss guilty? The question is funny because, of course, Puss can't answer it. Everybody knows you do not ask animals to account for their actions—everybody, that is, except two-year-olds like Charles, who do not yet realize that animals lack speech. "Puss cannot speak," and that ends the discussion. We smile at Mother (or perhaps it is at Charles) earnestly moralizing to Puss, and as we do so—indeed, *because* we do so—we realize that Barbauld has just quietly linked morality to the faculty of language. No language, no morality, she is saying by way of the most straight-faced irony, voicing the child's innocent question.[15]

Charles, on the other hand, has obligations toward Puss, even if Puss may have none toward rabbits. He must not pull her tail, for that hurts her, and he must stroke her fur the right way. These obligations are enjoined in the pages immediately following the one in which he begins to read his book—another way in which Barbauld associates language with ethics. Mother is a classical humanist. She is going to teach Charles that the power of language distinguishes him from all other animals. Although in some ways he resembles other animals (he is a biological being like them in that he, like them, eats food and grows [1: 11; 2: 65], and they are "cultural" beings like him in that they, like him, have, at least metaphorically, "houses" and "wear clothing" [1: 20, 2: 51]), Charles is nevertheless unique in being endowed with the power of language, and this endowment confers obligations on those who possess it, humans.[16]

The morality of *Lessons* is not enforced by any reference to God or religious sanction. That would be much too abstract: "spiritual . . . ideas," Crabb declares, ". . . have never been produced in the mind of man but by the progress of cultivation" (38). Unlike earlier primers, which often lead the child straight from word-lists to catechisms ("Who made you?" "Who redeemed you?" they ask[17]), *Lessons* is entirely free of religious doctrine; it is entirely secular, with no suggestion of any power transcending the empirically known natural world. (Barbauld reserved that for *Hymns in Prose*.) The do's and don'ts of human ethics are enforced, then, by human means: Mother's approval or disapproval, promises of rewards (such as having a garden of one's own to grow [2: 62–63]), Mother's teasing mockery (1: 45–46), or—very occasionally—tales telling of punishments or rewards to other boys who did wrong or did right. Such a tale, the very first regular story in *Lessons* (2: 73–77), tells of a boy who cruelly mistreated a robin, pulling out its feathers and starving it to death. This boy—whose name, significantly, Mother does not remember (except that it was not Charles)—soon finds himself abandoned by his parents and shunned by his neighbors: "we do not love cruel, naughty boys." Being too young to look after himself, he wanders into the woods and disappears; Mother believes he was eaten by bears. The boy is punished, in short, by exile from the human community, and in exile he cannot survive. The story may be blunt in its message, but its moral realism is unimpeachable. For the human, there is no alternative to being a socialized creature except extinction. There are, Wordsworth to the contrary notwithstanding, no Boys of Winander; every human being needs other human beings in order to live. Humans are communal entities, or, in a phrase favored by the young Karl Marx, "species beings."[18]

I quote Marx to suggest that the idea of society represented by *Lessons* belongs to that strain of middle-class Enlightenment humanist ethics which eventuated in Marx. Barbauld herself knew it from the ethical writings of James Harris and Francis Hutcheson, who each promote an ethics of human relatedness ("the natural affections of the social kind," as Hutcheson calls them [41]).[19] There is no question, in *Lessons* as in Harris, Hutcheson, and Marx, of the Romantic individual glorying in some transcendental solitude; people always live together, in some form of mutual dependence. ("For . . . without society with . . . our fellows, their mutual aids, and an intercourse of friendly offices, mankind could neither be brought to life nor preserved in it": Hutcheson 113.) Charles is given a proof of human interdependence—as well as a lesson in political economy—when he demands bread and butter, and is then asked where the bread and butter are to come from: twelve people, plying as many trades, must set to work to satisfy Charles's appetite (3: 27–31). *The Wealth of Nations*, with its famous illustration of division of labor in pin-making, had been published the year before Charles joined the Barbauld household, but Barbauld was probably recalling a passage in "Concerning Happiness, A Dialogue" (1744) by Harris. There Harris leads his interlocutor to admit that getting the bare necessities of civilized life requires the labor of at least twenty different arts and industries (150–52). Thus another of *Lessons's* ethical imperatives is *work*: "Every body works, but little babies; they cannot work" (2: 62). Everyone must *share*, as well. Given some raisins, Charles is directed to share them with Billy and Sally (1: 32); in a tale about three schoolboys, each of whom receives a cake from home, the model boy is the one who shares his cake with friends, and then gives some to a beggar (4: 13–31).

Consistently with a middle-class liberal idea of human relations, *Lessons* assumes that within the embrace of the social and natural orders, creatures follow their own individual agendas. The butterfly in the garden does not answer Charles's questions, will not let us catch it, and flies off (1: 18). The bee "will not sting you if you let it alone" (1: 19). Mother has work to do, so Charles must go away (1: 24). A man on horseback is going somewhere else and does not notice us (1: 27). Another man is plowing a field, going about his own business (2: 12). And Charles himself gradually individuates, at first sitting on Mother's lap to read and then, as he grows older, using a little stool. One can even trace his separation from Mother in the fabric of the dialogues themselves: in Volume 1 of *Lessons* it is not always clear which of them is speaking, so that at times one has the impression of a merged or shared subjectivity (Myers, "Of Mice and Mothers" 268), whereas in later volumes they are more easily distinguished. The lessons themselves develop clearer, firmer outlines, becoming more formal and more systematic as Charles matures.

As he grows, Charles learns that external reality does not always behave as he wishes. In the middle-class liberalism enacted by *Lessons*, we can see the origins of Freud's "reality principle." "I want my dinner, I want pudding," Charles demands in one lesson, and moreover, "I want some wine." But his demand for dinner has to wait until dinner is ready, and his demand for wine must wait until he is a much bigger boy; in the meantime, "here is water" (1: 21–23).[20] In another lesson Charles bumps into a table and gets mad at it for having hit him; to which Mother replies, "No, not naughty table, silly boy! The table did not run against Charles, Charles ran against the table" (1: 44). Here Barbauld is retelling wisdom from the Stoic Epictetus. In Elizabeth Carter's translation (1758), Epictetus chides the practice of blaming others for one's misfortunes by instancing a nanny who scolds the stone over which her child trips—instead of scolding the child for not watching his step (164). In one of the most famous lessons, Charles and Mother travel to France, where Charles, rather like an American tourist, confidently expects people to understand what he says to them in English, and thus meets a new kind of social limit to his wishes: incomprehension, inability to make others understand what he wants. Instead, he is laughed at for his ignorance, and retreats home baffled (4: 66–71).

But reality as imagined in *Lessons* is not simply a site of stubbed egos. It is equally a site of *pleasure*, of keen enjoyment of daily sensations. Despite a vague reputation for being grimly Presbyterian, Barbauld was in fact an advocate of pleasure. She has Mother engage Charles in play, hiding him under Mother's apron while Papa looks for him, pretending that Papa's walking stick is a horse (1: 12), running out in the snow to make snowballs (1: 34), promising that he will learn to slide on the ice, to skate, and to swim (1: 39; 2: 9–10). One standing topic of complaint in histories of children's books, especially Geoffrey Summerfield's *Fantasy and Reason*, is the injunctions of "rationalists" such as John Locke to guard children from servants, who are thought to corrupt them with old wives' tales and sundry bad habits (9–10, 79–80). In *Lessons*, the servant Betty brings Charles some gifts from a local fair: a toy gun and a sword. This act could have made trouble; Barbauld inclined toward pacifism. Does Mother therefore rebuff Betty's gifts? Not at all. She thanks Betty for them and encourages Charles to "charge your gun. Now let it off. Pop!" (1: 47–48). Here Barbauld allows play to take precedence even over principle.

She is also alive to the pleasures of sense. Some of the finest passages in *Lessons* are those in which Mother solicits Charles's attention to a sight or smell of the world around them—to snow ("how white it is, and how soft it is" [1: 34]), to a rainbow ("O what fine colours! Pretty bright rainbow!" [2: 14–15]), to a nosegay of flowers ("Smell! it is very sweet" [2: 17]). But for sheer sensuousness we can choose between the one in which she offers him a strawberry:

> Do you love strawberries and cream? Let us go then and gather some strawberries. They are ripe now. Here is a very large one. It is almost too big to go into your mouth. (2: 22–23)

or the passage describing a cake made for Harry, a schoolboy:

> It was very large, and stuffed full of plums and sweetmeats, orange and citron; and it was iced all over with sugar: it was white and smooth on the top like snow. (4: 15–16)

Even unpleasant experiences, such as a cold day or "dark, dismal November," can be made into scenes of pleasure: "we will sit by the fire, and read, and tell stories" (2: 37–38). If conditions deny pleasure now, there are also the compensations of fantasy. Thus when it is too dirty for Charles to walk outside, Mother encourages him to look ahead to the day when "he shall have breeches, and a little pair of boots, and then he shall go in the dirt" (1: 36). Even when she is teaching Charles something "useful," Mother tends to notice its aesthetic or amusement value. So, when introducing him at the end of Volume 1 to money (50–52), she observes the following order in treating the subject. She shows him a guinea, a crown, a half crown, a shilling, and a sixpence. The first thing she does is to spin the guinea on the tabletop, that is, to play with it. Only after that does she say what money is used for: to buy food. And finally, she has Charles give some to a beggar. Thus a hierarchy is implied: play, utility, ethics.

The practical aim of *Lessons* is to prepare Charles to be a capable schoolboy. *Lessons* offers, indeed, the rudiments of an entire school curriculum, or what John Newbery called "The Circle of the Sciences." In the course of teaching Charles to read, *Lessons* introduces him to botany, zoology, numbers, change of state in chemistry (by way of melting snow), the money system, the calendar, geography, meteorology, agriculture, political economy, geology, astronomy. In keeping with her always recursive, incremental method, Mother introduces each at first just as a hint, a glance in the passing flux of Charles's experience, and then more formally later on, when he is older. It was, to be sure, precisely the scientific-minded child that Wordsworth deplored in *The Prelude*, and his complaint has tarred *Lessons* along with the Edgeworths and other writers for children who were influenced by Barbauld's infant pedagogy. But Wordsworth and the historians mesmerized by him should have read *Lessons* more attentively. Natural and social sciences are not all that it inculcates. It aims as well to foster in Charles the sensibility of a poet, and it does so by a number of means.

To begin with, the very language of *Lessons* has always been praised, even by commentators hostile to its program, for its lucid simplicity, for sheer idiom. So potentially poetic has it been found to be that passages from it have even been printed as poetry, as I discovered some years ago on a visit to Ireland. Hanging on the wall at William Butler Yeats's tower, Thoor Ballylee, were two prints featuring texts from *Lessons for Children* arranged as free verse and illustrated by Pamela Coleman Smith. They were Nos. 9 and 12 in a series of "Broad Sheets" by one of Yeats's publishers, Elkin Mathews of London.

I will return to the poetry of *Lessons*, but first let us notice some particular moves that Barbauld makes to encourage Charles to feel and to think poetically. She models sensibility when she has Mother express pleasure at the beauty of something ("Pretty bright rainbow!"). She prompts Charles toward thinking poetically by making Mother point out analogies between things, analogies that can become metaphors. A snail's shell is its "house" (1: 20), a lamb's wool is its "petticoat" (2: 51). The most formalized such lesson occurs when Charles and Mother go outdoors to take tea (3: 15–18). But where is a table? Ah, a tree-stump will be a table. What to sit on? Let this turf and bank be our chairs. And we even have a carpet! Where? asks Charles; the carpet is in the house. The *grass*, answers Mother, "is the carpet out of doors." In technical terms, Mother has disposed Charles to think metaphorically by giving him both tenor and vehicle for the first two figures, then only the vehicle for the third (carpet). When, puzzled, he thinks of the literal (indoor) carpet, she initiates him into metaphor by explaining the likeness of grass to carpet. Crabb describes her method: "As a figure of speech is founded upon some analogy between two objects, it will be necessary only to point out these analogies, in order to render them intelligible" (51–52).

Finally, Barbauld goes so far as to indulge in the traditional fable device of making objects and animals speak—in contradiction to her prevailing theme that only humans have language, a contradiction that vexed one of the book's first reviewers, Thomas Bentley, business partner of Josiah Wedgwood the potter:

> Why will this good Lady go contrary to Nature, and persist in making dumb creatures speak?—However innocently and usefully fabulous, allegorical, and poetic language may be applied to animate natural descriptions, and to enforce the lessons of wisdom when addressed to persons of riper years; we humbly conceive that as the bodies of children should be nourished with the food of nature, so their tender minds should be fed and replenished with simplicity and truth. (488)[21]

Bentley's objections, flat-footed in their attachment to verisimilitude and even literal truth, nevertheless recognize what Barbauld is doing. She initiates Charles into the fictive, allegorical, animistic discourse often associated with poetry, and into tropes and symbols that are staples of poetry. It is in prose poetry that *Lessons* bids farewell to Charles, with two contrasting vignettes, Sun and Moon. Sun speaks first, declaring its own might and majesty, its domination and nurture of all things, describing its crown of rays and its blinding brightness, and naming the birds who associate with it in poetry, the Eagle and the Lark (4: 95–104). Sun is a male power, the absolute monarch that poetic figuration often makes it (cf. Louis XIV, the "Sun King"). Moon speaks last, declaring its gentleness, kindness, and quiet beauty:

> The Moon says My name is Moon; I shine to give you light in the night when the sun is set. I am very beautiful and white like silver. You may look at me always, for I am not so bright as to dazzle your eyes, and I never scorch you. I am mild and gentle. I let even the little glow-worms shine, which are quite dark by day. The stars shine all around me, but I am larger and brighter than the stars, and I look like a large pearl amongst a great many small sparkling diamonds. When you are asleep I shine through your curtains with my gentle beams, and I say Sleep on, poor little tired boy, and I will not disturb you. The nightingale sings to me, who sings better than all the birds of the air. She sits upon a thorn and sings melodiously all night long, while the dew lies upon the grass, and every thing is still and silent all around. (4: 105–08)

Moon is female, pluralist, and democratic. The passage is at once political allegory and a child's version of one of Barbauld's own finest poems, "A Summer Evening's Meditation," a poem that opens with a description of the mild Moon displacing "her brother" the Sun, "the sultry tyrant of the south," in the evening sky (*Poems* 81). Charles is being prepared to appreciate his mother's art. More broadly, every middle-class child is being prepared to be a poet, in sensibility if not in practice.

A mother who can do all that *Lessons* does, who is at once a poet, a student of the sciences, a philosophical moralist; who has a wide fund of information and knows exactly at what pace to impart it to a small child; who has a proto-Wittgensteinian understanding of language, a proto-Marxian concept of social ethics, a proto-Freudian idea of the individual's relation to the real world: such a mother would seem to be a theoretical ideal, a Utopian figure. Barbauld herself was such a mother in reality, for she was a person of rare intellect. (Her contemporaries honored her power of mind, after their fashion, by calling it "masculine.") Yet *Lessons*, for all the realism of its vocabulary, does have a Utopian aspect. Its representation of Mother is Utopian in the way that much feminist writing of the seventeenth and eighteenth centuries is necessarily Utopian: it represents a woman as she could be if social conditions allowed her to develop and employ her intellect. Barbauld's philosophical mother is simply a well-educated woman, but, because serious formal education was a thing denied to most middle-class women in Barbauld's time, she is *ipso facto* a Utopian figure, what a middle-class woman could be if she were well educated.

And yet this Mother of All Discourses is also, touchingly, a perfectly ordinary middle-class woman, one whose acts and speech sometimes seem to be sheer transcription from Barbauld's daily life. She is affectionate to Charles, but her affection is sometimes abrupt and impulsive: "Come and give mamma three kisses," one lesson begins, a trifle imperiously (1: 13). She exhibits what her contemporary Edward Gibbon would call, in one of his favorite phrases, "humane inconsistency," though a strict rationalist might call it "self-contradiction." Thus, having informed Charles that Butterfly won't answer him when he speaks to it, she nevertheless indulges his innocent animism by saying "Good night" to Snail (1: 18, 20). Having, like a good "rational parent," treated Charles's fall as harmless ("Never mind it," she tells him), she then turns around and kisses his scratched arm: "There, now it is well" (1: 43). Having taught

Charles the right way to stroke Puss's fur, she directs him (in a lesson added to a later edition) deliberately to stroke it the wrong way, to make it throw a spark on a cold night (1808 ed., 2: 7). Having almost broken our hearts by her description of a hare hounded to death and torn apart by dogs, she nevertheless does not scruple to point out that the corpse can be eaten (4: 84–88).

Though obviously attentive and affectionate, Mother is capable of being irritable with Charles, and Barbauld is not ashamed to represent her irritability. A "showing-the-features" game between them turns peevish when Mother asks "what are legs for," Charles answers "To walk with," and Mother brings him up short: "Then do not make mamma carry you. Walk yourself. Here are two good legs" (1: 26). Remembering that these lessons probably do transcribe interactions between Barbauld and her adopted son, it is worth noting that Barbauld did impress her intimates as showing, from time to time, "certain indications of temper" (Aikin [53])—as, of course, anyone does, but in late eighteenth-century social expectations about gender, women were supposed not to manifest temper.[22] Likewise, Mother is allowed to show a mix of anger and alarm when Charles seems about to eat a pin: "O do not put it in your mouth, that is a very, very naughty trick," she exclaims, without explaining, as a rational parent might be expected to do, *why* he should not eat a pin (1: 32).[23]

And finally, Mother, like everyone else in *Lessons*, is allowed to have agendas which preclude attention to Charles. One lesson ends with a blunt dismissal: "Go away now, I am busy" (1: 24). Another ends with Charles's plaintive request to her to lay aside her sewing and play with him, but his request is left hanging, unanswered (1: 33).

It has been customary for feminist commentators on late eighteenth-century women's texts to deplore their "domestication" of the female, that is, their inscription of the woman as Mother or as otherwise confined to the home.[24] That Barbauld regarded mothering as an important and valuable activity is written all over *Lessons*, and in that sense *Lessons* does certainly "domesticate" the female. But if "domestic" means "narrowed," "confined," "restricted," Mother in *Lessons* is none of these things. It seems to me that one of the signal achievements of *Lessons for Children* is the Utopian realism by which it is able to propose a mother who is both philosopher and ordinary woman, both Mother of All Discourses and—to borrow a phrase from current popular psychology—a "good-enough" mother.

NOTES

1. On the nineteenth-century popularity of "Little Charles," see Yonge 234: "Probably three-fourths of the gentry of the last three generations have learnt to read by his assistance." *Little Charles* is the title of one American edition from the 1830s that, like many nineteenth-century editions, rewrote and versified selections from *Lessons*. On nineteenth-century reprints see the *British Library Catalogue of Printed Books* and the *National Union Catalogue*; between them they list some 53 editions of *Hymns in Prose* between 1801 and 1905, and some 27 editions of *Lessons for Children* between 1801 and 1878 (these numbers do not include translations). Moreover, the *Archives of the House of Longman* indicate four more editions each of *Hymns* and *Lessons* not shown in either the *BLC* or the *NUC* (Impression Books, 1835–1865, 1841–1873, 1832, and 1852 [Reels 37 and 40]); the number of copies printed is always 1,000, 2,000, or 2,500.

2. The 1808 edition of *Lessons* includes new passages and was the one, presumably, on which all subsequent editions were based. (I have collated with 1808 only the texts of London 1812 and London 1821 [vol. 1] and 1825 [vols. 2–4].) See note 9 for additional information on my quotations from *Lessons*.

3. For the history of Barbauld's posthumous reception, see McCarthy, "A 'High-Minded Christian Lady.'" For an example of reviling her, see Hazard 33–37.

4. See also Summerfield. Peter Hunt remarks that "the most common view of the history of children's literature is that the books have progressed steadily from didacticism to freedom. . . . But as history it is false because children's books can never be free of didacticism or adult ideological freight" (xii). This sensible view is a bit compromised by the sentence that follows it: "But it is important to see children's books as the site of a good deal of anarchy."

5. Wordsworth celebrates the Boy of Winander, one of "A race of real children; not too wise, / Too learned, or too good," in *The Prelude*, 5: 364–425. This wild boy is proposed as a wholesome contrast to the alleged product of the "modern system" of education, satirized in 293–330. The "parent hen" (246) is Wordsworth's metaphor for the mother who, "through a grace / Of modest meekness [and] simple-mindedness" (290–91), makes no conscious effort to educate her child.

6. In the use of large type and wide margins she seems to have been preceded by one J. G., who in 1694 published *A Play-Book for Children to allure them to Read as soon as they can speak plain* (Sloane 211). By 1778 J. G. had probably been long forgotten; Sarah Trimmer, at any rate, concurred with Barbauld's claim: "infant readers are farther indebted to her for the happy thought of printing *first books*, in a large clear type. These useful hints given by Mrs. B. have been generally adopted by her cotemporaries" (64). For an account of one such contemporary,

Ellenor Fenn, see Immel: in 1783 Fenn followed Barbauld in calling for large type and wide margins, giving the same reason that Barbauld had given, the weakness of the child's eyes.

7. For Crabb's identity see McCarthy, "Celebrated Academy" 351. When he attended Palgrave is not known; it may have been after Barbauld's departure.

8. Ann Robley is listed in 1821 as occupant of a house in St. Mary's Parish, Stoke Newington (Land-Tax Assessment Book, MS 4517, Hackney Archives, London).

9. Quotations come mainly from the composite set of *Lessons* (British Library C.121.aa.16), of which Vol. 1 (*Lessons for Children, from two to three years old*) is 1787 and Vols. 2–4 (*Lessons for Children of three years old*, Parts 1 and 2, and *Lessons for Children from three to four years old*) are 1788. Quotations from 1: 51ff (lacking in BL) are from the Bodleian Library copy (Opie Collection). Barbauld responded to a test printing of *Lessons* in January 1778 (*Works* 2: 19–20). Dates of publication for Vols. 1–3 come from entries in *Records of the . . . Company of Stationers*, Part 1: Entries of Copies, 1770–1812.

One indication of the originally private character of *Lessons* and of its survival in the published books can be seen at 1: 41, where Charles is asked "Who is that lady?" and told to give her a kiss; the lady is never identified, and the text at that point appears allusive in the manner of a private document.

10. The same view of Mother is taken by Robbins. Like Myers's "Of Mice and Mothers," this is a splendid essay, with which my reading of *Lessons* entirely concurs.

11. For my understanding of schema theory, I depend on Crawford and Chaffin 4–6. The ice cream example is theirs.

12. This analytic turn in Barbauld's work is found again in her life of novelist Samuel Richardson (1804), where she analytically discriminates different kinds of narrative viewpoint—omniscient, continuous first-person, and epistolary—and discusses the advantages and disadvantages of each. This discussion was a novelty at the time, and one reviewer ridiculed it as "childish" (*Edinburgh Review* 24)—an accurate, albeit hostile, perception that Barbauld was applying her analytical powers to a pedagogical end here, just as she had in *Lessons*.

13. In the postmodern critical climate of deep suspicion of claims for the coherence of different "levels" within texts, it may appear naive (or worse) to propose that *Lessons* achieves congruence between its "child" and "adult" meanings. I am happy, therefore, to be able to cite similar claims by theorists who cannot be accused of naivete, Knoepflmacher and Myers: "Authors who write for children inevitably create a colloquy between past and present selves. Yet such conversations are neither unconscious nor necessarily riven by strife. . . . Most of the writers, artists, and editors we consider in this volume manage to integrate the conflicting voices they heed. Their constructs involve interplay and cross-fertilization rather than a hostile internal cross fire" (vii).

14. The Yale copy (1794) is Beinecke Library Ib 94/t2/v.1. For Barbauld's disapproval of bowdlerized books for the young, see "On the Uses of History": "If a young person were to read only the Beauties of History, or . . . stories and characters in which all that was vicious should be left out, he might as well, for any real acquaintance with life he would gain, have been reading all the while Sir Charles Grandison or the Princess of Cleves" (134).

15. Richard Lovell Edgeworth, who wrote a lengthy commentary on *Lessons* as soon as it was published, objected to Barbauld's raising the issues of death and animal "morality": "The Idea of killing is in itself very complex and if explained serves only to excite terror. And how can a child be made to comprehend why a Cat should catch mice & not kill Rabbits; indeed I know of no reason why this species of Honesty is to be expected from an Animal of Prey" (f54v), quoted with permission of the Bodleian Library. Edgeworth seems either unaware of or unwilling to entertain the possibility that Barbauld wrote ironically.

16. Barbauld's emphasis on speech as the distinguishing feature of the human goes back to Aristotle's *Politics*. In a later work Barbauld refines her distinction between animals and humans: "Your cattle cannot discourse; they like each other's company, they herd together, they have a variety of tones by which they can make each other sensible when they are pleased, angry, or in pain, but they cannot discourse. To discourse is to communicate ideas, that is thoughts, to compare, to reason upon them. This is the privilege of man" (*Civic Sermons* 4).

Elsewhere in *Lessons* (2: 54–56), Barbauld treats human language as simultaneously biological and cultural, a sophisticated and very "modern" understanding of it. She achieves this by setting up a long series of parallel sentences, beginning, "The dog barks. The hog grunts. The pig squeaks. The horse neighs," and so on through twenty-nine animals and their utterances, to end with "Charles talks." The syntactical parallels between "Charles talks" and the preceding sentences place "talks" on a par with "barks," "grunts," and "squeaks," i.e., "biologize" it; while the difference between the proper name "Charles" and the generic names "the dog," "the hog," and so on distinguishes him from them as a cultural being. The passage adumbrates one of Wittgenstein's remarks: "Commanding, questioning, recounting, chatting, are as much a part of our *natural* history as walking, eating, drinking, playing" (12 [my emphasis]).

17. *Tom Thumb's Play-Book* 20. Another catechism appears in *The Royal Primer* 23ff. If not catechisms, the books print "Scripture lessons" or simplified psalms; in one form or another, God makes his appearance not long after page twenty.

18. The term "species-being" (*gattungswesen*) came to Marx from Ludwig Feuerbach (Tucker 33n); for examples of Marx's use of it, see Tucker 43 (where Marx equates "species-life" with "society") and 76 (where he identifies the collective activity of producing culture in the very broadest sense of that word as proof that humans are "conscious species being[s]"). Barbauld's linking of

morality with language (above), though derived from Aristotle, also approximates Marx, who calls language "practical consciousness" (158).

Apparent exceptions to the necessary sociality of human beings were the feral children who occasionally came to notice in the eighteenth century. The "Wild Boy of Aveyron," for example, had lived for some twelve years in the woods, learning to feed himself on raw tubers. His behavior, when discovered, was not at all social, and there was considerable debate over how to classify him (Lane).

19. For Barbauld's knowledge of Hutcheson, see McCarthy and Kraft 14, 18. She read "Concerning Happiness" by James Harris at age sixteen, "with great edification" (*Works* 2: 126).

20. In this lesson dinner is linked to clock time, and this does bear out the contentions of Foucaultians like Alan Richardson about the creation of "self-regulating subjects" to the extent that Charles must regulate his appetite by clock time. See Richardson 28–30.

21. This review is attributed to Bentley by Nangle.

22. Aikin's manuscript is quoted by permission of Mr. Simon Martyn. Arguing against indulgence in anger, Hester Chapone, a widely admired writer on women's education, devotes a chapter of her *Letters on the Improvement of the Mind* (1773) to "the Government of the Temper": "Gentleness, meekness, and patience, are [woman's] peculiar distinctions; and an enraged woman is one of the most disgusting sights in nature"; "peevishness, though not so violent . . . in its immediate effects, is still more unamiable than passion" (76, 79). Barbauld herself shocked contemporaries by showing anger in her political pamphlet, *An Address to the Opposers of the Repeal of the Corporation and Test Acts* (1790). Horace Walpole condemned her as a "virago" (11: 169), and William Keate, throwing up his hands in dismay, could only fall back on a quotation from Pope: "And in soft bosoms dwells such mighty rage?" (64).

23. In some theories, the "rational parent" was supposed to allow the child to experience the natural consequences of its acts instead of being "prejudiced" by parental indoctrination. In a later essay "On Prejudice" (1800) Barbauld tests the limits of such ultra-empiricist dogma: "A child may be allowed to find out for himself that boiling water will scald his fingers, and mustard bite his tongue; but he must be *prejudiced* against ratsbane, because the experiment would be too costly" (*Works* 2: 336).

24. A forceful example of the argument that eighteenth-century culture made motherhood into a trap is Bowers. In view of Rousseau's notorious insistence in *Émile* that women resign their public amusements and "return" to their "natural" obligations as mothers (a view which, as Bowers shows, did not originate with Rousseau), it is understandable that today's feminist commentators would distrust texts that advocated or inscribed domesticity for women. Still, domesticity was not a topic that Rousseau or anyone else owned; rather, it was

a subject of contest among competing viewpoints, some of which were recognizably feminist. I'm suggesting that Barbauld's inscription of domesticity, at least in *Lessons*, was one of its feminist treatments.

WORKS CITED

Aikin, Lucy. Family History. Ms. Microfilm. *The Archives of the House of Longman.* Cambridge: Chadwyck-Healey, 1978.

[Barbauld, Anna Letitia.] *Civic Sermons to the People. Number 1.* London: Johnson, 1792.

[———]. *Hymns in Prose for Children.* London: J. Johnson, 1781.

[———]. *Lessons for Children.* 4 vols. London: J. Johnson, 1787–88.

———. "On the Uses of History." *A Legacy for Young Ladies.* Ed. Lucy Aikin. London: Longman, 1826. 117–64.

———. *The Poems of Anna Letitia Barbauld.* Ed. William McCarthy and Elizabeth Kraft. Athens: U of Georgia P, 1994.

———. *Works.* Ed. Lucy Aikin. 2 vols. London: Longman, 1825.

[Bentley, Thomas]. Rev. of *Lessons for Children. Monthly Review* 59 (1778): 25–28.

Bowers, Toni. *The Politics of Motherhood: British Writing and Culture 1680–1760.* Cambridge: Cambridge UP, 1996.

Browning, Elizabeth Barrett. *The Letters of Elizabeth Barrett Browning to Mary Russell Mitford, 1836–1854.* Ed. Meredith B. Raymond and Mary Rose Sullivan. 3 vols. Np. Armstrong Browning Library of Baylor U, Browning Institute, Wedgestone P, and Wellesley College, 1983.

Burney, Frances. *The Journals and Letters of Fanny Burney (Madame d'Arblay).* Ed. Joyce Hemlow, et al. 12 vols. Oxford: Clarendon, 1972–1984.

Chapone, Hester Mulso. *The Works of Mrs. Chapone.* New ed. Edinburgh: John Thomson, 1807.

The Child's New Play-Thing: Being a Spelling-Book Intended to make the Learning to Read, a Diversion instead of a Task. 8th ed. London, 1763.

Rev. of *The Correspondence of Samuel Richardson,* by Anna Letitia Barbauld. *Edinburgh Review* 5 (1805): 23–44.

Crabb, George. *The Order and Method of Instructing Children, with Strictures on the Modern System of Education.* London: Longman, 1801.

Crawford, Mary, and Roger Chaffin. "The Reader's Construction of Meaning: Cognitive Research on Gender and Comprehension." *Gender and Reading: Essays on Readers, Texts, and Contexts.* Ed. Elizabeth A. Flynn and Patrocinio P. Schweickart. Baltimore: Johns Hopkins UP, 1986. 3–30.

Darton, F. J. Harvey. *Children's Books in England: Five Centuries of Social Life.* Cambridge: Cambridge UP, 1932.

Edgeworth, Richard Lovell. Commentary on *Lessons for Children.* MS Eng. misc. c. 895. Bodleian Library, Oxford.

Eliot, T. S. *Collected Poems 1909–1962.* New York: Harcourt, 1963.

Epictetus. *Moral Discourses.* Trans. Elizabeth Carter. 1758. London: Dent, 1957.

Harris, James. "Concerning Happiness: A Dialogue." *Three Treatises.* 5th ed. London, 1792.

Hazard, Paul. *Books, Children and Men.* Trans. Marguerite Mitchell. Boston: Horn Book, 1944.

Hunt, Peter. Editor's Preface. *Children's Literature: An Illustrated History.* Ed. Peter Hunt. Oxford: Oxford UP, 1995.

Hutcheson, Francis. *A Short Introduction to Moral Philosophy.* 1747. Dublin, 1787.

Immel, Andrea. "'Mistress of Infantine Language': Lady Ellenor Fenn, Her Set of Toys, and the 'Education of Each Moment.'" *Children's Literature* 25 (1997): 215–28.

Keate, William. *A Free Examination of Dr. Price's and Dr. Priestly's Sermons.* London: J. Dodsley, 1790.

Knoepflmacher, U. C., and Mitzi Myers. "From the Editors: 'Cross-Writing' and the Reconceptualizing of Children's Literary Studies." *Children's Literature* 25 (1997): vii–xvii.

Lane, Harlan. *The Wild Boy of Aveyron.* Cambridge: Harvard UP, 1976.

[LeBreton, Anna Letitia]. *Memories of Seventy Years, by one of a Literary Family.* Ed. Mrs. Herbert Martin. London: Griffith, 1883.

Lemann, Nicholas. "The Reading Wars." *Atlantic Monthly* Nov. 1997: 128–34.

Rev. of *Lessons for Children,* by Anna Letitia Barbauld. *Critical Review* 46 (1778): 160.

McCarthy, William. "The Celebrated Academy at Palgrave: A Documentary History of Anna Letitia Barbauld's School." *Age of Johnson* 8 (1997): 279–392.

———. "A 'High-Minded Christian Lady': The Posthumous Reception of Anna Letitia Barbauld." *Romanticism and Women Poets: Opening the Doors of Reception.* Ed. Harriet Linkin and Stephen Behrendt. UP of Kentucky, 1999. 165–91.

———, and Elizabeth Kraft. Introduction. *Selected Poetry and Prose.* By Anna Letitia Barbauld. Peterborough, ON: Broadview, 2001. 11–32.

Myers, Mitzi. "Gender, Genres, Generations: Artist–Mothers and the Scripting of Girls' Lives." *NWSA Journal* 2 (1990): 273–81.

———. "Little Girls Lost: Rewriting Romantic Childhood, Righting Gender and Genre." *Teaching Children's Literature: Issues, Pedagogy, Resources.* Ed. Glenn Edward Sadler. New York: MLA, 1992. 131–42.

———. "Of Mice and Mothers: Mrs. Barbauld's 'New Walk' and Gendered Codes in Children's Literature." *Feminine Principles and Women's Experience in*

American Composition and Rhetoric. Ed. Louise Wetherbee Phelps and Janet Emig. Pittsburgh: U of Pittsburgh P, 1995. 255–88.

Nangle, Benjamin C. *The Monthly Review, First Series, 1749–1789: Indexes of Contributors and Articles.* Oxford: Clarendon, 1934.

Nesbit, E[dith]. *Wet Magic.* 1913. London: Ernest Benn, 1958.

Pickering, Sam. "Mrs. Barbauld's *Hymns in Prose*: 'An Air-Blown Particle' of Romanticism?" *Southern Humanities Review* 9 (1975): 259–68.

Records of the Worshipful Company of Stationers 1554–1920. Ed. Robin Myers. Microfilm. Cambridge: Chadwyck-Healey, 1985.

Richardson, Alan. *Literature, Education, and Romanticism: Reading as Social Practice, 1780–1832.* Cambridge: Cambridge UP, 1994.

[Ritchie, Anne Thackeray]. "Mrs. Barbauld." *Cornhill Magazine* 44 (1881): 581–603.

Robbins, Sarah. "*Lessons for Children* and Teaching Mothers: Mrs. Barbauld's Primer for the Textual Construction of Middle-Class Domestic Pedagogy." *Lion and the Unicorn* 17 (1993): 135–51.

Rousseau, Jean-Jacques. *Émile; or On Education.* Trans. Allan Bloom. New York: Basic, 1979.

The Royal Primer. London: J. Newbery, [c. 1776].

S. A. A. "Notable North Londoners. No. VI. Anna Letitia Barbauld." *North Londoner* 13 March 1869: 83.

Sloane, William. *Children's Books in England and America in the Seventeenth Century.* New York: King's Crown, 1955.

Summerfield, Geoffrey. *Fantasy and Reason: Children's Literature in the Eighteenth Century.* Athens: U of Georgia P, 1985.

Tom Thumb's Play-Book. Boston: A. Barclay, [c. 1760].

Trimmer, Sarah. "Observations on the Changes which have taken place in Books for Children and Young Persons." *Guardian of Education* 1 (1803): 61–66.

Tucker, Robert C., ed. *The Marx-Engels Reader.* 2nd ed. New York: Norton, 1978.

Walpole, Horace. *Correspondence.* Ed. W. S. Lewis, et al. 48 vols. New Haven: Yale UP, 1937–1983.

Wittgenstein, Ludwig. *Philosophical Investigations: The English Text of the Third Edition.* Trans. G. E. M. Anscombe. New York: Macmillan, 1968.

Wordsworth, William. *The Prelude: A Parallel Text.* Ed. J. C. Maxwell. Harmondsworth: Penguin, 1971.

Yonge, Charlotte. "Children's Literature of the Last Century. I. Nursery Books of the Eighteenth Century." *Macmillan's Magazine* 20 (1869): 229–37.

Zall, P. M. "Wordsworth's 'Ode' and Mrs. Barbauld's *Hymns.*" *Wordsworth Circle* 1 (1970): 177–79.

• 5 •

Gender, Nationalism, and Science in Hannah More's Pedagogical Plays for Children

Marjean D. Purinton

$\mathscr{I}$n "Hannah More's Tracts for the Times: Social Fiction and Female Ideology," Mitzi Myers challenges us to think beyond the popular novel and consider didactic genres intended to socialize juvenile and lower-class readers, discourses in which "female authors evaded cultural silencing to speak with teacherly force and sometimes with technical innovation" (264–65). Although Myers nods specifically to Hannah More's *Cheap Repository Tracts* (1795–1798) as that didactic discourse expressing "teacherly force" and "technical innovation," an examination of More's early pedagogical dramas, *Sacred Dramas* (1782) and "The Search After Happiness: A Pastoral Drama for Young Ladies" (1762), yields similarly important insights about More's pedagogical responses to the cultural, class, gender, and religious changes in Great Britain at the end of the eighteenth century. Often dismissed as juvenilia composed early in her career before her conversion to the Evangelical movement, *Sacred Dramas* is doubly significant: first, in what it reveals about the function of drama in More's own process of scripting her public voice and social-literary role; and second, in what is contributes to our understanding of the cultural and political issues with which young women were engaged during the Georgian period. *Sacred Dramas* deploys gender as a contested category through which to interrogate issues of nationalism and science.

While *Sacred Dramas* has, in the limited criticism it has received, generally been seen as a series of purely didactic retellings of Old Testament stories, I want to suggest that *Sacred Dramas* tells us much about the cultural and political issues with which More and other iconoclastic female thinkers of the period were engaged. *Sacred Dramas* portrays the larger issues of late eighteenth-century English society that reach beyond the religiosity of the Evangelical circle or the pedagogical morality of female education. In particular, *Sacred Dramas* is concerned with issues central to Romantic thought, negotiations of nationalism and imperialism, and of the supernatural and science, all of which are displaced onto and articulated through gender. As a category, gender mediates private passions and public actions, and defines emerging bourgeois ideology with domestic ideals. *Sacred Dramas* is therefore a simultaneously moral and political enactment, suggesting a powerful relationship between the governance of the nation and the regulation of the passions. *Sacred Dramas* consequently infuses passions with multiple meanings, significations resonating with the period's moral, political, and scientific pursuits designed to regulate bodies and behaviors.

SCRIPTING A PUBLIC VOICE

Like other women writers of her day, More expressed conflicted views about the theater as a pedagogical site. On the one hand, she recognized its pedagogical potential, as both *Sacred Dramas* and "The Search After Happiness" illustrate; on the other hand, she feared its artificiality and spectacle as antithetical to the reforms in female manners that she envisioned. More was surrounded by theatrical celebrities, the Sheridans, the Garricks, and Sarah Siddons. She saw David Garrick act on twenty-seven nights during one season, and it was while she was staying at the Garricks' villa in Hampton, in a room set aside for her writing and in the companionship of his widow, that More wrote *Sacred Dramas* (Meakin 110, 136–50). Jane Williams reports that More had a strong predilection for dramatic exhibitions, cherishing the belief that the stage might be made a powerful instrument in effecting the moral improvement of society (317). According to Annette Meakin, More envisioned purifying the stage with her *Sacred Dramas*, its pedagogical potential capable of reaching the audience as well as the theater itself (150–51).

Despite the antitheatrical position of Christian leaders, the young Hannah embraced the potential offered by the changing attitudes about theater's function in society. More avidly read drama and frequently attended the theater. She envisioned her dramas for young women as a vehicle for preparing them for roles as philanthropic social workers, as informed mothers and wives, and she wrote them specifically for private, educational settings rather than for the public venues deemed dangerous for women. In the Preface to "The Search After Happiness," More expresses an earnest wish "to furnish a substitute for the improper custom of allowing plays, and those not always of the purest kind, to be acted by young ladies in boarding schools" (110–11). Although "The Search After Happiness" was commonly performed at girls' boarding schools throughout Britain as a replacement for "those more dangerous amusements" (Preface to "Search After Happiness" 111), More was cautiously aware that acting in fickle and fashionable roles and playing morally suspect characters could undermine the girls' personal integrity (Ford 8).[1] *Sacred Dramas*, in fact, was intended for private readings rather than performance, although it was acted by children at the Park Street girls' school managed by the More sisters before being published in 1782 (Harland 84, Jones 15).

More was particularly suspicious of the influences of foreign drama. In her 1799 *Strictures on the Modern System of Female Education*, More criticizes Gothic drama, specifically German drama. She sees Schiller's tragedy *The Robbers* as detrimental to religious principles for women and "is *now acting in England by persons of quality!*" (1: 39). She is especially critical of the German drama *Stranger* that features an adultress who is "presented to our view in the most pleasing and fascinating colours" (1: 46). More contends that the playwright has been far too successful "in making the audience consider the husband as an unrelenting savage" (1: 47).[2] While these spectacles are clearly dangerous dramas, More nonetheless acknowledges the effectiveness of drama as an instructional strategy. She advises teachers that performance and enactments give knowledge meaning and shape: "Confine not your instructions to mere verbal rituals and dry systems; but instruct their feelings; by lively images, and by a warm practical application of what they read to their own hearts and circumstances " (1: 246). At the same time, More remains cautious about the potential temptation for women to transfer the dramas of the classroom to their decorum in adulthood, for the theatrical "show" is not proper for the emergent bourgeois morality: "Talents which have *display* for their object despise the narrow stage of home: they demand mankind for their spectators, and the world for their theatre" (2: 163).

Later in her life, in 1830, More wrote a "Preface to the Tragedies," a prose discourse to accompany her three early five-act dramas produced in the patent theaters, *The Invincible Captive* (1774), *Percy* (1777), and *The Fatal Falsehood* (1779). Here she recants some of her youthful enthusiasm for drama and the theater but nonetheless remains conflicted about its harmfulness or usefulness to pedagogy. She acknowledges that the stage possesses a superiority of mental pleasure "over every other species of public entertainment," and she hopes that "under certain restrictions, and under an improved form, it might be made to contribute to instruction as well as to pleasure" (502).[3] Nevertheless, More alleges that "the English dramatic poets are in general more licentious than those of most other countries" and that "the stage attained its highest degree of dissoluteness" despite David Garrick's efforts toward its purification (503). She expresses her concern for the ways in which the theater influences its young and impressionable spectators. For women theatergoers, the passion that is the most alluring and dangerous is love. More asserts that for the innocent young girl who is already attracted to romance and poetry, frequenting the theater is likely to cause feelings to be "transplanted from the theatre to the closet; they are made to become a standard of action, and are brought home as the regulators of life and manners" (507). More's concerns are displaced onto and articulated by Cleora, the young woman of distinction in "The Search After Happiness," who seeks pleasure and satisfaction in literature, especially drama. More fears that an obsession with drama, like that boasted of by Cleora, will plague other impressionable young women and men.[4] According to More's "Preface," the stage is a scene of "temptation and seduction, of overwrought voluptuousness and unnerving pleasure" (508), and therefore "a pernicious force" (508) capable of making deep and strong impressions on the mind, "stronger and deeper, perhaps, than are made by any other amusement" (510). Thus, despite the fact that More had come to embrace the theater as generally hostile to Christianity, she continued to believe in its potential for both amusement and instruction.[5]

Despite More's ambivalence about the morality of drama, it nonetheless played a significant role in her professional development. More's negotiations with cultural attitudes that denigrated drama and her personal inclination to write it for literary and pedagogical purposes tell us something about the constraints and pressures under which female playwrights struggled at the end of the eighteenth century. For More, drama was the genre uniquely conducive to the performative, enabling her to play with characters' voices, to enact fictional scenarios, and to rehearse her emergent role as social reformer and pedagogical philanthropist.[6] Furthermore, as an inherently public venue, drama offered More a vehicle to investigate how a private English woman could assume a respectable but authoritative public role in a society undergoing political and social changes. Some women writers, like Joanna Baillie and Elizabeth Inchbald, embraced the genre as the one best suited to their literary and social missions; however, for others, like More and Jane Austen, drama functioned in kind of "invention" capacity, a form in which they could discover a public persona that complemented their sociopolitical agendas and set the stage for their later innovative fiction.[7] These women playwrights' activities point to ways in which the boundaries between private and public were permeable and blurred. More, like other women playwrights of her day, perceived how theater could be used by women to shape the public sphere, even when their own drama was part of what Tracy Davis identifies as an "associative public sphere," a non-market public sphere.[8] Alison Twells notes that in blurring the boundaries between the "separate spheres" of male and female activity, reformist women, like More, became "carriers of civilization," involved in wider power dynamics than the home (26–27).[9]

More's *Sacred Dramas* and "The Search After Happiness" help us to recognize the central role that drama played in the repositioning of women's roles in the new social order. Seen in the context of More's professional development, drama played a more vital function than pedagogical tool; drama served as a structure instrumental in the ideological changes that marked Romantic culture's bourgeois family and expanded nation. This key role of Romantic drama can be discerned from the ways in which it facilitated More's literary career as well as the epistemological center it occupied as a cross-classed site of cultural production, the public forum for the making and disseminating of cultural knowledge. As a site for potential oppositional meanings, drama could enact a critique of epistemology itself. For the stage, as More's comments about the theater clearly reveal, created a world in which reality was suspended and alternatives displayed so as to expose the fictionality of the presumed reality of the moment. With reality exposed as artificial, contrived, and acted, the playwright could reasonably hope to encourage audiences to think about ways in which culture might be differently scripted. After all, drama accommodates multiple voices with seeming "innocence."[10] Here was the space for pedagogical and ideological differences; here was the space for women writers to make significant contributions in the education of audiences and the reformation of societies. I suspect that it was this epistemological opportunity, paradoxically available to aspiring women writers, that a young More perceived to be the potential "good" drama might render, particularly for private and pedagogical settings.

As writing dramas helped More to discover her literary voice, so pedagogical dramas could prepare young women to find their "calling" for roles as philanthropic social workers and educators. Importantly, drama, whether staged or read to children, is actually addressing a double-layered audience: the child reader/performer and the adult reader/spectator, what Mitzi Myers has identified as "cross-writing," a characteristic of all children's literature that deploys a dialogic mix of older and younger voices, or a colloquy between a writer's past and present selves ("Cross-Writing" vii). According to Myers, cross-writing represents "a transgressive and creative miscegenation of public and private spaces, gender and generational issues, domestic and national politics" ("Canonical 'Orphans'" 119). Myers's concept points to the way that More's dramas are always and already cross-read and adult/child double voiced. Drama can, then, be as much about critiquing the status quo as about inculcating it, and sometimes it can accomplish both simultaneously as it appropriates and resists prevailing ideological tenets. Drama draws its young audience into the meaning-making process and invites children to "authorize" their own meanings and interpretations. Playacting encourages children to engage in critical thinking, elevating their cognitive abilities beyond that to which adults frequently sought to limit them. The independently thinking child existed as an alternative to the eighteenth-century child of sensibility, dutiful and submissive, rooted in material and emotional dependency on adults.[11] Drama thus can render multiple layers of meaning: a didactic manifest content, often promoted by adult audiences, and an ironically subversive subtext, depicted from the perspectives of children.[12] It is possible that the potentially subversive subtexts of didactic dramas are what promoted censure of theater for young audiences. According to Mary Jackson, the subject of plays for children was especially prickly in Evangelical circles during the eighteenth century, the exception being More's *Sacred Dramas*, which were often acted and popular as reading plays, and "The Search After Happiness," which bestowed "a mantle of respectability to dramatic performance" (242–43).

Sacred Dramas consists of four dramas followed by a soliloquy: "Moses in the Bulrushes," "David and Goliath," "Belshazzar," "Daniel," plus "Reflections of King Hezekiah in His Sickness." These particular Old Testament stories reflect thematic and ideological commonalities. All the stories are familiar. They all offer vivid characters whose personal decisions have national consequences. They all involve cultures under siege and involved in war, repressed by imperialist usurpations and occupations. As such, they constitute interesting choices for More to dramatize at a time when her own government was intent on expanding its commercial interests abroad and acquiring colonies. They are all rescue dramas in which magical, supernatural, and proto-scientific forces figure significantly. They all enact conflicts in which gender-bending occurs and in which characters mimic or challenge performative gender roles.

It is in their "Introduction" that we receive indications that *Sacred Dramas* might yield more than a rescripting of biblical texts. First, the dramas constitute familial and national stories. Aside from their biblical source, they take on the qualities of myth, fable, and folktale, all popular if controversial children's genres because of their potentially subversive content.[13] For More, the folktale in dramatic form was conducive to her message and appropriate for her audience. More justifies recasting her biblical stories in mythical contexts, saying that they share "the fair romance / Of high imagination" and "the bright dream / Of thy pure fancy" (76). In the "Introduction," More asserts that biblical stories, framed in such a telling, have the glamour, adventure, and alluring fancy of classic tales. In another conflation of the sacred and secular, she invokes the energy of Isaiah and Milton, their "magic pow'rs," and "melody's sweet maze" (76). Finally, while the content of her drama is derived from biblical texts, the motive, she announces, is pleasure. She seeks to create a "soul-enchanting song" with the techniques of "Strong imagery," " bold figure," "apt metaphor," and "Divine simplicity" (76). Possibly, More turns to the acceptable Old Testament source for the content of her *Sacred Dramas* but retells and transforms the stories dramatically as folktales so that they might magically and imaginatively open onto the controversial and potentially subversive issues of her day.

Gender is the vehicle through which colonizing postures and positions are exposed and examined, analyzed and questioned in *Sacred Dramas*. The dramas are simultaneously about the national anxieties generated by gender politics accompanying class and social transformations and about expansionist ideologies created by colonial activities accompanying commercial, territorial, and cultural conquests. Both categories involve assumed "natural" structures of hierarchies and superiorities exposed in the dramas as constructions, myths and fables themselves. *Sacred Dramas* consistently associates the terms of male sexuality and masculine gender with acts of violence, conquest, and oppression, and it shows how those essentialized terms, and the ideas or ideals with which they are associated, can be seen in variant, but not necessarily deviant, forms. A critique of this masculine gender opens up spaces for More's promotion of the female and maternal role in the cultural project of nation building and reforming. What emerges from this conflation of gender and nationalism is the possibility of a feminine alternative to the prevailing masculine power, but a feminine alternative that is not necessarily maternal. Female passions are cast as moralizing forces, and female or feminized characters are portrayed as agents of change.

INTERROGATING NATIONALISM AND IMPERIALISM

More's dramatic portrayals represent a shift from the practice of earlier eighteenth-century drama that cast male heroes exclusively in the role of moral agents and national exemplars. In this way *Sacred Dramas* contributes to first-wave feminist efforts to redefine female subjectivity in terms other than those dictated by male norms, terms that generally universalized subjectivity (as masculine) or that essentialized female subjectivity as male-determined femininity.[14] Given More's young age as well as that of her audiences, it is possible that she was disposed to identify and develop feminine qualities not necessarily synonymous with the domestic or maternal role that she later came to encourage. In *Sacred Dramas*, we see female agency that is both maternal and not necessarily maternal portrayed as an essential pedagogical force for the new English nation and its colonies. We see the portrayal of a civil, female identity that asserts herself *within* the patriarchal world, but as an *alternative* to masculinist leadership. We see the acting out of a relational paradigm that could constitute the basis of a newly structured English family and nation.

Of the four "acts" or stories of the *Sacred Dramas*, only "Moses in the Bulrushes" involves female parts exclusively. Despite its male-specific title, "Moses in the Bulrushes" requires an all-female cast, a curious way to explore gender relations as a trope for nationalism. The other dramas require major male roles and might have represented an opportunity to perform cross-dressing, certainly cross-gendering, for students in the all-female boarding schools of the late eighteenth century.[15] In "Moses in the Bulrushes," More works through an early model of the domestic reformations that would come to characterize her later pedagogical writings, "a pattern of female domestic heroism, an image of activity, strength, fortitude, and ethical maturity, of self-denial, purity, and truth" (Myers, "Reform or Ruin" 204). This pattern develops in "Moses in the Bulrushes," particularly in the characterization of female intersubjectivity and in the depiction of the cohabitation of different women connected by maternal love. More's work attempts to produce middle-class female subjectivity, Cannon Schmitt argues, in nationalistic terms that demonstrate women helping to shape national character (30), and of all the *Sacred Dramas*, "Moses in the Bulrushes" conflates nationalism and female subjectivity most blatantly.

The play promotes relationality and understanding of otherness, even through partial connections. Together Jochebed, Miriam, and the Pharaoh's daughter enact a feminine alternative to the masculinist world that seeks to assert power with might and control with violence. When Egypt's Pharaoh decrees that all Hebrew male children will be killed, his daughter makes it possible not only for infant Moses to be spared but also for Jochebed, as Hebrew nurse and teacher, to continue to perform her motherly role. Although Jochebed is convinced that her sorrows can be consoled only by another mother, the Princess demonstrates that it is possible for women who are not biological mothers to adopt a maternal ideology capable of reforming conditions for children and governance of the nation. This maternal model enables people to live together in harmony because of woman's unchanging passion and hope: "A mother's fondness reigns / Without a rival, and without an end" (78). The maternal model of governance relinquishes competition so characteristic of male leadership, and it does not justify the means, infanticide, necessary to accomplish a nationalist/imperialist victory.

Both young Miriam and the Princess portray female leadership to which More's audiences might aspire, for, as Miriam comes to learn, the Princess does not "resemble her inhuman sire" and is instead "most merciful and mild" (79). The Princess, in fact, surmises that the infant she discovers might belong to some unhappy Hebrew woman who has attempted "to evade / The stern decree of my too cruel sire" (79). Her empathy transcends her nation's politics as she laments, "Unhappy mothers! Oft my heart has bled / In secret anguish o'er your slaughter'd sons, / Powerless to save, yet hating to destroy" (79). More's drama demonstrates that the price of national security need not be human blood. The Princess rejects the masculine rule of might: "Too much our house has crush'd their alien race. / Is't not enough that cruel task-masters / Grind them by hard oppression? Not enough / That iron bondage bows their spirits down?" (79). Characterizing the prevailing political policy as "crime," the Princess asks, "And shall I / Sanction the sin I hate? Forbid it, Mercy!" (79). The Princess explicitly challenges national policy as decreed by her father, and in taking this bold, private stance, she demonstrates how women can transfer domestic ideology to national issues.

As More's own reformist politics would later assert, the Princess, as an exemplar of this female subjectivity, asserts an alternative domestic ideology for the destructive and hateful policies of her father's government. While the Princess refers to Egypt's intolerance and fear of Hebrew difference, her censorious words also apply to British strategies of nationalization at the end of the eighteenth century. While the manifest meaning of her words seems to support the prevailing eighteenth-century notions of masculine superiority, her actions nonetheless enact a female agency that can reform the powerful machinery of masculine politics, a conflicted characterization that More herself later came to embody. The Princess remarks:

> So weak, so unprotected is our sex,
> So constantly expos'd, so very helpless,
> That did Heaven itself enjoin compassion,
> Yet human policy should make us kind,
> Lest in the rapid turn of Fortune's wheel,
> We live to need the pity we refuse. (80)

Ironically, in saving the infant Moses, the Princess comes to save a people and a nation, so potentially powerful is the compassion of this maternal paradigm.[16] Just as Jochebed will nurse and teach her son, and presumably lessons of peace and love, so this drama instructs its audience not to accept a passive and weak femininity, but to assert an active female role, with compassion and strength, and to seek change that results in harmonious human relations.

It is similarly possible to read the "David and Goliath" drama as another enactment of gender relations in which female agency is endorsed, despite its all-male cast, as an alternative to that masculine model that defined civic leadership. By portraying variant gender subjectivities, More's *Sacred Dramas* suggests that the nation benefits from diverse contributions from its citizenry. In More's David and Goliath story, two nations, represented by different styles of masculinity, are pitted against each other. David is a youth and, as such, a feminized character, particularly in contrast to the hypermasculinized Philistian giant, Goliath. David's father, Jesse, likewise resists essentialized masculinity and promotes a feminized anti-war posture. He warns his son not to assume that heaven approves "The active merit and the busy toil / Of heroes, statesmen, and the bustling sons / Of public care" (84). Likewise, King Saul's masculinity is questioned in his lamentation about being made king, his loss of peace of mind and virtue, and his forfeiture of his shepherd's life, with its domestic joys and simple happiness. He would rather meditate than fight.

The national hero of this drama is a feminized and youthful David. Against the background of war, we discover David performing the typically feminine activity of playing a harp and singing devotionals, and when he travels to the camp seeking news from the frontlines, his brothers mock their father's "darling," "charming," " peaceful," and "eloquent son" (85). They tease David for having left his flock, the domestic task to which he is much better suited than the challenges of war. Of course, it is this weak, feminized shepherd, the one "trained in peaceful deeds" (87), who courageously faces Goliath. From Goliath's perspective, David is the most feminized of an effeminate race, as he says: "Give me a man, if your effeminate bands / A man can boast" (86). Goliath makes it clear that he does not "war with boys" (90).

The drama's gender-bending spaces are where class and national issues are staged. At first, Saul is incredulous that David, a meager shepherd of low birth, has volunteered to fight Goliath, and warns his general Abner to tell such a story to

> weak believing women;
> They love what e'er is marvelous, and dote
> On deeds prodigious and incredible,
> Which sober sense rejects. (87)

This gendered relational paradigm illustrates how class and gender denigration constitute the same ideological basis as that which engenders one nation's seeking of another's enslavement. The women to whom Saul refers exhibit the stereotypical femininity that the drama rejects and against which Saul, Jesse, and David are contrasted. David does not allow Goliath's insulting taunts, brute strength, or enormous size to deter his rational and perceptive intellect, for ultimately, David out-smarts and out-talks the giant. David's deed, in turn, saves thousands who would have lost their lives in the extended war. David single-handedly saves his nation.

Yet David's character, feminized and a model of domestic, maternal leadership, is not without its faults, and in this respect, he lacks the paradigmatic potency of Jochebed, Miriam, and the Princess from "Moses in the Bulrushes." David is attracted to war, finds it alluring, and even aspires to become a warrior willing to sacrifice his life "at the height of life" (89). He is commodified as the prize to Saul's daughter for defeating Goliath and bringing the giant's head to the Israelite camp. Furthermore, when David compares Goliath, an "uncircumcis'd Philistine" and the "idolater" (88), with "the famish'd lion" and "panting monster" bear, he betrays an imperialist imagination that generally characterized the colonized "other" as primitive, beastly, and monstrous. As mental preparation for fighting Goliath, David dehumanizes his foe, characterizing him as a "vast colossal statue," "mere magnitude of form, / Without proportion'd intellect and valour" (89).[17] In this respect, David is really no better than Goliath whose name-calling of David as "curled minion," and "light boy" (90) represents a strategy to emasculate him.

"David and Goliath" performs gender-bending as a site where gendered qualities of leadership might be examined, but it fails to validate any alternative to the civil identity fashioned under the status quo. Ironically, at the end of the play, it is the two feminized Hebrew leaders, Saul and David, who are represented as potential rivals. In an aside, Saul complains about the elaborate procession staged in David's honor: "A rival's praise / Is discord to my ear!" (92). "David and Goliath" thus comes up short in its endorsement of its cross-gendered models of domestic leadership, for Saul and David ultimately fall victims themselves to the imperialist and masculinist ideology that they had temporarily suspended. More asks her audiences to engage in a more complex analysis of gender relations in "David and Goliath" than she stages in "Moses in the

Bulrushes," demonstrating how difficult it is, especially for men, to sustain an alternative to the powerful status quo, but at least nodding to the possibility for both men and women to think and to behave differently.

"Belshazzar" is a sacred drama that brings together male and female characters in another complex analysis of gender relations and national leadership. In this enactment, Belshazzar enacts a feminized masculinity, a corrupted gender that More would want her audience to eschew. Like the masculinities in "Daniel and Goliath," then, "Belshazzar" demonstrates that which is intended to be critically analyzed but not emulated. Belshazzar leads to a slovenly lifestyle at his wanton court, a result of Babylon's defeat and exploitation of Judah. Belshazzar has looted precious relics and artifacts from Judah's temple, profaning them with secular use, and he has pressed the Hebrew people into slavery. Haughty Belshazzar asks:

> What is empire?
> The privilege to punish and to enjoy:
> To feel our pow'r in making others fear it;
> To taste of Pleasure's cup till we grow giddy,
> And think ourselves immortal! This is empire! (96)

Babylon's pleasures and power are derived from human suffering, the conquest of peoples, the "undone," "outcast people" (96) who are commodified for colonial exploitation. Herein lies a powerful lesson for the emergent imperial imaginary of Great Britain.

Although war threatens, Belshazzar does not take civic responsibility, and instead, he holds a feast to Belus, the Babylonian god. Belshazzar, as Daniel reports, has come to see himself in deified terms, surrounded by "impious" and "lew'd parasites" who "justify his vices and extol / His boastful phrase, as if he were some god " (94). A hedonist, Belshazzar boasts that the pleasures of life should be enjoyed in the immediate moment and at the expense of those over whom he exerts authority. His sycophant courtiers kneel and drink to him, saying, "we are likest gods / When we have pow'r, and use it" (96). Fueled by indulgent drinking and specious praise, an intoxicated Belshazzar proclaims: "War and famine threat in vain, / While this demi-god shall reign!" (96). His presumption is, of course, his downfall. This scene reveals an ironic level of gendered meaning when we recall that its drinkers, sinners, and Orientals would have been performed by schoolgirls who already knew well, perhaps, the marginalization of being female in a patriarchal world.

Painfully, Belshazzar comes to realize that he is not a god, not even a king, but a weak man, "a helpless man, / Subject to pain, and sin, and death, like others!" (98). Refusing to listen to Daniel's wisdom, Belshazzar mocks the prophecy that might have saved his life. Belshazzar resembles the corrupt and dissolute class of British aristocrats who, as many feared, had grown effeminate in their manners and thinking, and had become ineffectual leaders for the nation and its colonies. It is ironic that it is the Old Testament Near East that functions paradigmatically in "Belshazzar" as the geography upon which the cautionary and pedagogic tale is enacted, for the eighteenth-century commercial/colonial enterprise in which British supremacy is being staged occurs in the Orient, in expeditions to the Near and Far East. More's drama suggests that nations, ancient and contemporary, East and West, might coexist in mutual peace and prosperity if they operated relationally, like a family, a domestic space in which men and women perform different but equally worthy and valuable roles.

Daniel is featured in his own sacred drama as the captive favorite of Darius, King of Media and Babylon. Like Belshazzar, hyperfeminized Darius falls victim to hubris, his presumption of deity being encouraged by his courtiers Pharnaces and Soranus. His ill-conceived new law against public prayer represents an effort to entrap Daniel in renouncing his religious beliefs. Daniel's steadfast piety and honor are depicted in a stark contrast to Darius's fickle and capricious power. Although the king begs Pharnaces to devise some way to redeem venerable Daniel's life, the wicked courtier protests that the law is irrevocable. Darius expresses the pedagogical message of this drama, the hope that future kings will learn from this crime and never delegate power to weak or wicked hands. God rescues Daniel from the mouths of hungry lions, but when Darius seeks to substitute his courtiers and their families in the lions' den, Daniel implores the king not to seek revenge. Daniel's request is too late, however, as the rash Darius has already ordered the deaths of those who so ill advised him. Like "David and Goliath," "Daniel" stages the fate of nations that promote civic irresponsibility, greed, and might. It also depicts the consequences that nations face when their governance is not based on a domestic-defined ideal that situates love and connectedness at its center.

INTERROGATING SCIENCE AND THE SUPERNATURAL

While variant genders open up spaces in More's *Sacred Dramas,* by which leadership issues linked to nationalism and imperialism could be displaced and enacted, gender is also the category through which the period's preoccupation with the supernatural and science were transposed and expressed. The soliloquy "Reflection of King Hezekiah in His Sickness," an addendum to *Sacred Dramas,* demonstrates how gender facilitated an examination of both nationalism and science. On his sickbed, King Hezekiah contemplates, perhaps for the first time, what it means to die, and as a mortally sick patient, Hezekiah functions as a synecdoche for a sick and dying nation. The diseased body became a popular metaphor of the French Revolution, but here, More applies it to the national crisis with which Britain is engaged. Mitzi Myers notes that More perceived her own society as one infected with fashionable corruption and that she diagnosed England's moral illness, offering female-derived reform as its antidote ("Reform or Ruin" 211). It is important to acknowledge that More selects biblical stories that record instances of ill advice, sickly leadership, and nations' health at risk as the basis for her *Sacred Dramas.* Like Hezekiah, the English nation at the end of the eighteenth century might ask: "*Is* all in order set, my house, my heart?" (109). Like Hezekiah, the English nation might ask what is the worth of wealth, pomp, and fame, "glitt'ring treasures," "gold and gems," acquisitions from colonization, if the body is not well (109). Hezekiah contemplates the human price of his success:

> Did I unjustly seek to build my name
> On the pil'd ruins of another's fame?
> Did I abhor, as hell, the insidious lie,
> The low deceit, the unmanly calumny? (109)

The calumny that Hezekiah comes to acknowledge is "unmanly," indicating a correlation between slander and female passions, but it is a deceit that has been engendered from an imperial ideology that embraces the masculine passion for conquest and possession. Hezekiah's "monstrous pride," like that displayed by Belshazzar and Darius, contribute to a nation built on the exploitation and oppression of others. Hezekiah confesses that of all the "mental strife / of warring passions" and "raging fires / Of furious appetites and mad desires," the strangest one is "That man is proud of what is not his own!" (109). The appetites and desires that drive colonial enterprises similarly drive sexual conquests, and both, the soliloquy suggests, result in a sick body.

Medicine and quackery, the scientific and the supernatural, and Eastern and Western epistemology are conflated in "Belshazzar," displaced and articulated through gender. Daniel has received "all the various learning of the East" but refrained from "acquiring the foibles of the East," an education that enables him to apply scientific, masculine rationality to the mysteries of a feminized supernatural. According to a Jewish captive, Belshazzar's weak, feminine leadership has been affected by the "magic poppies" of war whose "delicates opiates" charm him into "fatal slumbers" (94). Belshazzar's banquet includes the richest spices of the East: "The od'rous cassia and the dropping myrrh, / The liquid amber and the fragrant gums" (95), spices that possess magical and intoxicating effects. A Babylonian courtier ironically accuses the Jews of being superstitious in their reverence for their Temple's reliques as symbols of their faith, their "holy trumpery" (97). Seeming differences expressed between East and West, between the supernatural and the scientific, between feminine and masculine are exposed as fictional, interpretative, and fabulous, each side of the dialogical exchange claiming cultural and natural superiority.

The most amazing analysis of the supernatural–scientific dialogic occurs in "Belshazzar" in the banquet when the thunder claps loudly and the semblance of a shadowy hand writes on the wall the unintelligible words "Mene, mene, tekel, upharsin" (97). This spectacle of "transcendant horror" (97) terrifies all, but especially the fear-struck king whose "startling eyes / Roll horribly. Thrice he essay'd to speak, / And thrice his tongue refus'd" (97). In other words, Belshazzar swoons like a hysterical woman. Elizabeth Kowaleski-Wallace points out that More herself suffered from childhood devastating illnesses that were popularly believed to have their origins in nervous sensibility (91–92). These so-called bouts with mad enthusiasm were conventionally associated with female anatomy. More's illness was characterized by headaches, toothaches, severe fevers, even deliriums, symptoms that she could, with great authority, transcribe to Belshazzar's body at the moment he faces a mysterious experience that science seeks to explain. The king speculates about whether he is hallucinating, dreaming, or intoxicated: "Perhaps 'tis fancy all, or the wild dream, / Of made distemperature, the fumes of wine!" (97). After some thought, he asks: "Ye wild fantastic images, what are ye?" (97), and he orders them to explain their "dark intent" (97). But the wise astrologers for whom Belshazzar sends cannot interpret the mystic characters, and angrily, he curses their "lying science" (98).

Similarly, in "Daniel," neither science nor the supernatural can explain the mysterious force that charms the hungry lions. Both science and the supernatural are indicted as pretending to profess knowledge (culturally gendered masculine) that gives them power over those who do not possess such knowledge (culturally gendered feminine). As science and medicine became increasingly professionalized and masculinized during the Romantic period, it became another public venue for the assertion of male privilege and power, one that More's dramas cast as provisionally strong, justified, and sanctioned by the myths that it generates about itself.

Several characters of *Sacred Dramas* rely on the assistance of supernatural elements associated with the East and spurned by post-Enlightenment Britain. King Saul of "David and Goliath" turns to what is culturally defined as feminized Eastern arts when his military science fails to accomplish victory in battle. In a soliloquy he cries: "Oh! that I knew the black and midnight arts / Of wizard sorcery! . . . / Or, like the Chaldean sages, could foreknow / Th' event of things unacted!" (90). His desire to see the future, to conjure a drama in which he is presently not acting is further envisioned in Gothic terms as he covets to know "arts obscene, which foul diviners use" (90). His melancholy has fueled his superstition, and he has succumbed to its charms. Similarly, Eastern, feminized, gothicized arts conflated with scientific enquiry appear in "Moses in the Bulrushes" and are mocked by Miriam as unable to locate a baby in a cradle floating upon the river (78). Jochebed invokes the supernatural as maternal defense against masculine power, for she maintains that the ark in which her infant son rests is charmed "with incantations Pharaoh ne'er employ'd / With spells, which impious Egypt never knew" (79). Here the mysteries of maternal affection are conflated with beliefs in the Judeo–Christian tradition, but they out-Herod the sciences of Egypt so as to question the legitimacy of any oppressive power that claimed its justification was derived from intelligent forms—whether scientific or supernatural. More effectively suggests in this scene that the pagan beliefs of Egypt are masculinized and so the epistemological basis for gendered supernatural or scientific thinking is put into question. *Sacred Dramas* furthermore invites women to play an active, central role in the applications of scientific thinking for the moral improvement of the nation.

Sacred Dramas echoes critical thinking about the role of gendered science in the nation that is rehearsed in More's earlier pastoral drama, "The Search After Happiness."[18] Cleora's search for happiness has led her to the study of science, which, as she explains, seeks to limit her sex to matters of appearance and beauty. Cleora offers a representational girl who bursts "female bonds" (114) so as to engage her mind critically in the discursive debates of the day. More's drama suggests that science, like the supernatural, can impose limitations on human thinking and activity, limitations that not only deter happiness but also progress. Cleora ventures into those sciences promoted as especially masculine: astronomy, math, philosophy, chemistry, and physics. She turns away from the conventional avenues pursued by women who dabble in science, the beauties offered through poetical and taxonomical botany, for example, and determines to learn more about the facts and demonstrations, the causes and effects of natural phenomenon, the domain of male science:

> The schoolmen's systems now my mind employ'd,
> Their crystal Spheres, their Atoms, and their Void;
> Newton and Halley all my soul inspir'd,
> And numbers less than calculations fir'd;
> Decartes and Euclid, shar'd my varying breast,
> And plans and problems all my soul possess'd. (114)

Cleora's fatal flaw is not that she boldly ventures into scientific studies culturally restricted to her gender, but that she becomes like the male scientist in her thinking and being. Science becomes a tool for egotistical self-aggrandizement rather than the means through which humankind might become morally and physically reformed. The danger that More's drama depicts is not the science, but the application of science toward masculinist goals and in male-centered ways. In her pursuit of science, Cleora betrays compassion, an essential component of the female reformers that More encourages her audiences to become. The wise and ancient shepherdess Urania teaches Cleora to temper knowledge with humility, and she encourages her young charge to abandon the posture assumed by male scientists and intellects: "Let the proud sex possess their vaunted pow'rs: / Be other triumphs, other glories ours!" (118). While she maintains that woman shines in her "proper sphere," Urania nonetheless maintains that in her betterment of the home, woman contributes to the larger public sphere in which nation building is engaged.[19] At the end of the pastoral drama, the characters recite the poem "Ode to Charity," and its second verse emphasizes that the period's emergent science should serve useful and beneficial purposes rather than become, like superstition and religion before it, another weapon for domination, whether gendered or national (119). The happiness of the individual and the happiness of the nation depend on the charitable application of science for all human beings.

More's reputation and her contributions to the literary and feminist arenas of Romantic culture have been re-examined and reassessed during the last twenty years, and it is Mitzi Myers to whom we are indebted for this resurgence in scholarly attention to this complicated and extraordinary woman.[20] Myers asserts that More was "a female crusader infinitely more successful than Wollstonecraft or any other" woman of her day, and it was Myers who uncovered the submerged power and energy in More's writing ("Reform or Ruin" 209). Myers says that More's "work exemplifies how women could translate female ideology's didactic imperative into an authoritative voice capable of documenting and interpreting historical realities" ("Hannah More's Tracts" 268). More's *Sacred Dramas* and "The Search after Happiness," I have argued here, are important works in our understanding of the role that drama played in the literary development of women writers and how they used drama and the theater to examine, even challenge, prevailing social and political positions. Pedagogical plays for children powerfully enabled young women who wrote, performed, and read them to discover the performative and ephemeral nature of female conduct and to realize that they could play active roles in both private and public spaces of a changing British culture.

NOTES

1. According to Jane Williams, female boarding-schools occasionally represented plays that might be considered inappropriate for young women (317).

2. Mona Scheurmann explains that More was shocked by the playwright's insistence that the husband of the adulteress was in the wrong and a "savage." More

feared the drama's ability to inculcate this notion to spectators who were not literate (215).

3. More's later-life perspective maintains that seeing a play is more dangerous than reading a play because of its semblance to reality and its splendor of spectacle. Jacqueline Pearson notes that similar rules governed drama-reading as playgoing; however, despite the ambivalence surrounding the image of the play-reading woman, respectable, elite, middle- and even laboring-class women read plays in significant numbers (61).

4. More exposed the compelling attraction of drama and theater in her poem "The Puppet Show: A Tale." A nobleman buys the puppet Punch, and he is disappointed when it fails to perform its magic without the machinery, manipulations, and voices of a puppeteer. More's poem suggests her familiarity with the period's popular entertainment for children and perhaps Henry Fielding's play *The Author's Farce*, staged from 1729–1737. In Fielding's play, a troop performs a life-size puppet show entitled "The Pleasures of the Town." According to Lisa Freeman, Fielding's farce deploys the metaphor of a puppet show to suggest theater was a tool of political propaganda (61). More's poem connects the children's entertainment to gender politics demonstrating her recognition of the ways in which theater served politics.

5. More's "Preface to the Tragedies" has been variously interpreted as explanation for More's renunciation of play writing. Elisabeth Jay connects More's departure from the stage to her association with the Evangelical Clapham party (193). According to Annette Meakin and Marion Harland, Thomas Cadell's comment about *The Fatal Falsehood* and David Garrick's death in 1779 were the causes (Meakin 129; Harland 74–75). M. G. Jones and Charles Ford point to More's controversy with Hannah Cowley as well as More's recognition that she could not reform the theater (Jones 38–39; Ford 43). See also Anne Stott (22–69).

6. More may have seen the potential of eighteenth-century theater as one that, as Freeman argues, "provided an alarming opportunity for the fluidity of character and the proliferation of identities and thus threatened to disrupt the severe economy of social roles that was beginning to take shape" during the period (68).

7. Jane Austen's three short plays "The Visit," "The Mystery," and "The First Act of a Comedy" (1787–1790) constitute satire and parody and function heuristically for the dialogue that would come to characterize her later fiction. Like More, Austen was ambivalent about the propriety of drama for women. John McAleer reports that the favorite Austen family entertainment was the reading aloud or enacting of plays. Between 1782–1790, the family produced at least nine private theatricals (14–15). See also Ellen E. Martin (91–92), Gay Penny (4–11), and George Holbert Tucker (87–92).

8. Tracy Davis asserts, "the authoring of a play necessarily implicated public-ity (publicness) whether it was bound for publication, home theatricals, profes-

sional production—or even utter obscurity." The Evangelical Movement, explains Catherine Hall, created links between the private and public through its application of religion as domestic virtues to both spheres (84–86).

9. Meakin reports that Sir Alexander Johnstone, the Chief Justice of Ceylon, asked More permission to translate *Sacred Dramas* into Cingalese and Tamil so that the dramas might be performed at festivals celebrating the liberation and education of Cingalese slaves belonging to Dutch masters, beginning in 1816. Interestingly, Joanna Baillie's drama *The Martyr* (1826) was, as she tells us in the "Preface" to *The Bride* (1836), intended for translation into Cingalese "as a work which might have some effects upon a people of strong passions, emerging from a state of comparative barbarism, and whose most effectual mode of receiving instruction is frequently that of dramatic representation, according to the fashion of their country" (665). Baillie, in fact, wrote *The Bride* following Johnstone's invitation to write a play that would have a moral effect on the inhabitants of Ceylon. Clearly More's and Baillie's dramas played a role in the civilizing mission of Great Britain, an important pedagogical function that reached well beyond the domestic sphere.

10. Cannon Schmitt reads More's pedagogy rather narrowly when she maintains that More was skeptical of the role of imagination for the well-educated woman, adding that the idea of childhood innocence was a dangerous myth (29). On the other hand, Angela Keane points to More's belief that works of imagination served pedagogical and utilitarian functions (122–29).

11. Mary Jackson describes this eighteenth-century child of sensibility as one who lingered in "a fondly sentimentalized state of childishness" and who was "eagerly obedient or lavishly repentant" and "who seldom made important decisions without parental approval" (131). Judith Plotz's recent study cautions that the category of childhood was itself vastly amorphous as it was simultaneously deployed as an important Romantic trope (xii–xiii).

12. In "De-Romanticizing the Subject," Myers offers a feminist reconfiguration of the Romantic-period child as written and mythologized by women. Myers discovers a progressive female tradition of prose fiction, such as Maria Edgeworth's short story "The Bracelets," that works toward a different metanarrative of literary childhood than that written by men. I am arguing that it is possible for us to discover a similarly alternative Romantic child in drama written by young women, like More's *Sacred Dramas* and "The Search After Happiness."

13. Folktales, explains Alison Lurie, are among the most subversive texts in children's literature, and they are a middle- and working-class genre (16–19). Other critics, such as Alan Richardson, have identified reactionary and conservative uses of folk and fairy tales in the Romantic era.

14. More's contributions to first-wave feminism have been variously disputed by recent scholars. Lucinda Cole asserts that More grants women the power of influence but strictly within acceptable late eighteenth-century parameters that

define women as charming and passive companions of men. In More's Christian hierarchy, Cole argues, there can be no mutual sympathy between men and women (124–25). Myers alternatively claims that More was among the didactic women who shaped the new ideal of the educated and responsible woman ("Hannah More's Tracts" 265–66).

15. Mary Shelley's dramas *Midas* and *Proserpine*, as I have demonstrated, rely on single-sexed casts to challenge the binary categories of sexuality, to question the pervasive nature of masculine authority, to connect familial and national matters ("Polysexualities" 385–411).

16. According to Dorice Williams Elliott, "More implicitly makes the home the controlling metaphor for all human activity, including the state" in *Cheap Repository Tracts* ("'Care of the Poor'" 195). I assert that we can see More's similar use of the home metaphor in *Sacred Dramas*.

17. Goliath is cast by David as a Techno-Gothic grotesque, the term I use to describe the dramatic manifestation of an aberration, a freak, with which nascent science and tautology were both fascinated at the end of the eighteenth century. See "Theatricalized Bodies," 134–55.

18. "The Search After Happiness" was written in 1762 and published in 1773; by 1787, it was issued in its ninth edition and had sold nearly 10,000 copies (Ford 7–8).

19. According to Linda Colley, More's interpretation of women's sphere included ample space for women to have a greater sense of purpose and an opportunity for action relevant for society at large (276).

20. Anne Mellor asserts, "Hannah More was the most influential women living in England in the Romantic era" (13). For Marlon Ross, More "more than any other establishes the nineteenth-century woman writer as the conscience of culture" (202). Elliott argues that thousands of Englishwomen followed More's advice in the early decades of the nineteenth century (*Angel Out of the House* 81). Anne Stott concludes that More was an invaluable role model for women who came later; she was "the 'mother' of Victorianism" (336).

WORKS CITED

Austin, Linda M. "Children of Childhood: Nostalgia and the Romantic Legacy." *Studies in Romanticism* 42.1 (Spring 2003): 75–98.

Baillie, Joanna. "Preface." *The Bride. The Dramatic and Poetical Works of Joanna Baillie Complete in One Edition*. 2nd ed. London: Longman, 1851. 665–66.

Colley, Linda. *Britons: Forging the Nation 1707–1837*. New Haven: Yale UP, 1992.

Cole, Lucinda. "(Anti)Feminist Sympathies: The Politics of Relationships in Smith, Wollstonecraft, and More." *ELH* 58 (1991): 107–40.

Davis, Tracy C. "The Sociable Playwright and Representative Citizen." *Romanticism On the Net* 12 (November 1998). 11 June 2003, http://users.ox.ac.uk/~scat0385/bwpcitizen.html

Elliott, Dorice Williams. *The Angel Out of the House: Philanthropy and Gender in Nineteenth-Century England.* Charlottesville: UP of Virginia, 2002.

———. "'The Care of the Poor Is Her Profession': Hannah More and Women's Philanthropic Work." *Nineteenth-Century Contexts* 19.2 (1995): 179–204.

Freeman, Lisa A. *Character's Theatre: Genre and Identity on the Eighteenth-Century English Stage.* Philadelphia: U of Pennsylvania P, 2002.

Ford, Charles Howard. *Hannah More: A Critical Biography.* New York: Peter Lang, 1996.

Gay, Penny. *Jane Austen and the Theatre.* Cambridge: Cambridge UP, 2002.

Hall, Catherine. *White, Male and Middle Class: Explorations in Feminism and History.* New York: Routledge, 1992.

Harland, Marion [Terhune, Mary Virginia (Hawes)]. *Hannah More.* New York: Putnam, 1900.

Jackson, Mary V. *Engines of Instruction, Mischief, and Magic: Children's Literature in England from Its Beginnings to 1839.* Lincoln: U of Nebraska P, 1989.

Jay, Elisabeth. *The Religion of the Heart: Anglican Evangelicalism and the Nineteenth-Century Novel.* Oxford: Clarendon, 1979.

Jones, M. G. *Hannah More.* Cambridge: Cambridge UP, 1952.

Kowaleski–Wallace, Elizabeth. *Their Father's Daughters: Hannah More, Maria Edgeworth, and Patriarchal Complicity.* New York: Oxford UP, 1991.

Lurie, Alison. *Don't Tell the Grown-ups: Subversive Children's Literature.* Boston: Little, 1990.

McAleer, John. "What a Biographer Can Learn about Jane Austen from Her Juvenilia." *Jane Austen's Beginnings: The Juvenilia and* Lady Susan. Ed. J. David Grey. Ann Arbor: UMI, 1989. 7–27.

Meakin, Annette M. B. *Hannah More: A Biographical Study.* 1911. 2nd ed. London: John Murray, 1919.

Mellor, Anne K. *Mothers of the Nation: Women's Political Writing in England, 1780–1830.* Bloomington: Indiana UP, 2000.

More, Hannah. *The Complete Works of Hannah More.* New York: Harper, 1838.

———. *Strictures on the Modern System of Female Education.* 2 vols. 3rd ed. London, 1799. Facsim. ed. Oxford: Woodstock, 1995.

Myers, Mitzi. "Canonical 'Orphans' and Critical *Ennui*: Rereading Edgeworth's Cross-Writing." *Children's Literature* 25 (1997): 116–36.

———. "De-Romanticizing the Subject: Maria Edgeworth's 'The Bracelets,' Mythologies of Origin, and the Daughter's Coming to Writing." *Romantic*

Women Writers: Voices and Countervoices. Ed. Paula R. Feldman and Theresa M. Kelley. Hanover: UP of New England, 1995. 88–110.

————. "Hannah More's Tracts for the Times: Social Fiction and Female Ideology." *Fetter'd or Free? British Women Novelists, 1670–1815.* Ed. Mary Anne Schofield and Cecilia Macheski. Athens: Ohio UP, 1986. 264–84.

————. "'Reform or Ruin': A Revolution in Female Manners." *Studies in Eighteenth-Century Culture.* Vol. 11. Ed. Harry C. Payne. Madison: U of Wisconsin P, 1982. 199–216.

Myers, Mitzi, and U. C. Knoepflmacher. "'Cross-Writing' and the Reconceptualizing of Children's Literary Studies." *Children's Literature* 25 (1997): vii–xvi.

Pearson, Jacqueline. *Women's Reading in Britain 1750–1835: A Dangerous Recreation.* Cambridge: Cambridge UP, 1999.

Plotz, Judith. *Romanticism and the Vocation of Childhood.* New York: Palgrave, 2001.

Purinton, Marjean D. "Polysexualities and Romantic Generations in Mary Shelley's Mythological Dramas *Midas* and *Proserpine*." *Women's Writing* 6.3 (1999): 385–411.

————. "Theatricalized Bodies and Spirits: Gothic as Performance in Romantic Drama." *Gothic Studies* 3.2 (2001): 134–55.

Richardson, Alan. *Literature, Education, and Romanticism: Reading as Social Practice, 1780–1831.* Cambridge: Cambridge UP, 1994.

Ross, Marlon B. *The Contours of Masculine Desire: Romanticism and the Rise of Women's Poetry.* New York: Oxford UP, 1989.

Schmitt, Cannon. *Alien Nation: Nineteenth-Century Gothic Fictions and English Nationality.* Philadelphia: U of Pennsylvania P, 1997.

Schuermann, Mona. *In Praise of Poverty: Hannah More Counters Thomas Paine and the Radical Threat.* Lexington: UP of Kentucky, 2002.

Stott, Anne. *Hannah More: The First Victorian.* Oxford: Oxford UP, 2003.

Sutherland, Kathryn. "Hannah More's Counter-Revolutionary Feminisms." *Revolution in Writing: British Literary Responses to the French Revolution.* Ed. Kelvin Everest. Philadelphia: Open UP, 1991. 27–64.

Tucker, George Holbert. *Jane Austen the Woman: Some Biographical Insights.* London: Robert Hale, 1994.

Twells, Alison. "'Let Us Begin Well at Home': Class, Ethnicity, and Christian Motherhood in the Writing of Hannah Kilham, 1774–1832." *Radical Femininity: Women's Self-Representation in the Public Sphere.* Ed. Eileen Janes Yeo. Manchester: Manchester UP, 1998. 25–51.

Williams, Jane. *The Literary Women of England including a Biographical Epitome of All the Most Eminent to the Year 1700; and Sketches of the Poetesses to the Year 1850; with Extracts from their Works and Critical Remarks.* London: Saunders, Otley, 1861.

"A Conservative Woman
Doing Radical Things"
Sarah Trimmer and The Guardian of Education

M. O. Grenby

$\int$ arah Trimmer was perhaps the most important individual influence on late eighteenth- and early nineteenth-century British children's literature. This claim rests not so much on her writing for children, though she wrote several exceedingly successful children's books and has a fair claim to be regarded as the most saleable children's author of her day,[1] as on her sustained critical analysis of this rapidly developing genre. Taking the form of both short, practical reviews and lengthy, theoretical essays, this criticism appeared most fully in her final work, a periodical entitled *The Guardian of Education*. It was published monthly, then quarterly, from June 1802 until September 1806 and, as far as we know, was written entirely by Trimmer. By the time of its closure, due to Trimmer's ill-health, not any lack of demand,[2] the *Guardian* had apparently become a bible for those parents and teachers who supervised children's reading. It told them clearly what was and was not suitable for their charges. As Sidney Smith crossly acknowledged in the *Edinburgh Review* in the year that the *Guardian* closed, Trimmer had become "dearer to mothers and aunts than any other author who pours the milk of science into the mouths of babes and sucklings" (177).[3] After her death, four years later in 1810, one correspondent to the *Gentleman's Magazine* suggested that a "national monument" be built in St. Paul's Cathedral to honor Trimmer's memory.[4] The monument was never built, but the correspondent's certainty that the necessary money would easily be raised gives some indication of the vast gap that exists between Trimmer's consequence to her contemporaries and her position on the margins of literary history today.

However, Trimmer's rehabilitation has now begun. A number of recent essays have tried hard to appreciate Trimmer's achievements, challenging her reputation as the gorgon of early British children's literature.[5] The *Guardian* has just been republished in facsimile, a separate index having already been compiled by Andrea Immel.[6] To this index Mitzi Myers supplied an introduction. Here, she recognized Trimmer's periodical as "the most venturesome of all her pioneering projects" and announced that a commentary on the *Guardian* would soon be produced to accompany Immel's index (x). Regrettably, the commentary never appeared, and we are left to speculate on the approach she would have taken. Myers did, however, leave one or two clues. Chief among these is her suggestive assertion that Trimmer was "a conservative woman doing radical things" (xiii). It is from this statement that the current essay takes its lead.

The first half of the statement—that Trimmer was a reactionary—seems an easy thing to demonstrate. Trimmer's conservatism is perhaps more nuanced than might at first be thought, though, so this essay will begin with a brief analysis of her sociopolitical, religious, and pedagogic views. After this analysis, we will have to consider just how such ardent anti-Jacobinism could possibly coexist with any kind of radical agenda. Recent critical revisions of women's writing, by Myers and others, have suggested how the conservative–radical oxymoron might be resolved. In Trimmer's case, though, these readings are not always wholly convincing. The final section of this essay, then, will suggest fresh reasons to position Trimmer as someone who, in the final analysis, did more to change attitudes, social structures and, above all, children's print culture, than to keep them the same.

Inasmuch as *The Guardian of Education* is known today at all, it is as the first work to review children's books. In fact, children's literature was reviewed surprisingly fully in the general periodical press of the period. Major new children's books, including those by Trimmer, were usually discussed in the *Monthly*, the *Critical*, and the *Analytical* reviews, as well as in several less eminent journals (Grenby, Introduction xiv). Andrea Immel has also pointed out that there was at least one earlier attempt to review British children's literature ("James Pettit"). Despite all this, Trimmer can be congratulated for being the first to adopt a sustained, systematic, and unpatronizing approach. She developed a clear and consistent set of criteria for her reviews. She took into account the different ages of readers. She did not promote, or "puff," her own books, a practice which was endemic in children's publishing. She also strove to review every published children's book, both past and present, although inevitably she failed in this overambitious task. In fact, just a handful of books from before the late 1790s were reviewed (mostly from the firm of Newbery), along with only around half of those books published during the *Guardian's* run.[7] In total, the *Guardian* contained almost four hundred reviews. This number was in itself an enormous achievement, and an expression of confidence in this relatively new literary form that must have done much to legitimize children's literature as a whole.

But the *Guardian* was much more than just the sum of its reviews. Almost all the numbers contained four principal sections. The reviews always came last. Before them came Trimmer's own "Essay on Christian Education," which set out her thoughts on educational best practice from birth to the end of adolescence; an "Extracts" section, in which she copied out lengthy sections of texts that had impressed her; and a section entitled "Systems of Education Examined," in which she appraised recent books of educational theory and praxis. At first, the extracts came at the front of each issue, but when the *Guardian* changed from a monthly to a quarterly in January 1804, Trimmer repositioned her own "Essay" at the beginning of each number. It is tempting to think that this slight alteration represents the replacement of Trimmer's early, modest conviction that the primary purpose of the *Guardian* was to provide readers with a digest of worthy works, with an awareness that it was, in fact, her own opinions that were proving the work's most popular feature. Certainly, the "Essay on Christian Education" was popular enough to be republished on its own, posthumously, in 1812. It covered 339 octavo pages, giving a good indication of how substantial Trimmer's whole undertaking was.

What the "Essay," the extracts, and the reviews all share are Trimmer's unambiguous religious, social, and political values. Each section contributed to what her friend Jane West's verse obituary was to call her "faithful service to the Church and Throne" ("To the Memory" 261). It is her service to the Anglican Church, above all else, that dominates the *Guardian*. Trimmer was essentially a religious fundamentalist. Her primary loyalty was to the word of God, as expressed in the Scriptures and as interpreted by the Church of England. She insisted on the unwavering use of the standard Anglican liturgy, for instance, and she loathed any attempt to alter the catechism or the prescribed hours and forms of prayers, even if the aim was to help young children to become good

Christians.[8] Even when she found herself bridling at the severity of biblical edicts, she felt compelled to approve them. She admitted, for example, that she disliked corporal punishment, but she nevertheless advocated its use because King Solomon had "expressly named the Rod as the proper instrument of correction" (1: 356).

Trimmer's veneration for the Bible also directed her literary criticism. Throughout the *Guardian* she reserved her deepest invective for any text that attempted to amend or abridge the Scriptures.[9] Thus she condemned John Milton's *Paradise Lost*, just as she condemned the work of Evangelicals, whose eagerness to spread the word of God led them into attempts to popularize or simplify the Bible. For the same reason, she denounced William Godwin's *Bible Stories*, a retelling of certain Old Testament narratives that aimed to optimize their potential to instruct and entertain (1: 244–64 and 3: 372–75). The second of these articles on Godwin's *Bible Stories* has become one of the most well known in the *Guardian*, partly because it was so substantial, partly because Godwin included a preface denouncing much recent children's literature as likely to suffocate children's imaginations, and partly because its author was a noted "Jacobin" (though there is no indication that Trimmer knew this, since Godwin used the pseudonym "William Scolfield"). Rather than seeing Trimmer's response as part of an assault on Jacobinism or the Romantic imagination, it is more accurate to see Trimmer's attack as part of her campaign against those who might easily, but erroneously, be classed as Trimmer's allies: those dedicated to propagating Christianity to children, but whom she regarded as mutilators of God's word.[10] Above all, then, Trimmer's fundamentalism was based on a deep respect for text, which explains why she dedicated five years of her life, running herself into ill health, to a periodical designed to patrol the texts that children were receiving.

Interestingly, this respect for the sanctity and nonnegotiability of original texts did not apply only to the Bible. Trimmer was convinced, for instance, that Godwin spoiled Samuel Croxall's early eighteenth-century edition of *Aesop's Fables* "by endeavouring to improve it" (5: 292). Likewise, she worried that Elizabeth Hamilton, whose work she favored in other contexts, could only "invalidate the truths of History" by using fiction to enliven an account of the Roman heroine, Agrippina (4: 383). Such fundamentalism is deeply conservative, of course, and clearly ties in with Trimmer's secular politics, which can be most easily characterized by the word "reactionary." Never does Trimmer criticize any existing social or political institutions, and this loyalism is always strongly bound up with her complete religious orthodoxy. When she came to review a book, she immediately asked, first, whether it was damaging to religion, and second, whether it was damaging to political loyalty. So sensitive was Trimmer to any infringement of political and religious rectitude that her judgment can sometimes seem rather persnickety, not to say obsessive. She censured Elizabeth Somerville's innocuous *Preludes to Knowledge*, for example, because it included an unsympathetic description of the sixteenth-century cleric and politician, Cardinal Wolsey. This description might, Trimmer feared, lead children "into prejudices against Churchmen and Prime Ministers in general" (4: 169). For Trimmer, such careless talk was hardly a trivial matter. She genuinely believed that "there is not a species of Books for Children or Youth . . . which has not been made in some way or other an engine of mischief" (2: 409), and that "books of a dangerous tendency were daily making their appearance" (*Some Account* 1: 57). This being the case, her strict literary policing had to be meticulous and unstinting.

Trimmer was far from alone in this almost paranoid fear of a politically radical and anti-Christian insurgency. During the crisis inaugurated by the French Revolution and sustained by the support that it garnered in Britain and Ireland, the menace of "Jacobinism" was the constant theme of pamphleteers, novelists, playwrights, and poets, as well as prelates and politicians. This sense of crisis reached its climax in the very last years of the 1790s and the very first years of the nineteenth century—curiously, since radicalism was actually at its height in Britain at the beginning of the 1790s. For Trimmer, as for most of her allies, "Jacobinism" was never precisely defined, though it certainly incorporated both a secular and a spiritual threat.[11] Thomas Paine's attack on organized religion, *The Age of Reason* (1794–96), published shortly after his clarion call for more social and political liberty, *The Rights of Man* (1791–92), seemed to draw the two threads together. The publication of several exposés of a grand conspiracy behind the French Revolution and assaults on religion and the political status quo around Europe seemed to confirm the link. Trimmer was particularly influenced by the Abbé Augustin Barruel's *Memoirs, Illustrating the History of Jacobinism* (1797–98). From it came the first extract that Trimmer included in the *Guardian*, and she continued to quote from Barruel, either directly or indirectly, throughout much of the rest of the work. His conspiracy theory can appear rather outlandish to modern eyes, positing as it does the existence of a secret sect, the Illuminati, who worked with the Freemasons and the French philosophes, to plot the downfall of Christian society.[12] What struck Trimmer as the most horrific element of the conspiracy was its determination to usurp control of educational institutions and thereby to poison the minds of the young. The conspiracy, she wrote, was "endeavouring to infect the minds of the rising generation, through the medium of Books of Education and Children's Books" (1: 2). Chief among the conspirators was Jean-Jacques Rousseau, whose educational theory, as she read it, excluded the formal teaching of Christianity to children. Trimmer was convinced that to follow such a course would not only result in the permanent infidelity of children, a terrible evil in itself, but would also lay Britain open to certain insurrection. It was the conviction that Jacobinism was targeting education and children's literature as an effective means of overturning the social, political, and religious order that persuaded Trimmer of the pressing need for an antidote: *The Guardian of Education*.

The first half of Myers's characterization of Trimmer is not in doubt then: she was incontrovertibly a conservative. For many commentators she has been the paradigmatic conservative, not so much an individual writer as a tendency. Mary V. Jackson, for example, has written of the "Trimmerites" and of "Trimmer's minions" (124, 249), and Samuel F. Pickering of Trimmer and "the crew associated with her" (176). Even such an acute commentator as F. J. Harvey Darton spoke blithely of "The Trimmers of that age" (159). Often she has been differentiated from the anti-Jacobin gang only so that she may be identified as the chief demagogue at its core. Thus Geoffrey Summerfield pronounces that "Of all the morally shrill women active in the late eighteenth and early nineteenth centuries, she was probably the shrillest" (188). Her anti-Jacobinism has been regarded as a given, and a half-sentence summary of her contribution to children's culture has usually been thought sufficient. She has been labeled "a belligerent moralist and educationalist of conservative views," for example, and she has been blamed for appropriating children's books "to the service of conservative bourgeois ideals" (Townsend 44; Jackson 249). Moreover, accusations of anti-Jacobinism have been fused with charges of hostility to literary progress. She has been cast as a representative of those "political conservatives" who condemned and suppressed the supposedly less restrictive, less earnest children's books of the mid-eighteenth century, as a member of "the anti-fairy-tale brigade," and as one who "ruthlessly hunted down frivolity and fantasy" (Jackson 124, 127; Moon, "Tabart" 5; Wood 221).[13]

How then, one wonders, could Myers have found room for any radicalism on Trimmer's part? Perhaps the most immediately attractive possibility is that behind Trimmer's overt anti-Jacobinism existed an almost submerged willingness to question the status quo and to sympathize with the revolutionary project. This sort of analysis found favor in the late 1980s and early 1990s, at the beginning of the flurry of scholarship that did so much to rehabilitate neglected women writers of the 1790s. In her book *Unsex'd Revolutionaries*, for example, Eleanor Ty detected an "underlying sympathy for revolutionary advocates" running in parallel with the much more explicit ideological orthodoxy in the work of several Georgian women writers, many of whom had previously been regarded as straightforwardly conservative. Ty suggested various means by which such a "double-voiced discourse" (to use Mikhail Bakhtin's term) might have been introduced into a text and could be extracted from it. For instance, Ty thought Elizabeth Hamilton's parodying of radical principles in her novel *Memoirs of Modern Philosophers* (1800) might not always have been at the expense of the parodied texts, but could "be read as a reworking rather than a condemnation of 'modern philosophy.'" Likewise, the ostensibly conservative novels of Jane Austen or Ann Radcliffe displayed "in their distrust of conventional literary forms, in their restrained use of teleological means of closure in their novels, or in their refusal to privilege the phallus" an "uneasiness with the masculine symbolic realm," and with "things as they are" more generally (Ty 28, 27, 25). The ideas of psycholinguistic critics like Luce Irigaray and Julia Kristeva were also employed to "suggest ways in which writers can subvert and challenge" patriarchal discourse (xv).

This kind of rereading has a substantial appeal. It endows neglected authors, especially women writers, with a radicalism that is far more exciting than a rather dowdy conservatism, and it makes the case for a reevaluation of their work that much more urgent. There are, though, two things to say here. First, conservatism need not be drab. The anti-Jacobin campaign brought forth graphic satires, political treatises, novels, poetry, pamphlets, and plays that were energetic, entertaining and artistically progressive, and show conservative culture to have been vibrant and multifaceted. The loyalism of respected men of letters like Edmund Burke and Isaac D'Israeli, of abusive satirists like James Gillray and the young George Canning, of moralists such as Hannah More and William Wilberforce, and of zealots like T. J. Mathias and William Gifford, varied hugely, as did their methods of propagating their views. They had as much to divide them as they had to unite them. Though no one has yet fully investigated the murky goings-on in the conservative half of Grub Street, it seems likely that the community of London anti-Jacobins formed as convoluted and sordid a community as that surveyed in Iain McCalman's study, *Radical Underground*. Moreover, given the number of anti-Jacobin publications, it is probably the conservative campaign that deserves the more credit for expanding the political constituency in the 1790s. The *Cheap Repository Tracts* and the anti-Jacobin novels outnumbered and outsold their radical equivalents, and even if their message was one of quiescence, they nevertheless brought political issues to audiences that had not been deliberately politicized before. It is almost certainly also true, though difficult to prove, that more women were involved in the production and consumption of anti-Jacobin material than its radical counterpart.

Second, Ty's suggestion that a thoroughgoing radicalism can lie behind an explicit conservatism does not easily fit Trimmer. For one thing, the sort of linguistic subversion and clever management of literary conventions that Ty detected might well undermine a superficial orthodoxy in a novel, but such tactics would be much more problematic in the sort of forthright nonfiction that appeared in *The Guardian of Education* (or, for that matter, in most of Trimmer's children's books). Furthermore, although Ty did not deal with Trimmer, she was clear that writers close to Trimmer, such as Jane West and Hannah More, spoke "from the position of the Father," defending the political and religious status quo and subscribing "to the ideological notion of female subservience to male authority" (Ty 15). There can be little doubt that Trimmer would have been in this camp too. One further problem with Ty's approach, when applied to Trimmer, is that it assumes that the radicalism that was hidden behind the conservative façade was actually the more genuine expression of the author's opinions and values, and that the conservatism was merely the dominant mode with which it was almost impossible not to comply.

If, as the argument goes, conservatism was the "default setting," then it ought not to be given too much credence. Indeed, it has been argued that certain writers adopted an overt loyalism as a cover for their more genuine, subversive attitudes. According to Ty's reading, both conservatism and radicalism could not exist at once, and we are asked to privilege the radicalism over the professed conservatism, and even to disregard the anti-Jacobinism entirely. With Trimmer, the anti-Jacobinism is so forthright that it is difficult to ignore. Thankfully, Myers's formulation of "a conservative doing radical things" does not demand that we do so. For Myers, conservatism and radicalism were not mutually exclusive.

Myers's most celebrated exemplar of the conservative–radical is Hannah More, the principal subject of her 1982 essay, "Reform or Ruin: 'A Revolution in Female Manners'" and her 1986 essay "Hannah More's Tracts for the Times." This "robust recuperation," as Anne Mellor has called it, argues that Evangelicals such as More "should be regarded as moral and social revolutionaries," as Gerald Newman had succinctly put it (Mellor 18; qtd. in Myers, "Reform" 203). Myers verified this hypothesis by comparing the opinions of More and Mary Wollstonecraft: Wollstonecraft functioning as a sort of radical touchstone, someone recognized right from the time of her death (though probably not before, as R. M. James notes) as a leading proponent of the radical critique of society. Like Wollstonecraft, Myers wrote, More preached "a militantly moral middle-class reform grounded in women's potentiality" ("Reform" 211). This potential was fulfilled when these writers began to produce children's literature. In books such as Wollstonecraft's *Original Stories* (1788), Myers argued in a subsequent essay, the reader can find "large strategic claims for female nature and capacities and for woman's ability to make a difference in her social world" ("Impeccable Governesses" 54). Whether loyalist or Jacobin, then, these women writers were all engaged in the same project of cultural reform, a project that wrested from the previously male-dominated educational establishment a new and important role for women. The question is, can Trimmer also be seen as part of this project? If so, Myers's apparent oxymoron finds an instant solution.

It seems likely that Myers would at least have begun to support her assertion of Trimmer's radicalism in this way. After all, she referred to Trimmer, fleetingly, in the same breath as More and Wollstonecraft, listing her as another of those "female educators of every stripe" who "vigorously attacked the deficiencies of fashionable training and values" and sought "to endow woman's role with more competence, dignity, and consequence" ("Reform" 201). It is not hard to see how Trimmer's life and work bear this contention out. She was apparently obsessed by educational praxis. Her son recorded that she "scarcely read a book upon any other topic" and "almost wearied her friends" by talking of little else (Some Account 1: 14). She founded one of the first Sunday schools in the kingdom, a model institution, patronized by Queen Charlotte. Three years later in 1789, she established a School of Industry to prepare young women, formerly denied an education, for self-sufficient lives in small-scale manufacturing industry.[14] Her books for children took up the very latest pedagogical practices. Her *Easy Introduction to the Knowledge of Nature* (1780), for instance, emulated Anna Laetitia Barbauld's ground-breaking *Lessons for Children* (1778) in its innovative, clear typography and its awareness that different texts were required for readers of different ages. Likewise, her many sets of copperplate prints of various historical and scriptural subjects, accompanied by descriptive texts, followed Madame de Genlis's strategy of advancing literacy and knowledge-retention by combining graphic and textual content, and by encouraging the use of these prints in card games (Pickering 189–91). As for *The Guardian of Education*, its very name (and its first sentence[15]) gives away Trimmer's determination to protect, to strengthen, and even to take control of educational theory and practice. We do not have to look further than the first page to see Trimmer, just like so many radical writers, attacking "the deficiencies of fashionable training and values" (Myers, "Reform" 201). The *Guardian's* Introduction lambastes equally parents' desires for "accomplishments"—music, drawing, dancing, "the Science of Dress" and so on—and schools' willingness to pander to these misguided wishes by providing this kind of debilitating curriculum (1: 2). The "Systems of Education Examined" sections, which appeared in all but four issues of the *Guardian*, also perfectly reflect the campaign Myers described. They make obvious the growing female control of educational discourse, for eleven of the twenty-six educational treatises reviewed were by women,[16] and they demonstrate Trimmer happily pontificating on these new pedagogic systems and overcoming her diffidence about engaging in public controversies. She confidently assessed how likely each system was to add the moral, religious, and political rigor that she thought so necessary for both the individual, especially girls, and society. On top of this assess-ment, Trimmer's "Essay on Christian Education" offered her own ped-agogic system: another contribution to the campaign to wrest away control of education from its traditional male regulators. No matter how crushingly Anglican Trimmer's system was, then, it can still be considered radical in its attempt to usurp the management of the na-tion's educational practice.

There are, however, several ways in which this re-envisaging of Trimmer as "doing radical things" by asserting female control of peda-gogic discourse might be criticized. First, Trimmer does not wholly fit Myers's paradigm. For one thing, she was not totally opposed to girls' "accomplishments." These arts might become the root of vices, she wrote in the *Guardian*, but they ought not to be banned from curricula. Rather, so long as such activities are carefully regulated, they ought to be encouraged (2: 400–06).[17] Second, however expedient it might be to see Trimmer, More, Wollstonecraft, and those other women writers whom Myers called "mentorias" ("Impeccable Governesses" 54) as contributing to the same campaign, there were substantial differences between them. Whereas More was, for most intents and purposes, an Evangelical, Trim-mer was not.[18] Unlike the Evangelicals, says Aileen Fyfe, Trimmer "placed more emphasis on God the Father and Creator than on Christ the Redeemer" (456). She also openly condemned "those who call themselves, by way of distinction, Evangelical Christians" (1: 382). Above all, her fundamentalist respect for the literary truth and inerrancy of the Scriptures contrasted with the Evangelicals' much more pragmatic piety. This distinction might be thought a rather tiresome, theological point until we observe how these religious disparities affected political positions. Like many Evangelicals, More devoted much of her energy to attempting to reform the manners of the great, which naturally involved criticism of the social élite. Even though this criticism was fairly mild and was never meant to challenge the probity of social hierarchy, such a strategy would have appalled Trimmer. She had, we should remember, balked at something as apparently trivial as a slightly unflattering por-trayal of Cardinal Wolsey. She also criticized what was otherwise a fa-vorite book, John Newbery's *The Renowned History of Little Goody Two-Shoes*, for imputing the poverty and oppression of its heroine to members of the governing class. In these times, she wrote, "when such pains are taken to prejudice the poor against the higher orders . . . we

could wish to have a veil thrown over the faults of oppressive 'squires'"—
which was precisely what More and other Evangelicals were not doing
(1: 431). Trimmer's determination to protect the sociopolitical status quo
was more absolute than More's. This determination hints that, as a corol-
lary, her radicalism must necessarily have been different too.

In certain important respects, Trimmer's radicalism did go in different directions, and perhaps went further, than that which Myers claimed
for More and the other mentorias in her "Reform or Ruin" essay. Trimmer's whole conceptualization of childhood ran contrary to that of
many of her Evangelical contemporaries and was far more progressive.
she vehemently disagrees with her Evangelical contemporaries, who believe "that children are naturally disposed to wickedness," arguing "that
by the gift of the Holy Ghost bestowed upon them in Baptism, they are
disposed to goodness" (2: 468). She added that Christ himself taught "that
infancy is to be regarded as a state of innocence" and went so far as to
say that "Children are incapable of offending God to the degree for
which the greatest eternal punishment is threatened in his Holy Word"
(1: 169–70, 392). The surprising but inevitable conclusion is that, in this
respect at least, Trimmer was making common cause with Rousseau and
the Romantics who also urged the innocence of childhood (even if their
concept of childhood innocence was practical rather than theological).
Corroboration of this unlikely alliance can be taken from Trimmer's refusal to countenance the politicization of childhood. Alan Richardson
has demonstrated that Wordsworth too was horrified by the idea that
childhood innocence, and children's literature, should be contaminated
by politics (*Literature* 109–66). It is much more surprising that Trimmer
should feel the same way, given her contention that the Jacobin conspiracy was deliberately attempting to infuse children's literature with its ne-
farious values. The temptation "to repel the enemy's insidious attacks
with similar weapons," as Trimmer's friend Jane West had put it in justi-
fying her anti-Jacobin novels, must have been hard to resist (Tale 3:
386–87). That Trimmer never included anything more than the most
mild and general political opinions in her children's books, and did not
promote such publications in the *Guardian,* testifies to an almost
Wordsworthian conviction that childhood must remain undefiled by
adult concerns.[19]

It is also surprising to find that Trimmer openly praised some of
the ideas of Rousseau, whom she elsewhere implicated in the grand Ja-

cobin conspiracy. His advocacy of direct parental involvement in the care and education of children, and his insistence on the importance of instruction beginning as early as possible and continuing into adulthood, she thought exceedingly valuable (1: 184). Trimmer apparently also sympathized with Rousseau's key idea, later taken up by Wordsworth and other Romantics, that children should not be forced to become adults too early. On this issue, she turned against one of the writers who had been most influential on her, and whose work she anthologized in the *Guardian*, Madame de Genlis. In reviewing her *New Method of Instruction for Children*, Trimmer reprobated de Genlis's scheme for hothousing children so that they would mature more quickly. De Genlis had proposed that children be encouraged to undertake adult activities for real rather than just in play: dealing with tradesmen, making medicines for the sick, traveling abroad, formally receiving company, and so on. Trimmer thought this absurd: "A family of children educated in this way would, in our opinion, be a set of ridiculous, unnatural, troublesome little creatures, fit only to live in an island by themselves" (3: 158). Furthermore, as Donelle Ruwe has pointed out, Trimmer's *An Easy Introduction to the Knowledge of Nature* had shown a distinctly Rousseauvian understanding that the countryside was the most fitting place for children to be brought up and that a Christian sensibility would be most successfully fostered through exposure to nature (9–10).[20] By and large, Trimmer's review of *Émile* was balanced and commendatory, and it was only in her reviews of books which she thought had been influenced by Rousseau that she engaged in invective. In the limited space of these reviews, Rousseau served as a sort of shorthand for the skeptical thought that Trimmer associated with the Illuminati and the conspiracy to overthrow Christian society. When she considered his work dispassionately, Trimmer actually approved of the most important of Rousseau's ideas.

Trimmer's opinions as an educationalist are also surprisingly liberal. She was certainly not the Gradgrindian we might infer from her posthumous reputation. She boasted of having made a lengthy enquiry into the new educational methodologies being proposed by "writers who treat of the philosophy of the human mind." As a result, she rejected rote learning, even of the Bible, preferring lessons carried out as dialogues between teacher and pupil that, she insisted, encouraged the child to think (2: 91, 289). Elsewhere in the *Guardian*, Trimmer offered practical advice to parents, which often seemed distinctly enlightened and reformist. She joined her voice to the chorus advocating breast-feeding, and she gave advice on how to ensure the quality of breast milk; she cautioned against feeding a child except at those times fixed for its meals; she warned against too many sweets and cakes in a child's diet; and she insisted that a mother must never become too busy to attend to her child, "as by doing so, she may check the progress of the intellect" (1: 178, 293, 355, 183). Parenting should be a joint enterprise between both father and mother, she averred. It was a new and somewhat controversial position, as she acknowledged when she lamented that, as things were, too "many fathers deprive themselves of some of life's best joys, from an idea that young children cannot be pleasing to men till they are old enough to amuse them with their prattle" (1: 101, 352). She wanted infants to be taken out of their cradles and their nurses' arms and to be placed on the carpet, and "no further restraint should be laid upon him." Thus the child would acquire muscular strength and "useful experience" (1: 242). Like an early Dr. Spock, she condemned "the gilded and painted toys usually given to young children," advocating the use of "bits of wood of different sizes" (1: 421): toys that would strengthen the imagination.[21] Modern speech therapists would surely approve of her strictures on encouraging the development of language skills. After a child was six months old, everything "should be called by its right name with distinct articulation" and should be passed to the child for him or her to handle. This kind of rational and useful conversation would be far more suitable than using baby-talk (1: 242). All this advice is found in the first volume alone.

Even Trimmer's reviews of children's books argue that the main agenda of the *Guardian* was as forward-looking as it was reactionary. Her hostility to any attempt to frighten child readers into good behavior, as many of her Evangelical contemporaries were doing, seems very modern. A characteristic review criticized one writer for punishing the young protagonist of a moral tale who had persecuted birds by having a dog set on him that dragged him about by his leg. She was horrified when the same author suggested that the grave of a boy who had been wicked throughout his short life would forever be circled by carrion birds that might even dig up the boy's remains (1: 305–06). She disliked anything that might frighten a child. Ann and Jane Taylor and Adelaide O'Keeffe's *Original Poems for Infant Minds* was culpable for putting into children's minds notions of being "confined in a coffin" and "buried in the cold grave" (4: 79). Similarly blameworthy was the sort of tale brought to the pitch of perfection by the sisters Mary Martha Sherwood and Lucy Lyttleton Cameron, which ended with the pious death of the young hero or heroine and offered only the promise of heavenly bliss to satisfy the reader's desire for denouement. It would be far better, Trimmer wrote, to reward a virtuous protagonist with happiness in this world (1: 392–93).[22] Clearly Trimmer's more humane approach to the enforcement of the moral tale's morality was premised on her construction of childhood as a state of innocence, which contrasted with the Evangelicals' neo-Puritan insistence on the innate sinfulness of children. Her concern was practical as well as theological, though, and rested firmly on consideration for children's psychological welfare. Her liberal credentials might also be asserted on the basis of a campaign to foster social harmony. Writing in the *Edinburgh Review*, Sidney Smith, himself indulging in a bout of conservative nostalgia for the "good old days" of his own education, censured her for objecting to the disciplining of a child by forcing him to parade around a classroom shouting "Old Clothes" like a London tradesman. "The punishment is objected to on the part of Mrs. Trimmer, because it inculcates a dislike to Jews," Smith mocked (182). His attitude casts Trimmer in a role customarily denied her by literary history: the more enlightened party.

Trimmer also appears as something of a reformist when she is compared with those writers who have advocated fairy tales as the most suitable reading material for children. Notoriously, Trimmer did not care for fairy tales (although she was not entirely consistent in this opinion, and the few reviews in which she voiced it were very short and not particularly severe (1: 62; 4: 74–75, 94–95). As Nicholas Tucker has pointed out, champions of fairy tales—John Ruskin, C. S. Lewis, J. R. R. Tolkien—have tended to be political and social conservatives (113). According to Alan Richardson, who adds Wordsworth to this tradition, fairy tales were widely understood as an "'innocent' food for rural folk and children," a literary form that would return "the new mass readership to an apolitical, class-specific discourse." Fairy tales, in other words, would militate against the development of political consciousness and social change ("Wordsworth" 45). Read in this light, Trimmer's hostility to fairy tales suddenly appears to be a deliberate attempt to make children's literature relevant and socially useful rather than an ideological anesthetic. The idea that Trimmer regarded children's literature as a force that should change society, rather than as one that should be used to make it stay the same, is convincing, and could help to account for her low opinion of fairy tales. Even if this claim seems tendentious, Trimmer's hostility to fairy tales must nevertheless seem rather modern and not at all reactionary (as it is usually thought to be), when her actual reasons are examined. Nicholas Tucker has defended Trimmer on the basis that her chief aim was to protect children from all that was frightening in fairy tales, from that which savored of superstition and the irrational, and from the bawdy material that often appeared in chapbooks alongside fairy tales. These concerns seem not only eminently reasonable but are also still current, even in a world as enthusiastic about fairy tales as today's. Trimmer's concern seems particularly valid when we consider that shocking, brutal, and semipornographic tales such as "Blue Beard" were appearing alongside apparently more innocuous tales like "Cinderella" in editions of Charles Perrault's *Histories, or Tales of Past Times* (Tucker).

The denunciation of fairy tales also contributed to what was perhaps Trimmer's most radical ambition for *The Guardian of Education*: that it should imbue the corpus of children's literature which had already developed, and which was then expanding more rapidly than ever before, with a careful regulation and a consequent respectability, neither of which it had previously enjoyed. Trimmer knew that fairy tales had long been popular with children, but for her, they were associated with a body of popular literature which included ribald ballads, coarse chapbooks, and the servants' tales of "Sprites and Goblins," which Locke had inveighed against a century earlier in *Some Thoughts Concerning Education* (196). As well as being liable to damage a child psychologically (Trimmer's great fear according to Tucker), a more pressing concern to Trimmer was that such material could be thought to be bringing the whole children's literature project into disrepute, making the children's book no more than the written equivalent of the nursemaid's tale. The chief selling point of the new, post-Newbery children's literature was that it could enhance a child's life, economically, socially, morally, or spiritually. It was, in a word, improving. If it could entertain along the way, then it was so much the better, especially if the delight could assist the instruction. After all, an entertaining book could only increase sales, appealing to the actual end-users (children), as well as the likely purchasers of the books (adults). The majority of fairy tales, or at least those early examples written by Perrault and D'Aulnoy that Trimmer was thinking of when she issued her denunciation, did not support this agenda. They offered little in the way of instruction and, perhaps worse, were tainted with their association with servants and the popular culture of the hoi polloi, which was precisely what the new children's literature was attempting to take its readers away from. In the defense of what was still a new literary genre, struggling to be taken seriously, therefore, Trimmer attempted to detach fairy tales from the main body of children's books. Her condemnation of legendary tales, religious tracts, novels, and other forms of popular literature that might be mistaken for what she considered true children's literature can be considered as part of the same attempt to define the limits of the genre and eradicate anything that compromised its program (4: 75, 52–58; 2: 408).

It is not only in the attempt to remove unsuitable printed material from the children's library that one witnesses Trimmer's campaign to garner respectability and to secure economic viability for children's literature. The essay "Observations on the Changes Which Have Taken Place in Books for Children and Young Persons" in the opening volume of the *Guardian* was dedicated to the same objective. It established a canon of children's literature, the aim of which was to impress prospective book-buyers with the huge strides the genre had made and with the dignity and usefulness of modern children's books. The essay touched on the tales of Mother Goose but set them in an historical past: "the first period of Infantine and Juvenile Literature," an age when children's books were calculated to "entertain the imagination, rather than to improve the heart or cultivate the understanding." By the time she was writing, Trimmer concluded, such stuff had been superseded and "much that is sound and good is to be met with . . . and we trust the stock is still increasing from the most respectable sources" (1: 62–63, 65). In addition, Trimmer's reviews, spread out over all five volumes, contributed to the same campaign, identifying those books that were worthy of adding to the new children's literature, and those that were stuck in the past, offering nothing to benefit the reader. *Mince-Pies for Christmas*, for instance, a book of riddles, receives short shrift. Ostensibly this reaction was because it included some "exceptionable" jibes at monarchy ("What is majesty deprived of its externals?" The answer: "A Jest"—"majesty" without its first and last letters), but the volume also crossed the boundary between literature for adults and literature for children, and as such, like fairy tales, threatened to undermine the newly won sense of purpose carved out by Trimmer's generation of children's books (4: 97–101). Hence, its dressing-down.

If Trimmer was committed to detecting the rotten apples in the literature barrel, texts that compromised the respectability of children's literature because of their vulgar and unimproving content, she also designed the *Guardian* to protect book buyers from the more mundane and practical perils of the market. She signaled no ideological objection to the tales of Louis François Jauffret, for instance, but what she resented was the fact that "the same materials, chiefly imported from Germany and France, after undergoing the operation of translation into our native tongue, are worked up in a variety of forms, so as to be purchased over and over again; sometimes as articles in periodical works, sometimes as detached tales, and very often as parts of different collections" (4: 186). This kind of warning to prospective purchasers appeared frequently. Trimmer pointed out revisions of old works under new titles and exposed purportedly original volumes that included already published material. She castigated the use of false attributions of authorship to hoodwink the public (including the piracy of her own name), and she bemoaned the use of "plausible title-pages, handsome bindings, and attractive prints" to fool the consumer into unnecessary expenditure. She even railed at the ever-increasing price of children's books (3: 383–89; 2: 360–63; 3: 284; 4: 186; 5: 413). As all these things show, she was determined to be the consumer's friend. All her reviews, whatever their overt ideological import, were designed, at base, to save book buyers money by showing them what was worth their investment and what wasted their money.

The Guardian of Education was intended to enable consumers to navigate what had become an unregulated and frenzied market. Just at the period when Trimmer was compiling the *Guardian*, children's books were proliferating as never before. Formerly they had been scarce, and consumers had been forced to take what they could get. But by the turn of the nineteenth century, the more powerful agents in the market were the buyers, not the sellers. *The Guardian of Education* was designed to empower these consumers, giving them the knowledge to select their purchases wisely. It had other agendas of course—Trimmer's strident Christianity, her anti-Jacobinism, her campaign for educational best practice, her attempt to instill a progressive understanding of children's needs—but all her campaigns overlapped. Trimmer's insistence that different children's books were required for different age-groups, for example, was a pedagogic principle that she had espoused as early as her first books for children published in the 1780s. It was restated in the *Guardian*, her reviews being organized under separate headings—"Books for Children," "Books for Young Persons"—and some going so far as to specify that a particular book might suit, for instance, "a little boy of six or seven years" (4: 189). In the *Guardian*, though, she aimed simultaneously to save consumers money by pointing out precisely which books would suit their present needs, and thus to bring some discipline, trustworthiness, and creditability to a formerly unruly market. The two programs went hand in hand. Even Trimmer's anti-Jacobinism was bolstered by, and itself reinforced, Trimmer's conviction of the importance of children's books. What, after all, could cast the Jacobin conspiracy in a worse light than if it could be shown to be targeting children? And what could argue more strongly for the importance and respectability of children's literature than a conviction that it could be the most decisive battlefield in the fight against the Jacobin menace?

Trimmer can be called a radical for several reasons, then. As Myers suggested, her determination to wrest control of education away from its traditional male guardians was a quiet, but significant, act of subversion. So too was her implicit insistence that children, and especially girls, could become much more useful members of society, and more self-fulfilled too, if only they were properly educated. At the same time, her understanding of childhood was surprisingly modern and brought a distinctly Rousseauvian and Romantic agenda to the mainstream of British society. Her child-rearing program was also progressive, though it must be admitted, not always so. She believed strongly in partnership-parenting, for instance, but the shackles of patriarchy are still evident when she encourages a mother to tell her son that his father was "the person who supplies money to buy all the little boy wants" (1: 353). But above all, the most radical achievement of the *Guardian* was its attempt to raise the status of children's literature itself. By driving a wedge between children's books, and chapbooks, fairy tales, novels, and tracts, Trimmer was defining children's literature as a distinct branch of literature, and, moreover, a genre untarnished by associations with vulgar popular print culture. By identifying and excoriating unsuitable books—for whatever religious and political reasons—Trimmer contended that those which were left were valuable and beneficial to their readers: the chief selling point of the new children's literature. This faith in the power of children's literature to improve its readers was not wholly new, though in Trimmer's hands it gained a new potency. It had existed since Locke's *Some Thoughts Concerning Education* and his suggestion that the child was a tabula rasa upon which educators might inscribe what they wished. But Trimmer was willing to make an even bolder claim for the importance of children's literature, identifying it not only as the key to personal development, and by extension, to society's future, but also, potentially, constructing it as the safeguard of the nation in a time of crisis. This was a truly radical claim. Perceived threats to national security would come and go over the next centuries—Bonaparte, Nazism, Communism, terrorism—but never again would the importance of children's literature be so ardently asserted as when Trimmer invoked its power to save Britain from the Jacobin menace. Trimmer deliberately cast herself as the mother of the nation, the guardian of all British children's education and reading. The role was uncontested. Trimmer became hugely influential, and not only within her natural Anglican and loyalist constituency. When she began writing books for children, the genre was precarious and marginal. By the time *The Guardian of Education* had come to the end of its run, children's literature was a defined, regulated, and respectable genre, and it was valued for its importance to society as a whole, as well as for individual children. It had reached this flourishing maturity under Trimmer's strict but nurturing maternal supervision.

NOTES

1. An 1800 catalogue of titles for sale from the famous Newbery children's bookshop at the corner of St. Paul's Churchyard, London, offered over thirty works by Trimmer, more than by any other author (Pickering 61). The Newbery shop might not have carried many of Trimmer's works published by other firms.

2. Henry Scott Trimmer, Sarah Trimmer's son and the editor of her journals (hereafter cited as *Some Account*), suggested that the effort of producing the *Guardian* "was too great a fatigue, and at length brought on so serious an illness, that Mrs. Trimmer was obliged entirely to desist" (*Some Account* 1: 57–58). Almost a year after its final number, Trimmer was still insisting in her private correspondence that the *Guardian* would be resumed (Letter to Mrs. Cockle, 3 March 1807).

3. Jeremy Bentham went further, almost blasphemously complaining that "What the Blessed Virgin is to the Church of Rome, this *Blessed Matron*"—

meaning Trimmer—"is to the *Church of England.*" Her writings, Bentham felt, had eclipsed in importance the actual religion of Christ: "In the Mother," he explained, "the son finds a rival and that rival, is a preferred one" (19).

4. *Gentleman's Magazine* 81 (March 1811): 203; see also 81 (February 1811): 112.

5. For example, Nicholas Tucker and Donelle Ruwe.

6. Many of the arguments made in this essay are set out at greater length in Grenby's introduction to the 2002 facsimile edition of the *Guardian.*

7. It is difficult to assess the precise coverage of the *Guardian* since it is far from certain how many children's books were published in any given year. However, if we compare Trimmer's reviews with Marjorie Moon's very complete checklists of certain individual publishers ("John Harris" 168–76; "Benjamin Tabart" 172–74), we see that, on average, around 50 percent of the books published in a given year between 1802 and 1806 (whether new or repeated) were noticed in the *Guardian.* The figure is a little higher for John Harris, successor to the Newbery firm, and a little lower for works issued by the less respectable firm run by Benjamin Tabart.

8. See *The Guardian of Education* (1: 110–111). Hereafter, references to the *Guardian* will be given parenthetically in the text, enclosing volume and page numbers.

9. Extracts were acceptable, such as her own *Sacred History, selected from the Scriptures* (1782). A solitary exception to her decree against modifications of the Scriptures was made for Hannah More's *Sacred Dramas*, which Trimmer unaccountably praised both in the *Guardian* (2: 498–501) and in her private correspondence with More (W. Roberts 2: 59).

10. See Ruwe for a more substantial discussion of Trimmer's strictures on "Scolfield's" *Bible Stories.*

11. For analysis of manifestations of anti-Jacobinism, see Butler; De Montluzin; Dickinson; Grenby, "Anti-Jacobin"; Grieder; Hole, "British" and "Pulpits"; Philp; and Scott.

12. See Roberts for discussion of how John Robison and William Playfair also sought to expose the conspiracy.

13. For other similarly hostile assessments, see Stone (77) and Sandner, esp. chs. 2–3.

14. For details of Trimmer's life, the principal sources are her son's edition of her letters and biography (*Some Account*) along with Balfour, Bradley, Rodgers, Wills, and Yarde.

15. "Perhaps there never has been a time since the creation of the world, when the important business of EDUCATION was more an object of general concern in any civilized nation, than it is at the present day in our own" (1: 1).

16. The full lists of authors whose educational texts were reviewed is as follows: Elizabeth Hamilton; Maria Edgeworth (twice, once with Richard Lovell

Edgeworth); Stéphanie Félicité de Sillert Brulart de Genlis (twice); Hannah More (twice); Lady Mary Champion de Crespigny; Priscilla Wakefield; Charlotte Badger, Jane West; Jean-Jacques Rousseau; Edward Kendall; Joseph Lancaster; Johann Gottlieb Burckhardt; Anthony Florian Madinger Willich; David Williams; Joachim Heinrich Campe (twice); Andrew Cowan; Thomas Simons; Chirstian Fuerchtegott Gellert; Andrew Bell; J. Burton (gender unknown). Trimmer also reviewed one anthology and one anonymous text.

17. Typical are Trimmer's strictures on dancing: "dancing is now to be considered merely as an amusement, which may be innocently enjoyed within the bounds of moderation; and at reasonable hours; but which certainly becomes sinful when it is carried to excess, and allowed to break in upon the time that should be devoted to that sweet and calm reflection, which youth will naturally enjoy when the growing passions and appetites are kept in due subjection." Trimmer praised Hannah More's ideas of "Children's Balls" but condemned any attempt to express piety through dance, as had been suggested by Elizabeth Hamilton (2: 402 and notes).

18. The problems of identifying More as an Evangelical are discussed in Robert Hole's introduction to *Selected Writings of Hannah More* (xxii–xxiv).

19. See Grenby for a more substantial discussion of Trimmer's reluctance to politicize her writing for children ("Politicizing").

20. Deborah Wills expresses reservations about these similarities in her essay on Trimmer (158, 344).

21. Consulting *drspock.com* and its "message boards" reveals that many of the issues Trimmer raised are still being discussed and that numerous points of congruence exist between the influential mid-twentieth-century pediatrician Dr. Spock and Mrs. Trimmer. On the subject of toys, for instance, the Spock view reiterates what Trimmer had taught: "A good-size bag of wooden blocks of different shapes is worth 10 toys to any six-year-old" (Needleman).

22. See also Trimmer's complaints about Maria Edgeworth's famous tale, "The Purple Jar," which lament the author's overly cruel enforcement of the moral lesson (2: 235–37).

WORKS CITED

Balfour, Clara Lucas. *Working Women of the Last Half Century: The Lesson of Their Lives.* London: Cash, 1854.

Bentham, Jeremy. *Church of Englandism and Its Catechism Examined: Preceded by Strictures on the Exclusionary System as Pursued in the National Society's Schools.* London: Effingham, 1818.

Bradley, David G. "Sarah Trimmer (1741–1810). Guardian of Morals." Masters Diss. Loughborough U of Technology, 1986.

Butler, Marilyn, ed. Burke, *Paine, Godwin and the Revolution Controversy*. Cambridge: Cambridge UP, 1984.

Darton, F. J. Harvey. *Children's Books in England. Five Centuries of Social Life*. Ed. Brian Alderson. Rev. ed. Cambridge: Cambridge UP 1982.

De Montluzin, Emily Lorraine. *The Anti-Jacobins, 1798–1800. The Early Contributors to the "Anti-Jacobin Review."* Basingstoke: Macmillan, 1988.

Dickinson, H. T. "Popular Conservatism and Militant Loyalism 1789–1815." *Britain and the French Revolution 1789–1815*. Ed. H. T. Dickinson. Basingstoke: Macmillan, 1989. 104–25.

Fyfe, Aileen. "Reading Children's Books in Late Eighteenth-Century Dissenting Families." *Historical Journal* 43 (2000): 453–73.

Grenby, M. O. *The Anti-Jacobin Novel: British Conservatism and the French Revolution*. Cambridge: Cambridge UP, 2001.

———. Introduction. *The Guardian of Education: A Periodical Work*. By Sarah Trimmer. Bristol: Thoemmes, 2002.

———. "Politicizing the Nursery: British Children's Literature and the French Revolution." *Lion and the Unicorn* 27.1 (2003): 1–26.

Grieder, Theodore Godfrey, Jr. "The French Revolution in the British Drama: A Study in British Popular Literature of the Decade of Revolution." Diss. Stanford University, 1957.

Hole, Robert. "British Counter-Revolutionary Popular Propaganda in the 1790s." *Britain and Revolutionary France: Conflict, Subversion and Propaganda*. Ed. Colin Jones. Exeter: U of Exeter P, 1983. 53–68.

———. *Pulpits, Politics and Public Order in England 1760–1832*. Cambridge: Cambridge UP, 1989.

———, ed. *Selected Writings of Hannah More*. London: Pickering, 1996.

Immel, Andrea. *Revolutionary Reviewing: Sarah Trimmer's Guardian of Education and the Cultural Politics of Juvenile Literature*. An Index to "The Guardian." Occasional Papers 4. Los Angeles: Dept. of Special Collections, U of California Los Angeles, 1990.

———. "James Pettit Andrews's 'Books' (1790): The First Critical Survey of English Children's Literature." *Children's Literature* 28 (2000): 147–63.

Jackson, Mary V. *Engines of Instruction, Mischief, and Magic: Children's Literature from Its Beginnings to 1839*. Lincoln: U of Nebraska P, 1989.

James, R. M. "On the Reception of Mary Wollstonecraft's *A Vindication of the Rights of Woman*." *Journal of the History of Ideas* 39 (1978): 293–302.

Locke, John. *Some Thoughts Concerning Education*. Ed. John W. and Jean S. Yolton. Oxford: Clarendon, 1989.

McCalman, Iain. *Radical Underground: Prophets, Revolutionaries and Pornographers in London, 1795–1840*. Cambridge: Cambridge UP, 1988.

Mellor, Anne K. *Mothers of the Nation. Women's Political Writing in England, 1780–1830*. Bloomington: Indiana UP, 2002.

Moon, Marjorie. *John Harris's Books for Youth 1801–1843: A Check-list.* Winchester: St. Paul's Bibliographies, 1987.

———. *Benjamin Tabart's Juvenile Library: A Bibliography of Books for Children Published, Written, Edited and Sold by Mr. Tabart, 1801–1820.* Winchester: St. Paul's Bibliographies, 1990.

Myers, Mitzi. "Hannah More's Tracts for the Times: Social Fiction and Female Ideology." *Fetter'd or Free? British Women Novelists, 1670–1815.* Ed. Mary Anne Scofield and Cecelia Macheski. Athens: Ohio UP, 1986. 264–84.

———. "Impeccable Governesses, Rational Dames, and Moral Mothers: Mary Wollstonecraft and the Female Tradition in Georgian Children's Books." *Children's Literature* 14 (1986): 31–59.

———. Introduction. *Revolutionary Reviewing: Sarah Trimmer's Guardian of Education and the Cultural Politics of Juvenile Literature, An Index.* By Andrea Immel. Occasional Papers 4. Los Angeles: Dept. of Special Collections, U of California–Los Angeles, 1990. vii–xv.

———. "Reform or Ruin: 'A Revolution in Female Manners'" *Studies in Eighteenth-Century Culture* 11 (1982): 199–216.

Philp, Mark. "Vulgar Conservatism, 1792–93." *English Historical Review* 110 (1995): 42–69.

Pickering, Samuel F., Jr. *John Locke and Children's Books in Eighteenth-Century England.* Knoxville: U of Tennessee P, 1981.

Playfair, William. *The History of Jacobinism, Its Crimes, Cruelties and Perfidies, from the Commencement of the French Revolution, to the Death of Robespierre.* 2 vols. London: Wright, 1798.

Richardson, Alan. "Wordsworth, Fairy Tales, and the Politics of Children's Reading." *Romanticism and Children's Literature in Nineteenth-Century England.* Ed. James Holt McGavran, Jr. Athens: U of Georgia P, 1991. 34–53.

———. *Literature, Education, and Romanticism. Reading as Social Practice, 1780–1832.* Cambridge: Cambridge UP, 1994.

Roberts, J. M. *The Mythology of Secret Societies.* London: Secker, 1972.

Roberts, William. *Memoirs of the Life and Correspondence of Hannah More.* 4 vols. London: Seeley, 1834.

Robison, John. *Proofs of a Conspiracy Against All the Religions and Governments of Europe, Carried on in the Secret Meetings of Free-Masons, Illuminati and Reading Societies.* London: Cadell, 1797.

Rodgers, Betsy. *Cloak of Charity: Studies in Eighteenth-Century Philanthropy.* London: Methuen, 1949.

Ruwe, Donelle. "Guarding the British Bible from Rousseau: Sarah Trimmer, William Godwin, and the Pedagogical Periodical." *Children's Literature* 29 (2001): 1–17.

Sandner, David. *The Fantastic Sublime: Romanticism and Transcendence in Nineteenth-Century Children's Fantasy Literature.* Westport: Greenwood, 1996.

Scott, Iain Robertson. "'Things As They Are': The Literary Response to the French Revolution 1789–1815." *Britain and the French Revolution 1789–1815.* Ed. H. T. Dickinson. Basingstoke: Macmillan, 1989. 229–49.

Smith, Sidney. Rev. of *A Comparative View of the New Plan of Education Promulgated by Mr. Joseph*, by Sarah Trimmer. *Edinburgh Review* 9 (1806): 177–84.

Needleman, Robert. Rev. of *Baby and Child Care*. By Robert Spock. 1998. dr-spock.com. 19 February 2003 http://www.drspock.com/article/0,1510,5538,00.html.

Stone, Wilbur Macey. "Emasculated Juveniles." *American Book Collector: A Monthly Magazine for Book Lovers* 5 (1934): 77–80.

Summerfield, Geoffrey. *Fantasy and Reason: Children's Literature in the Eighteenth Century.* London: Methuen, 1984.

Townsend, John Rowe. *Written for Children: An Outline of English-Language Children's Literature.* Harmondsworth: Pelican, 1976.

Trimmer, Henry Scott, ed. *Some Account of the Life and Writings of Mrs. Trimmer, with Original Letters, and Meditations and Prayers, Selected from Her Journal.* 2 vols. London: Rivington, 1814.

Trimmer, Sarah. *The Guardian of Education. A Periodical Work. 1802–1806.* Facsim ed. Ed. M. O. Grenby. Bristol: Thoemmes, 2002.

———. *Letter to Mrs. Cockle*. 3 March 1807. British Lib., London. Mss. 18, 204, f 178.

Tucker, Nicholas. "Fairy Tales and Their Early Opponents. In Defence of Mrs. Trimmer." *Opening the Nursery Door. Reading, Writing and Childhood 1600–1900.* Ed. Mary Hilton, Morag Styles, and Victor Watson. London: Routledge, 1997. 104–16.

Ty, Eleanor. *Unsex'd Revolutionaries. Five Women Novelists of the 1790s.* Toronto: U of Toronto P, 1993.

West, Jane. *A Tale of the Times; By the Author of A Gossip's Story.* 3 vols. London: Longman, 1799.

———. "To the Memory of Mrs. Trimmer." *Gentleman's Magazine* 81 (1811): 261.

Wills, Deborah. "Sarah Trimmer." *DLB*. Vol. 158. Ed. Gary Kelly and Edd Applegate. Detroit: Gale, 1996. 340–48.

Wood, Marcus. *Radical Satires and Print Culture 1790–1822.* Oxford: Clarendon, 1994.

Yarde, D. M. *The Life and Works of Sarah Trimmer, a Lady of Brentford.* Bedfont, Middx.: Hounslow and District History Society, 1972.

———. *Sarah Trimmer of Brentford and Her Children: With Some of Her Early Writings 1780–1786.* Heston, Middx.: Hounslow and District History Society, 1990.

Part 3

THE POLITICS OF PEDAGOGY
AND THE CHILD

The Making and Unmaking of a Children's Classic
The Case of Scott's Ivanhoe

Bruce Beiderwell and Anita Hemphill McCormick

From the publication of *Waverley* in 1814 until his death in 1832, Walter Scott was an extraordinary literary presence. Of course, Scott had created a notable career well before his first novel appeared; he was an editor, a poet, and an antiquarian. But his novels in particular were—by the standards of his time—wildly popular, enthusiastically reviewed, and readily translated. Goethe admired them. Jane Austen mused that it was hardly fair that Scott the respected poet would turn not only to writing novels, but to writing good novels. A bit later, Balzac would boldly lay claim to the status of a French Walter Scott. And the young Dickens would plan on turning away from the serial form to complete a three-volume historical novel in the prestigious manner of Scott (the novel became *Barnaby Rudge*, but Dickens was never to break from serial publication).

Scott had, in a way unusual for a novelist of his time, a *serious* reputation. He was "The Great Unknown" (who was nevertheless known despite his official anonymity), the "Wizard of the North" (a title offered without irony); he was compared to Shakespeare (however much he discounted the comparison). The gap between Scott's grand stature in his own day and his thin claim on a modern readership has become to some extent a scholarly prompt. When Ina Ferris, for example, examines the material conditions that gave shape to Scott's career, she argues that the rise of journals in the early nineteenth century in some ways necessitated the emergence of Walter Scott, or more precisely *a* Walter Scott. The reviewers, after all, needed something to review that a broadly well-educated audience had an interest in reading. And these same reviewers could not lay claim to their own legitimacy if they had nothing substantial to review. Scott was the ideal available subject. A case for his seriousness as an artist could easily be made in the context of the literary values of the time: he was in effect pre-approved by virtue of his success as a poet (a more dignified identity than novelist). And by making history his subject, he surmounted common assumptions about the inconsequential nature of plain fiction. History was also, as Ferris convincingly argues, a thoroughly gendered discipline; it was a study for serious, adult males. In a time when the novel was oftentimes seen as neither serious nor male, ambitious critics needed Scott as much as he needed them (Ferris 19–59).

But if Scott arrived at the right time, it seems that the right time didn't last. Although it is not quite accurate to say as many have that "The Great Unknown" became "The Great Unread," Scott's critical reputation doesn't long hold steady beyond his death in 1832. Carlyle was presumptuous enough to announce the process of diminishment just six years later (345–73). Of course, Scott remained a figure of polite respect, but a specific form of diminishment is worth charting. For as the century moved forward, Scott became notable in a very different literary/cultural context. His medieval novels—and *Ivanhoe* in particular—took on a new identity as "children's classics" (arguably a new category). We will focus on how and to what purpose late Victorian and Edwardian readers reshaped *Ivanhoe*'s canonical status. In complex ways, that reshaping reveals how adult needs and anxieties are superimposed on books for children and the uses we make of such books.

In *Ivanhoe*'s case, the transition to children's fiction is anticipated by a move away from adult respect. Fifty years after Scott's death, Mark Twain did his darndest to sink metaphorically Scott's reputation in *Adventures of Huckleberry Finn*; the decrepit, abandoned steamboat named the *Walter Scott* breaks to pieces and goes under the waters of the Mississippi. A year earlier in *Life on the Mississippi* (1883), Twain had registered intense dislike, but no such assured dismissal of Scott's cultural importance. Indeed, Twain blamed "Sir Walter" for causing the Civil War: "Sir Walter" made every southern male a "colonel" or a "general" ready to defend "honor" on the field of battle (Twain 500–02). Of course, Twain possessed a special contempt for conventional attitudes toward tradition and authority, but the terms he invokes reveal an important transformation in Scott's reputation: for good or bad, the masculine qualities that had helped define Scott as "major" (i.e., masculine, vigorous, ambitious) began to characterize him as "boyish."

Twain was not the only (or even the first) to register a profound shift in the way Scott's fictions were perceived. Nor was he alone in reading Scott's medieval novels as most illustrative of that shift. In 1858, Walter Bagehot singled out *Ivanhoe* as a Scott novel of a distinctly juvenile and gendered appeal. The pageantry, the jousts, the repeated and physically enforced claims of honor constituted a simplistic vision uncluttered by reference to subtle moral or psychological reflections: "The charm of *Ivanhoe* is addressed to a simpler sort of imagination—to that kind of boyish fancy that idolizes medieval society as the 'fighting time.' Every boy has heard of tournaments, and has a firm persuasion that in an age of tournaments life was thoroughly well understood" (Bagehot 2: 149).

What Bagehot casually observes (an idealization of medieval society and order) is of course precisely what enrages Twain. It is also what inspires John Ruskin, who opens his *Præterita* (1885) by proclaiming what he had learned as a child from reading Scott's novels: "a most sincere love of kings and a dislike of everybody who attempted to disobey them" (14). From a variety of political, temperamental, and moral perspectives, it seems clear that in the last half of the nineteenth century, Scott had come to matter as a writer for children—and matter less as a serious, adult artist.

To some extent, becoming a children's book was a process of flat dismissal; for highly literate Edwardians, to matter as a writer for children meant to matter very little at all. In his *Aspects of the Novel* (1927), E. M. Forster diminishes Scott by associating him with childhood experiences. In fact, Forster maintains that any remnant of adult regard for Scott arises from fond memories of youthful encounters:

> Many of the elder generation had him read to them when they were young; he is entangled with happy sentimental memories, with holidays in or residence in Scotland. They love him indeed for the same reason that I loved and still love *The Swiss Family Robinson*. I could lecture to you now on *The Swiss Family Robinson* and it would be a glowing lecture, because of the emotions felt in boyhood. (31)

But as glowing as such memories may be, Forster leaves no doubt that they constitute scant basis for adult reflection: "Is he [Scott] really more than a reminder of early happiness? And until our brains . . . decay, must we not put all this aside when we attempt to understand books?" (32).

It is clear that "books" for Forster are complex and challenging. Books are characterized by feelings of ambivalence and unease. Real books such as these are for adults. Adults do not need, or should not want, their novels to entertain merely or, even worse perhaps, teach. Forster's "we" designates mature readers, who should not return to inferior pleasures of simple stories (or to a state of happiness) until their brains "decay." Forster's implied notion of child as a smiling intellectual dotard is perhaps not typical, but his association of moral clarity or assurance with youth (along with the paired notion of the progressive break from those qualities that arrives with age) relates to a common, if richly varied, theme of the special value—or peculiar dangers—of reading in childhood, as well as the place of Scott's novels in that reading.

Virginia Woolf links what she sees as the youthfulness of Scott's fiction to the decidedly less mature quality of an entire era. In *To the Lighthouse*, Mr. Ramsey is moved by reading Scott because he possesses an inchoate sense that something he valued in youth has passed (118–21). Woolf gives shape to the immature feeling of her character through his affection for the Waverley novels. To her mind, Scott's appeal lies in the confidence he has that his values are shared values. Scott's time allowed for a robust presentation of character and action in which modern/contemporary—and here I think we can equate "adult"—readers and writers can no longer believe (Woolf, *Common Reader* 238). Of course, Woolf's standards were notoriously high and decidedly "mature"; to her mind, George Eliot's *Middlemarch* stands almost alone among English novels in that it was written for "grown up people" (*Common Reader* 168). The distinction between children and adults comes to define aesthetic value along with moral/political realism.

To the extent that *Ivanhoe* remained an adult novel in the late nineteenth and early twentieth century, it did so as what we might call (with a bow to Forster) a "Leonard Bast novel." Bast is a character in Forster's *Howards End*—a bank clerk with longings for the kind of easy familiarity with "culture" that upper middle-class people like Helen and Margaret Schlegel exhibit and consume so gracefully. Trapped in his dead-end job and entangled with a ruthlessly vulgar woman, Bast cherishes the times he can read Ruskin or attend a concert, and some of his money goes to purchase books that give him the sensation that he is cultured, or that at least he is becoming cultured. And of course, it was an age when many women of various classes became interested in advancing their educations, too. In the later nineteenth century and early years of the twentieth, certain publishers' series enabled upwardly aspiring working-class and lower middle-class adults to discern what books better-educated people considered central to the canon: if *Ivanhoe* was in the "Ward & Lock Standard Novels" series (1880) and among "Sir John Lubbock's Hundred Books" (1891), then this market would be more likely to view them as worth purchasing and reading. Series like "The Burleigh Library" (1896) may allude to a then-familiar Tennyson poem, "The Lord of Burleigh"; this poem recounts the romance of a Lord of Burghley who, the story goes, courted a working-class girl without letting her know of his title. The poem's fantasy of upward mobility plays to the sorts of fantasies a Leonard Bast reader indulges in the very act of acquiring a library. Other commonplace features, such as an engraving of an exalted-looking Scott, illustrations by well-known artists, and markers of authenticity, could also signal to Leonard Bast readers a kind of high seriousness: the 1875 Routledge edition, for example, was marketed "with steel plates from designs by George Cruikshank and other artists" along "with the author's notes."

All of these editions suggest that, at some level, *Ivanhoe* was beginning to move downward in the hierarchical canon of serious literature. But *Ivanhoe* came on very strongly through the same period as a significant children's book. The rapid movement toward an identity as a late Victorian children's classic must be aligned with Britain's Education Act of 1870. To understand *Ivanhoe*'s newly defined cultural place, it is essential to think of the broad cultural impact of this large historical moment. The Education Act was a close follow-up to the Reform Act of 1867, which expanded suffrage dramatically, giving voting rights to untold numbers of British men who had no formal education. If more men were to vote, more should be educated to vote well. And if men were to vote well, they would need to be schooled in the virtues of an increasingly ambitious, commercially expansive culture.

Parliament moved quickly to ensure that in the near future voters would have at least an elementary education; Robert Lowe gave voice—albeit a bitter voice—to many Members' concerns when he said, "We must compel our future Masters to learn their letters." The Education Act of 1870 made universal elementary education mandatory for British children, and it required that every schoolchild in the thousands of new state schools have two reading books. At least one had to be a poetry book. And sometimes, it appears, the second reading book was *Ivanhoe*. One of the more subtle agendas behind the 1870 Education Act was a perceived need to encourage young Britons to feel a greater allegiance to their country, for during an imperialistic age Britain needed ordinary men as sailors, soldiers, and skilled workmen throughout the Empire. *Ivanhoe* must have seemed an appropriate choice, focusing as it does on an idealized British landscape, heroic Anglo–Saxons, and patriotic sentiments.

A careful consideration of the various editions of *Ivanhoe* in the British Library Public Catalogue demonstrates vividly how the book's readership had changed since the first edition of 1820. Virtually every edition published in Britain *before* the 1870s shares certain similarities: they are printed as octavo volumes; they are multivolume works; and they almost invariably stress their authenticity on the title page—attractive features for collectors and for some adult readers. In the 1870s, however, a massive change in the potential readership becomes apparent. *Ivanhoe* began to be marketed explicitly for children: it was included in publishers' lists of children's series, and it was sold as a school text. Students' guides to the novel—the nineteenth-century equivalent of Cliff's Notes—also appeared. Scott's seriousness took a new form for many educators: *Ivanhoe* offered an exciting, useful, and acceptable school text. It was used to promote an appealing myth of Englishness. It described a world in which Anglo–Saxon courage, decency, and moral superiority triumph over the superior strength of foreigners. It was offered as evidence that combat was the best means to enforce justice in the world.

As we have noted, most of these qualities speak to young boys, but *Ivanhoe* could be granted some real if subtle power as a girl's book, too. The Rebecca plot holds out the promise that a girl's innocence has the power to save her from sexually aggressive men. And Rebecca, virtuous and selflessly devoted to others, might seem more admirable than Rowena to girls who long for a destiny beyond marriage. Rebecca's story reworks the plot of Milton's *Comus*, a masque in which a young and innocent girl, the Lady, ventures alone into a dangerous wood where she encounters a sorcerer named Comus. The Lady's inviolate state is both a physical reality and a consequence of her spiritual purity; even the malicious Comus—"of Bacchus, and of Circe born"—is unable to seduce her to join in his beastly rites, for "Vertue may be assail'd, but never hurt, / Surpriz'd by unjust force, but not enthrall'ed" (2: 589–90). Like the Lady, Rebecca resists a man who attempts to seduce her; also like the Lady, Rebecca (who has no apparent defenses) holds fast against the man's power and allurements. In both texts, true virginity (virginity grounded in a woman's virtue and spirituality) can indeed move nature to protect her. Comus and Sir Brian are disarmed, both figuratively and literally, by girls—and heaven's care for girls—who embody "the sage / And serious doctrine of Virginity" (2: 786–87).

All children, of course, would be better able to enjoy *Ivanhoe* if it were edited in order to make it shorter and more accessible, and just this kind of edition begins to be published in Britain in the years after 1870. The version in the "Bell's Reading Books" series, for instance (1875), is "Abridged for use in schools" and illustrated. There were editions like W. P. Mimmo's of around 1876, "ed. By Rev. P Hately Waddell," which included material for class use: "Notes: Critical and Historical" and a "Glossary of Words and Phrases." There was also an edition of *Ivanhoe* in the "English Classics for Schools" series of 1891. And perhaps the most telling indicator of how dramatically *Ivanhoe* could be revised for a new audience is a ninety-six page book "from the novel by Sir Walter Scott" in "Nelson's Supplementary Readers" series.

Much of what we have described as characterizing the changing presentation of *Ivanhoe* in Great Britain can be observed happening in the United States as well. Of course, there are variations. Because *Ivanhoe* was not protected by copyright laws in the United States, early American editions trumpet their apparent authenticity much more stridently than English editions, often covering their piracy by asserting that they are "from the last revised edition." In the United States, however, publishers began to market *Ivanhoe* to an undifferentiated audience of adults and children fairly quickly. A copy from the 1830s is labeled the "People's edition," one from 1857 is a "Household edition," and one from the 1860s is "Peterson's cheap edition for the millions." Some versions, like the "Kensington edition" or the "Windermere edition," suggest the cachet of being real *English* editions (a strong appeal to the American counterparts of Leonard Bast).

Ivanhoe moved into the classroom comparatively late in America, perhaps because equivalents to England's Education Act happened gradually state by state; there was simply no sudden, dramatic need for a nationally adapted reading book. It is also possible that a nation that had been at war with Britain as recently as 1812 might have resisted embracing a book that so wholeheartedly admires British martial feats—although, as we have noted, Twain believed Southern gentlemen felt no such reservation. In any case, *Ivanhoe* was published in the United States specifically as a children's book for the first time only in 1886 as part of Ginn's "Classics for Children" series. This edition was introduced by Charlotte M. Yonge, whose earnest Anglican novels for children had won great respect in America. The first American abridged version appeared in the 1890s, as did the first American edition specifically marketed for schools (the American Book Company edition of 1892, in the "English Classics for Schools" series). Once in the classroom, *Ivanhoe* rapidly became happily at home, with eight different schoolroom editions published between 1897 and 1899 alone, and by the turn of the century *Ivanhoe* in America, like *Ivanhoe* in Britain, was published mainly for school use.

On either side of the Atlantic, radical abridgments such as "Nelson's" mentioned earlier or the 1907 American edition *Two Hours with Ivanhoe* (126 pages) could have served students as cheat sheets, a short cut through the labor of actually reading the whole book. More importantly, these abridgements inevitably had the effect of making aesthetic matters subordinate to broadly drawn outcomes, effects, and themes (the stirring of a boyhood feeling, the lessons of honor, the love of country, etc.); the specific qualities of a particular text (that is, details of plot, style, structure that are subject to serious criticism) become inconsequential. In other words, works like *Ivanhoe*—stories of adventure, of Robin Hood, of the return of King Richard, of historical pageantry, of jousts—become less distinct as novels and more generally a storehouse of narrative material that could (in any number of forms) entertain, excite, teach, inspire—and, more specifically, entertain, teach, and inspire children.

The broadening and flattening effects of these readings of *Ivanhoe* remain evident today in the ways we often "know" his medieval novels. It is through bits and pieces, through films and cartoons that highlight an amazing physical accomplishment (Robin Hood's splitting of the arrow at the archery contest), or a grand gesture (King Richard's unveiling), or an eloquent statement of principle (Ivanhoe's statements of honor or purpose that anticipate battle), or a stunning expression of moral clarity (Rebecca holding steady even at the point of death by fire).

Eventually, *Ivanhoe* came to exist almost exclusively as a source for such scenes; as a classic novel or even a significant one, it passes to near oblivion. Indeed, after 1918, British editions of *Ivanhoe* which are clearly intended for school use essentially stop appearing. Just as the Education Act of 1870 had prompted use of the text, the "Great War" sped its decline. As Paul Fussell explains in *The Great War and Modern Memory*, language that "worked" before the war quickly became archaic—even unseemly.[1] The bits and pieces from *Ivanhoe* that have continued to provide scenes or "inspiration" for later works began to show only in the most common popular forms of entertainment. By the 1950s, *Ivanhoe* was perhaps best known through a British television show starring a very young Roger Moore, who rode to the rescue of the needy on a weekly basis. This series mixed equal parts adventure with middle-class morality. Its plot lines are drawn as broadly as the silly illustrations that dominate the crudest modern revampings ("abridgments" becomes too limited a word to suggest the distance from the original text).

Now that children are no longer likely to read *Ivanhoe* at home or at school, it lives on in the American popular imagination for the most part as a quintessentially huge and boring school reading assignment or as an emblem of outdated values. Twain, no doubt, would be pleased that *Ivanhoe* makes an appearance in *Zits* (a daily newspaper comic strip popular with teenagers) as a symbol of all that is tedious and soporific in high school English classes (Scott and Borgman 113–14). *Ivanhoe* also appears as an important irrelevancy in *The Ballad of Lucy Whipple* by Newbery Award winner Karen Cushman. This novel (frequently assigned in American grade school classrooms) tells the tale of Lucy, a girl who is very angry when her family leaves the East to join in the California gold rush of 1849. Lucy cherishes her copy of *Ivanhoe* as a heavily freighted symbol of all that is good and civilized about life in New England. But in the climax of Cushman's book, when a fire whips through the little mining town where her family has settled, Lucy is only momentarily sad to think *Ivanhoe* has been destroyed. Its consumption is ultimately freeing. Lucy realizes that she has come to love her new friends and new life in California. When *Ivanhoe* goes, her allegiances to the East go too. Young readers are clearly meant to endorse Lucy's feeling that she can discard such cumbersome baggage as *Ivanhoe* and bloom where she has been planted. If a comic strip as popular as *Zits* as well as a Newbery Award–winning author both use *Ivanhoe* as a transparent code for irrelevant, outdated, and dull, then *Ivanhoe* must be well outside the current canon of children's literature.

We cannot close this discussion without noting that as much as *Ivanhoe* has become material to be mined for children's edification and entertainment (or mocked for its failure to provide either), a particular kind of modern professional reader has sustained a countervailing force. If Scott were to be a fit research subject for those sorts of academics likely to dismiss anything for children as unworthy of adult study, he would have to be rescued. He would, quite simply, need to be taken back from young readers who had encroached—with the help of teachers—on the sovereign territory of serious adult scholars who study only serious grown-up books. Yet the terms of such critical efforts have at times seemed strained by a consciousness of *Ivanhoe*'s compromised status. Edgar Johnson (in his massive biography from 1970) most dramatically as well as most inadvertently exposes the problematic divide between adult and children (in this case, between men and boys). Johnson starts by quickly cataloging many features that have made *Ivanhoe* a standard text and then just as quickly grows uneasy. It is as if Johnson fears that the things that inspire his enthusiasm are somehow the wrong things—the things that he feels must be dismissed if one is to protect *Ivanhoe* as a book suitable for mature study. Johnson has never been much admired for his criticism, and we do not mean to cite him as representing characteristic qualities of academics who write on Scott; nevertheless, the terms of his praise and defense of *Ivanhoe* are fascinating—first, in the context of late sixties, early seventies institutional anxieties over unruly youth, and second, in the context of a professional definition of a fit subject. After listing some of the "picturesque details" of medieval society that make *Ivanhoe* so compelling, Johnson turns to scenes of violence and nearly gets lost in his own boyish enthusiasm for such scenes:

> Still more is an enjoyment of physical violence, which—without approving it any more than we do—he [Scott] shares with most of mankind. *Ivanhoe* is full of the atmosphere and sound of violence—the clanging steel, shattered lances, and blood-soaked knights of Ashby-de-la-Zouche; the hissing arrows and ringing blades, the crashing walls, and the flaming towers of the siege of Torquilstone; the last thunderous shock of Ivanhoe and Bois-Guilbert at Templestowe. (737)

Note the parenthetical remark about not "approving" of violence. On one hand, Johnson seems to implicitly embrace the boy's adventure book, but on the other hand, he explicitly calls attention to an adult sensibility guiding the narrative. In the paragraph that follows the one quoted above, Johnson tries to correct for any possible misunderstanding. He first assures us that *Ivanhoe* is in fact not likely to interest modern boys for the curious reason that it is not violent enough. He then turns against what the youth of his contemporary culture have come to. It seems that Johnson the scholar thinks *Ivanhoe* is no boy's book (it is complex, layered, crafted), although Johnson the alarmed establishment citizen might wish it were (we need order, clarity, direction):

> These [hissing arrows, ringing blades, and so on] are among the things that have led later generations of critics to dismiss *Ivanhoe* as a boys' book, but it is doubtful if the story is violent enough to gratify that zest in either the present generation of boyhood or their elders. The gunsmoke of television, mass murders in the films, sadism in the novel; our political assassinations, shootings in the streets, clashes of police and university students from Berkeley to the Sorbonne and Madrid, and bombings of civilian cities—all these involve volumes of bloodshed that leave the violence in all of Scott's work tame by comparison. (737)

Johnson's tortured hedging over who reads *Ivanhoe* and how *Ivanhoe* is read reveal defensiveness about his subject that Scott's earliest critics did not feel. As we noted at the outset of this essay, Ferris shows us how male critics in the early nineteenth century were able to define "seriousness" around well-established, gendered conventions that Scott operated within. Without those conventions to refer to and build upon, a self-consciously adult seriousness may be called into question. Many of Johnson's contemporaries handle this difficulty with grace and sophistication (and of course some critics are mature enough to attend unapologetically to books children might read), but even the titles of prominent essays from the sixties and seventies suggest the degree to which Scott and *Ivanhoe* were being consciously repositioned to make a greater claim on adult readers: "The Rationalism of Sir Walter Scott"; "The Anti-Romantic in *Ivanhoe*"; "Scott, The Romantic Past and the Nineteenth Century" (Forbes; Duncan; Garside).

By now, it has become clear that *Ivanhoe* (as Scott wrote it) cannot settle into a place on the children's classic shelf; it is too difficult, too arcane, and too mannered. Recent college editions of *Ivanhoe* suggest a turn back to securely adult kinds of seriousness (albeit not back to a wide readership). Its redefined status may recall ironically the very context that first gave birth to the author of *Waverley*. A few professional critics and scholars still make their own seriousness depend upon the study of books conventionally accepted as mature. And now that children and their teachers have surrendered their claim on *Ivanhoe*, Walter Scott's romance of medieval England is again available to those few professionals.

Note: The authors would like to thank Nicholas McCormick, Hollis Beck, and Matthew Eakin, intrepid middle school research assistants; Donald McCormick of the University of Redlands; Alan W. Harris of the German Aerospace Center (DLR); and Roberto d'Affonseca Herbster Gusmão of *Universidade de Minas Gerais*, all of whom—from childhoods in different countries and in different languages—remember Roger Moore as Ivanhoe.

NOTE

1. The horrors of World War I had a less comprehensive effect in the United States; in fact, the "Great War" seems to have had no effect on the popularity of *Ivanhoe* as a school text. Many schoolroom abridgments and adaptations were printed well into the 1940s, but this run ended with the onset of World War II.

WORKS CITED

Bagehot, Walter. "The Waverley Novels." In *Literary Studies*. Vol. 2. New York: Dutton, 1950.

Carlyle, Thomas. Review of Lockhart's *Life of Sir Walter Scott*. In *Scott: The Critical Heritage*. Ed. John O. Hayden. New York: Barnes and Noble, 1970.

Cushman, Karen. *The Ballad of Lucy Whipple*. Boston: Clarion, 1999.

Duncan, Joseph E. "The Anti-Romantic in *Ivanhoe*." *Nineteenth-Century Fiction* 9 (1955): 293–300.

Ferris, Ina. *The Achievement of Literary Authority: Gender, History, and the Waverley Novels*. Ithaca: Cornell UP, 1991.

Forbes, Duncan. "The Rationalism of Sir Walter Scott." *Cambridge Journal* 7 (1953): 20–35.

Forster, E. M. *Aspects of the Novel*. San Diego: HBJ, 1955.

Fussell, Paul. *The Great War and Modern Memory*. Oxford: Oxford UP, 1975.

Garside, P. D. "Scott and the 'Philosophical' Historians." *Journal of the History of Ideas* 36 (1975): 497–512.

Johnson, Edgar. *Sir Walter Scott: The Great Unknown*. 2 vols. New York: Macmillan, 1970.

Milton, John. *Complete Poems and Major Prose*. Ed. Merrit Y. Hughes. Indianapolis: Odyssey, 1957.

Ruskin, John. *Præterita*. Vol. 35 of *The Works of John Ruskin*. Ed. E. T. Cook and Alexander Wedderburn. London: George Allen, 1908.

Scott, Jerry, and Jim Borgman. *Humongous Zits: A Zits Treasury*. Kansas City: Andrews McMeel, 2000.

Twain, Mark. *Mississippi Writings*. New York: Library of America, 1982.

Woolf, Virginia. *The Common Reader: First Series*. Ed. Andrew NcNeilie. San Diego: HBJ, 1984.

———. *To the Lighthouse*. San Diego: HBJ, 1989.

Heroism Reconsidered
Negotiating Autonomy in St. Nicholas Magazine *(1873–1914)*

Susan R. Gannon

"You read the story of a fine action or a heroic character—the death of Socrates, or the voyage of Columbus, or the sacrifice of Nathan Hale, or such a poem as "The Lady of the Lake"—not for information only, but to create in you a higher ideal of life, and to give you sympathy with your fellows and with noble purposes." (Warner 172)

"Not all the light that science brings to bear on ancient story, Can break the hold these myths have gained on childhood's love of glory." (Brooks 424)

". . . Most heroes and heroines of real life are thankful for the quiet weeks and months when they may be just ordinary men or women—nor are they the less heroic for that." ("Books and Reading for Young Folk" 360)

$\mathcal{B}$ecause formulaic fictions dealing with heroism explore the gap between the explanatory messages of canonical legend, and the lived experience of readers and writers, they tend to reveal fault lines in established cultural attitudes. *St. Nicholas Magazine*, America's premier children's periodical at the turn of the century, glorified traditional heroic models of conduct in its features and editorial commentary, while in its realistic fiction, it offered its dual audience of children and adults alternative—and to some extent revisionist—perspectives on the subject. The tropes and figures from heroic legend and the patterns of argument and ideology found in the magazine's editorial discourse and feature articles may have offered confident answers to compelling human questions, but translating legend into domestic fiction challenged these simple pieties "not because the authors are essentially dissenters . . . but because the language game they are playing returns us to gaps between experience and explanation" (Bercovitch 27).

In this essay I first comment on the way the *St. Nicholas* community used the stories of heroes and heroines like George Washington, Christopher Columbus, Nathan Hale, Betsy Ross, Molly Pitcher, and Lydia Darrah to understand, explain, and justify themselves to themselves in the last years of the nineteenth century. Then I examine the way formula fiction involving patriotic action offered families an opportunity to reconsider the implications of heroic paradigms of conduct in the light of their own experience of ordinary life.

1. THE *ST. NICHOLAS* "TAKE" ON HISTORY

What did *St. Nicholas* at the turn of the nineteenth/twentieth centuries expect historical features to do for its readers? In a piece on "Books and Reading" published in 1891, Charles Dudley Warner told them: "You do not read all books for facts or for information merely, but to be inspired, to have your thoughts lifted up to noble ideas, to have your sympathies touched, your ambition awakened to do some worthy or great thing, to become a man or a woman of character and consideration in the world" (891). American culture was well supplied with inspirational historical narratives conveying traditional values through the shape of the story, the familiar qualities of character assigned to the actors, and predictable moralizing commentary, sometimes enshrined in famous quotations or appropriate (if sometimes hard to verify) "last words." Yet as John Stephens and Robyn McCallum suggest, any particular retelling of a traditional story "may purport to transmit elements of a culture's formative traditions and even its sustaining beliefs and assumptions, but what it always discloses is some aspect of the attitudes and ideologies pertaining at the cultural moment in which that telling is produced" (ix). So it should not come as a surprise that the lives of the great were carefully tailored by writers for *St. Nicholas* to suit the ethical agenda of a magazine that aimed to inculcate in the young a complex of genteel virtues: courage, self-discipline, self-reliance, generosity, responsibility, and love of family and country, while adult readers were encouraged to take a sympathetic interest in their children's moral and intellectual development and to set them a good example.

The editors were quite aware that some familiar hero stories, "strong, familiar story shapes with already legitimized values and ideas about the world" (Stephens and McCallum x), though "improving," were just not true. But their attitudes about historical accuracy were mixed. Parson Weems's stilted and preachy book on George Washington was scoffed at, but the author's good intentions were praised. Elbridge S. Brooks, a frequent contributor of chatty anecdotal pieces on American history, wrote a little playlet for *St. Nicholas* in which Clio, the Muse of History, condemns certain mythic figures whose stories have not measured up to scientific scrutiny: Dido, Nero, Dick Whittington, Joan of Arc, William Tell, Evangeline, and Young George Washington with his hatchet. Clio complains: "Not all the light that science brings to bear on ancient story, / Can break the hold these myths have gained on childhood's love of glory." But a lawyer named Portia Pleadwell turns up to argue convincingly that "these myths, so-called," are "but tutors come to teach us . . . true lessons that "set forth with skill," may "help to the world's refining" (424).

So, though editor Mary Mapes Dodge had a tender conscience about matters of historical accuracy, there seems to have been a place in her magazine for stories that, while not *quite* true, might be said to teach useful lessons. Dodge did go out of her way to investigate what she thought to be doubtful accounts of historical events. Alice Balch Abbott's serial *The Frigate's Namesake* had featured a scene in which the heroine laid flowers at the monument to Captain Lawrence, whose last words were supposed to have been "Don't Give Up the Ship!" Unfortunately, a newspaper article questioning the historicity of the incident had appeared at the same time. The editors were torn between a desire to edify and pride in their reputation for accuracy. In the issue in which the story appeared, they say: "It is unpleasant to doubt that the brave Lawrence made use of the heroic words, and our readers will be glad to learn that the evidence is all in favor of the truth of the story." They cite the surgeon's mate of the *Chesapeake* who had testified that he was told by the captain "to go to the deck, and tell the men to fire faster, and not give up the ship," and conclude: "While this is not exactly proof that Captain Lawrence used the words before he was carried below decks, yet it shows that the idea and heroic resolve were in his mind, and, in connection with the tradition, make it seem probable that he did give the order as has been believed" (456).

The editors consciously solicited articles in order to fill what they regarded as gaps in history that needed to be filled. Elizabeth Cady Stanton commented once in the magazine that historians take little note of the doings of women and children. And *St. Nicholas* seems to have been very much aware that while history as we have it offers answers to questions that have already been asked and investigated, important but neglected topics remain to be investigated. A survey of the Index of the magazine reveals the extent of the editors' efforts to write children back into history. Historical fiction, imagining what the world might have looked like from children's perspective, presented an opportunity to raise questions overlooked or underplayed in the history books.

2. TRADITIONAL MODELS OF PATRIOTIC VIRTUE

The kind of classic hero tales Charles Dudley Warner commended as raising higher ideals of life tend to come pre-supplied with meaning. George Washington, who appeared in innumerable poems, plays, feature articles, and fictions, and was the subject of a full-scale serial biography by Horace Scudder, was the archetypal American patriot–hero. His legend as told to the readers of *St. Nicholas* reads like classic quest–adventure, complete with the call to action, a road of trials, the crossing of the waters to a realm of danger, definitive battles with the enemy, recognition by his compatriots, and selection as leader of the nation. Though Washington, in popular culture, had acquired the qualities of a kind of demigod, the Washington of Scudder's lengthy and exceedingly sober biography (serialized in 1886) was, though noble, a human being—capable on occasion of making mistakes, but brave under fire, humble, methodical, and "large-minded," "with the ripe and full judgment of a man whose one thought in his life had been to serve his country faithfully" (914). Wise and kind, a shrewd judge of people and circumstances, disciplined and self-sacrificing, he emerges as *St. Nicholas*'s image of the ideal father figure. Scudder's biography ends with the reflection that studying Washington's life is the best way for his countrymen to honor him. And perhaps it is not surprising to find that a similar Washington-figure appears in countless historical fictions, conveying their country's appreciation to those who have offered it brave and devoted service.

Christopher Columbus, though predictably celebrated in *St. Nicholas* every October for his daring voyage of discovery, and in Charles Dudley Warner's terms a "heroic figure" who performed "fine actions," was not invariably praised. The magazine published pieces expressing admiration for his achievements around the time of the Columbian Exposition in 1892, but five years later, when Spain's management of its colonial possessions was coming under criticism in the press, another view emerged. Frank Stockton suggested in a series called *Buccaneers of Our Coasts*, that once having gone " beyond the boundaries of civilization," Columbus also placed himself beyond the boundaries of civilized law. "Robbery, murder, and the destruction of property by the commanders of naval expeditions who have no warrant or commission for their conduct, is the same as piracy," and when Columbus "began to devastate the countries he had discovered, and to enslave and exterminate their peaceable natives, then he became a master in piracy, from whom the buccaneers afterward learned many a valuable lesson" (8). Stockton thinks it only just that the leader who committed such "atrocities" (8) should be sent back in chains to Spain. So Columbus serves to exemplify what could happen when a "heroic figure," however "fine" his achievements, fails to demonstrate the moral discernment and self-restraint of a Washington.

If Washington was the beloved "Father of his Country," and Columbus a sort of "Darth Vader," where were the models in history for the dutiful sons who might be called upon to put their lives on the line for their country and its values? One obvious choice for canonization by *St. Nicholas* was Yale man, feminist, scholar, and athlete Nathan Hale, America's military proto-martyr. In July of 1894, Mary S. Northrop wrote "A Young Hero," illustrated with a picture of the statue by Frederick McMonnies in New York's City Hall Park, showing Hale "pinioned, awaiting the gallows as he uttered his last words" (794). And this "bronze statue" is said to be "of a young man, the story of whose brief life thrills all patriotic hearts." "Americans" are said to "unite in admiration of his noble character, pride in his self-forgetful heroism, and grief over his untimely death. Every boy and girl in America should know by heart the life of Captain Nathan Hale" (794).

Hale's spying mission failed, of course, and he is remembered not for anything he accomplished militarily, but for the gallant way he died, and the cool style with which he tossed off what were said to be his last words, a paraphrase of lines from Addison's *Cato*. Northrop's retelling stresses the modesty of the young Hale, who undertook a dangerous and demeaning task because he felt it would be useful. She doesn't mention his initial reluctance to undertake the mission. "His only thought," she says, "seemed to be to serve his country" (795). In fact, when Washington's first call for volunteers was relayed to the elite corps of Knowlton's Rangers, the reaction was dead silence: nobody volunteered. Hale asked his good friend Captain (later General) Hull what he thought he should do. Hull urged him not to accept the assignment, since his frank and straightforward nature did not make him an ideal candidate for a course of action requiring lying and deception. For a gentleman, the propriety of such a course of conduct would be doubtful, and the death of a spy could be swift and ignominious. Northrop quotes Hale's rejoinder to Hull: "Every kind of service necessary to the public good becomes honorable by being necessary." And she then describes how the brutal British commander refused Hale a Bible and clerical attendance, and tore up the letters he had been allowed to write. But Hale's courage in his last moments and his famous final words, "I only regret that I have but one life to lose for my country" are the triumphant central focus of the article (795).

Nathan Hale's story as passed on to school children "ardent for some desperate glory" was a kind of saint's legend, a "literary crystallization of the perceptions of a collective conscience" (Jacques Fontaine, qtd. de Certeau 270) designed to edify through "'exemplarity'" (de Certeau 269). And particularly as it was so universally reverenced, Hale's was a very powerful example for the young. The sacrificial death of the soldier hero who puts his life and his conscience on the line for his country was treated as a beautiful and significant action in the world of *St. Nicholas*, and such deaths were recounted with awe and respect.

American historical legend is full of stories in which clever and capable women have come to the aid of their country in time of need. The stories of three women—Betsy Ross, Molly Pitcher, and Lydia Darrah—who were remembered as heroines of the American Revolution, were retold in *St. Nicholas*, suggesting three different ways women might serve their country: by putting some special expertise at the service of the community, by serving beside men in combat, or by working surreptitiously to subvert the enemy on the home front. Betsy Ross, the accomplished seamstress and upholsterer to whom Washington is said to have turned to make the first American flag, is credited in popular legend with suggesting the five-pointed star to him because she could create one with one snip of the scissors. The extent of the magazine's idealization of things military is admirably documented by the recent work of Marilynn Strasser Olson. *St. Nicholas* published quite a few pieces in the nineties celebrating the flag; for example, in July of 1892 it told Ross's story in "The Five Pointed Star," by C. F. Jenkins. In June of 1900 *St. Nicholas* offered readers a rousing (though wildly inaccurate) poem by Laura E. Richards on the brave service of Mary Ludwig Hays MacCauley, popularly known as Molly Pitcher. For Richards, Molly was a woman avenging her husband's death, a woman who, because she "has played a man's full part" is said by Washington to deserve a "man's reward for her loyal heart," as he grants her the rank of a sergeant in the army (719). Only a couple of lines refer to the water-bringing that gave Molly her nickname, the poem being structured to show the difference between the service of the young man—who loved a fight for its own sake—and that of the loyal wife who becomes an avenging fury "with streaming hair, with eyes of flame" only after her husband has been shot.

A less famous heroine, Lydia Darrah, was honored by having her story told twice in *St. Nicholas*. General Howe's Adjutant-General had taken up headquarters in the home of Darrah and her Quaker husband. When a secret council to plan an attack on nearby rebel forces was called, Mrs. Darrah listened at the door, "a piece of eavesdropping which the zealous woman no doubt felt was entirely justified as a war expedient" (Ogden 336). Mrs. Darrah "dared not even consult her husband," but later that night slipped out on a supposed errand and passed the word to Washington's men.

Skill in traditional women's work, courage, and cool-headedness are overtly praised in these women, and these are virtues often urged upon young women of the *St. Nicholas* reading community. But the lightly fictionalized stories spun out of the few facts that might have been available about these women perhaps inadvertently manage to underline the way in which their achievements would have been impossible without transgressive behavior. The ability to speak up to as awesome an authority figure as George Washington; to embrace a bloody course of revenge on the battlefield; to eavesdrop, to deceive not only the "enemy" but a spouse, and shamelessly to trade on one's sex and noncombatant status are also implicitly commended to the young in the example of these women, "every kind of service necessary to the public good" becoming "honorable" when "necessary" (Hale, qtd. in Northrop 795).

3. FORMULA FICTION ABOUT YOUNG HEROES

It would be easy to dismiss many of the formulaic stories published in *St. Nicholas Magazine* in the last decades of the nineteenth century as thin, flat, stereotypical. Yet contemporary accounts attest to the rapt attention given them by young and old. Though R. Gordon Kelly has suggested that formulaic fiction in American periodicals of this time functioned primarily to pass on traditional values in a time of rapid social and economic change, the stories in *St. Nicholas* were not simply didactic instruments of an older generation seeking to shape the values of the young. Restoring such texts "to their political and literary matrix" (Myers, "Child's Play" 28) lets us see them as expressive responses to immediate problems that allowed writers and readers to think imaginatively about their options and negotiate the inevitable differences parents and children might have about what might be "necessary" and "honorable" behavior in difficult circumstances.

Mitzi Myers once pointed out that:

> However different the literary kinds that they choose or the historical periods within which they write, most authors who take seriously the responsibility of writing to and about children understand that childhood is about power, balancing the young person's need for autonomy and world-knowledge . . . and the need for home, for a haven to return to: the conflicting yet interrelated juvenile rights to individual agency and communal protection that we still struggle to resolve. ("'Anecdotes'" 227)

Students of the art of negotiation suggest that focusing on positions—as most disputants do— makes it hard to perceive the underlying concerns driving the participants, and these concerns can constitute a treacherous hidden agenda. A good mediator helps opponents to listen empathetically, to imagine alternative ways to resolve problems, to invent together options that will be mutually helpful. And a key stage in the mediation comes when opponents can work out together or accept from the mediator a reframing of their dispute that will acknowledge (and therefore give them a chance to meet) the unspoken needs that impelled them to disagree. Through a variety of narrative strategies, fictions involving heroic choices in *St. Nicholas* offered readers, young and old, creative ways to reframe intergenerational conflict at the needs and interests level so as to move beyond conflict to collaborative action in the face of difficulty. In the course of this negotiation, the young might earn a degree of autonomy, though often, as the best of the stories make clear, at considerable cost.

Much more accessible models for young America than George Washington and Nathan Hale were the patriotic children who appeared in story after story, making things happen: galloping off on midnight rides, bringing water to the wounded, or hiding escaped prisoners. Such patriotic fiction offered *St. Nicholas*'s dual readership of children and adults a space in which traditional heroic paradigms of behavior could be reconsidered, and differing visions of child–adult relations could be figured, tested, and explored. I focus on two closely related story patterns involving patriotic valor: the home/rescue story usually told about girls, and the military initiation story told primarily about boys. In each of these, the young protagonist undergoes separation from parental authority, encounters danger and perhaps must defeat an enemy, and then returns to the home. In the girl's story, the separation is often more psychological than physical. It does not necessarily involve an arduous journey, or the physical combat usual in the boys' stories. Instead, there is a bold assumption of responsibility. Often the girl initiates a tricky rescue or support operation, and if combat with an enemy is involved, it is more likely to be carried out by guile or moral example than force.

In both the home/rescue and the military initiation story, questions of dependency versus autonomy are central. The first move is a key one: a child must break out of the normal situation of dependence on a parent. In proposing various ways this might happen, such fictions invite the readership to think about some unsettling questions. In what circumstances is it justifiable to take risky action without parental permission or approval? When an action that seems necessary also seems wrong, how might one resolve scruples of conscience? May permission to do something risky be obtained through dubious means? Begged for? Are there times when a little cheating is expected? What if parents disagree? What if it is the parent who asks a child to lie, deceive, commit an act of violence, or face almost certain death? In a few stories the issue of parental responsibility is evaded by using some "casting off" device: the child has been left alone at home and has no one to ask, or is an abandoned orphan, or the parents are incompetent. A number of stories present absent or ill fathers and mothers overburdened with responsibilities. But often a basic conflict over a child's right to take risky action is the initial problem presented in a story. At the end of the girl's story there is often, though not always, explicit recognition by parents or other authority figures (George Washington appears with relentless frequency in this role) that—however unorthodox the action taken might have been—the decision to undertake it was proper, and the task carried out well.

Older people in many stories are more committed to traditional ways of looking at things than the young, though the stories are designed for a dual audience and are susceptible of being read—as I have suggested elsewhere—differently by readers with different life experiences (Gannon 160–61). In E. W. Demerritt's "How the Tories Broke up the Meeting," Molly is a very young bride, whose husband is away with the army. To her mother's despair, she insists on living alone in a coastal Connecticut town that is subject to frequent raids by British troops. Though pressed repeatedly to return to the relative safety of her parents' inland farm, Molly is determined to live independently and protect her new homestead. One Sunday she chooses to take her little sister to a religious service at her local meeting house, and, as predicted, the British arrive, kidnapping the minister and terrorizing the congregation. Molly prudently surrenders her gold necklace to them but decides not to let them steal her valuable horse, tethered outside. So she slips out of the building and gallops off with her little sister on her lap, offering the little girl a thrilling adventure as well as a powerful model of female agency. The parents who feared that Molly's independence might put her in harm's way are shown to have been right, but they also come to accept that the same self-sufficiency, together with her exceptional nerve and competence, made her triumphant escape possible. And, in a move repeated in many such stories, final closure comes when the larger community indicates its approval of her unconventional behavior as well. The proudest day of her life, and of her family's, comes during a triumphal parade after peace is declared: the superb horse she gave to the Continental army at her soldier husband's request—a horse whose matchless spirit her father compares to her own—is chosen as the personal mount of General Washington.

Mitzi Myers observed once that feminist thinkers have seen "wars, especially internecine struggles," as tending to "destabilize binary oppositions and dissolve psychic as well as physical boundaries." She quoted Virginia Woolf's comment that when

> "the public world very notably invade[s] the private," . . . cultural constructions of gender come to the fore, either reified (the protected "feminine" who embodies the values fought for) or inverted (female figures, even little girls, who transgress established political ideologies by explicit critique or alternative Utopia). ("Child's Play" 28)

In many of the stories of heroic rescue in *St. Nicholas*, innocent young girls do embody the values fought for, yet they find themselves driven to transgress the boundaries of convention, challenge their elders, and undertake risky and occasionally morally dubious action in the course of protecting those values or asserting their worth.

In the girls' rescue story, the home is often a sacred space whose protection has been left to a young and inexperienced heroine who personifies domestic virtue. Children in these tales seem innocently confident they will not be harmed by the enemy, though fear for their own physical safety may be displaced onto fears for their homes. In Lillian Price's "Laetitia and the Redcoats," the terror of the townspeople is focused on "rough soldiers clanking about the house with devastating hands." They fully expect their homes to be burned, their treasured dishes smashed, the fields and flower beds trampled. And so the usually obedient and truthful Laetitia, aged fourteen, is moved to set aside the rules of conduct and expectations of behavior with which she has been raised. She makes a false excuse and runs back from a safe refuge into the path of danger, in order to pin notes on the front and back doors of her home, begging the invaders to think of their own children and homes and spare hers, which they do. At a key moment at the end of the story, her grandmother sees that it was Laetitia's ability to touch the hearts of the enemy by evoking shared values that saved their home. Had Laetitia asked for permission to post the notes, it would certainly have been denied, but in the end her grandmother admits her line of action to have been correct, calling her an obedient daughter after all.

Often, as in this story, a little girl's power over adults resides in the innocence and single-minded purity of purpose with which she forces adults to think twice about what they are about to do. In Ethel Parton's "Rhyme of the Tory Tollevers," little Prue's family sends her to warn their Tory neighbors that a lynch mob is on its way to hang Mr. Tollever. The Tollevers flee in panic, leaving a sleeping baby behind. When Prue goes back for the baby, she is caught by the mob, but she faces them down, telling them that he is too little a Tory to hang.

The story's illustrations stress the brawn and menace of the armed mob. The crowd is first depicted with raised fists, guns, clubs, and a massive sledgehammer to break in the door, and one holds the rope they hope to use on Mr. Tollever. But they find just the little girl and the baby in the fire-lit room. Taken by surprise, softened and moved by the baby's smiles and laughter, they are then shown hoisting the two children on their shoulders when they carry them off to Prue's home, vastly relieved—now that the moment is past—that they have not done what they planned to do. Members of the crowd, now jolly and fatherly looking, celebrate their own deliverance from bloodguilt as they carry the children off in the final illustration, where the only fist raised is that of the smiling baby. The picture here of patriotic zeal is highly unflattering; but the relief of the mob suggests that the ferocious partisan feeling that drove them was not the whole story: other human feelings were pulling them in another direction and just needed to be awakened by a little girl's witness to values they shared.

In many stories, young girls living in occupied territory are called upon to protect the wounded or weak, or to carry important messages. Much interest is centered on their choice of mission, its moral implications, and the way even successful performance may disturb established gender roles and intergenerational relations. Lillian Price's "The Bulb of the Crimson Tulip" tells of a girl, home alone, who hides her brother, a wounded soldier with the inevitable message for Washington. She so competently handles the situation that when her mother returns, the girl casually orders her to change her brother's hiding place, and the mother, recognizing her daughter's achieved authority, meekly obeys. In another story, "The Black Duck," parents strongly disagree about whether to send their daughter off to complete her injured father's dangerous task— bringing that same inevitable message to General Washington. This time the girl has moral qualms about undertaking a course of action which might require her to do things that will offend her conscience. She finally decides that because her father is a good man, and he had undertaken this commitment, she can safely carry it out. But she takes great care to deceive the enemy while telling them nothing that is not "technically" true. And as a pretty girl, she is able to beguile a flustered young sentry who might well have challenged and shot her father. Both her cautious mother and daring father are proud of their daughter's success, though neither is completely reconciled to her newfound outspokenness, particularly her insistence on always having the last word—even with General Washington, when she finally gets to meet him.

When parents deliberately put a child in danger, no matter how noble their aim may be, the experience can be traumatic for all concerned. "The Girl Who Saved the General" is based on a true incident in the American Revolution in which a mother chose to send her eldest daughter into a hail of bullets to rescue a baby cousin. Though the girl volunteers to go, and the baby is safely rescued, the parents remain distraught about what they have been driven to do. They, and their daughter, are only consoled by their conviction that she must have been divinely protected on her mission: thus, their decision to allow her to face almost certain death must have been part of God's plan. Reader confidence in such an interpretation of the facts might have been bolstered by the information given in the story's last line: the providential result of the girl's daring was that the baby she saved would grow up to become General John Fenwick, hero of the War of 1812.

The boys' initiation story involves separation from parents and home, with particular emphasis on the breaking of the relationship with the father and entrance into a confused and hostile wartime world. Boys often encounter alternative father figures, face deadly violence, return home wiser, stronger, more experienced, and either are reconciled with the father or adopted by a more adequate parent. Issues arising in these fictions resemble those in the female rescue formulas, but the stakes are higher in terms of physical and moral danger. When the return home is a triumphant one, the boy is well on his way to being a man, with a career and sponsorship for his future assured. Should he die, he is a martyr, a model for others like Nathan Hale, and is mourned by those close to him.

S. K. Wiley's "Maurice and His Father: A Romance of the American Revolution" centers on the experience of an English father and son visiting the Colonies, who witness an atrocity of war. Major Banastre

Tarleton's men burn and pillage a private home simply because its owner is a rebel. Sir Lawrence Terraine protests the soldiers' terrorism as "unmanly, un-soldierly, and un-Christian" (710). There is a skirmish, and Maurice is captured by the guerilla forces of General Francis Marion, the "Swamp Fox." Marion's ragtag forces wage war in unconventional ways, but they are gentlemen, not terrorists. At the outset of the story both father and son seem to assume that their interests are aligned with those of the British forces, but experiences during his captivity lead Maurice, almost against his will, to admire Marion and Washington. The story raises difficult questions about the true nature of loyalty, the sort of reasons that might justify going to war, and how war should be waged. Neither the rebels nor the redcoats are idealized: Tarleton is a brute, and Benedict Arnold breaks Washington's heart when he defects. When father and son are re-united, Maurice discovers that they have not been divided by his sympathy for the Colonials. Their shared principles and personal experience have led them to similar conclusions: his father is now a trusted aide of General Washington.

In contrast to the uncertainties that beset Maurice and his father, in Molly Seawell's serial fictionalizing of the careers of Stephen Decatur and Richard Somers, the protagonists, well-known national heroes, are committed to a very traditional ideal of civic heroism. Yet the brave naval officers have humanly mixed feelings, too, for their tender Achilles–Patroklos relationship ends tragically when Somers volunteers for what proves to be a suicide mission. Built into the story for young readers is the parallel adventure of a lively boy sailor, Israel Pickle, who in his eagerness for glory joins Somers, leaving Decatur with two graves to visit. This story celebrates the bravery of the naval officers, who were iconic national heroes whose careers would be well-known to adult readers, but the ending underlines what Israel's naïve eagerness to follow their example cost. Though his death is in the Hale tradition and is honored, the ending of the story is saturated with Decatur's grief over the loss of his irreplaceable comrade—and the rash and disobedient little boy who idolized him. Adult readers may have been moved by Decatur's plight here, but Israel's joining Somers in death must have particularly affected the many young readers who had enjoyed his lively antics, with little expectation of the fate that awaited him.

Marilynn Olson has documented the consistency with which *St. Nicholas* promoted an ardent patriotism in its young readers and presented soldiering to them as a noble calling. Though the death of the young in battle is a distressing subject, all the more difficult to handle when the scene takes place in the present or recent past, a number of stories about boy soldiers were set on the battlefields of the Civil War or the Spanish–American War. And some of the most vivid of these were written by army officers drawing on personal knowledge of life in the field. "A Little Contraband," for example, reads like a rather tormented confession by a parental figure who has been unable to protect a young and eager boy from the cruelty of war. An army captain rehearses the story of a little slave his outfit had adopted during the Civil War, who died waving his white shirt at the enemy, sure it would protect him and his friend the wounded Captain. The narrator tells himself there was nothing he could have done to save the boy, but he doesn't seem convinced. The shock of the little boy's death is especially strong, since the story begins as an affectionate account of all the mischief and trouble he caused in camp, and the effect of his sudden death is disturbing, inviting readers to share the narrator's sense of unresolved pain and loss.

Letters to the editor reprinted in *St. Nicholas* give ample testimony that readers, young and old, prepared to understand a war and heroism by reading the kind of formula fiction described here, and that they were justifiably impressed by the mature complexities of the most extensive war narrative the magazine ever printed, Harry Kieffer's autobiographical "Recollections of a Drummer-Boy," serialized in 1881–82. Kieffer's memoir, based on detailed journals and letters home during three hard years in the army, is sober and realistic, a thoughtful older man's reflections on his experiences as a boy. He presents his own separation narrative—conceived and told in terms reminiscent of the sort of fiction he had probably read as a boy—with extraordinary sympathy for the father who agonized over letting him go. Though Harry was a delicate and scholarly boy of sixteen, "war-fever" had taken hold among the students in his school, and many were going off to war, led by their teacher. His father tried to accept Harry's desire to go, but just couldn't. Finally he went with Harry to look things over at the camp, and as they were at the station heading back home, Mr. Kieffer choked out his final position: the boy could still come home with him, but if he wanted to enlist with his friends, he could. Young Harry was off like a shot. But looking back, he sees that he *and* his father were both seized with "war-fever." And it seems as if he almost wishes his father had held out against him. As a noncombatant, Harry reports no experiences in which he shot at or killed the enemy, or performed any outstanding feats of bravery, though he was constantly in danger, ill, exhausted. It is clear that he enjoyed the comradeship of his mates, especially his closest friend, Andy. But the exhilarating struggle with the forces of darkness, the recognition as an outstanding soldier, all the usual touches in the fictive stories of boy soldiers are missing.

There is a devastating description of Gettysburg and the horrors of walking the field afterward. Kieffer notes that many readers of *St. Nicholas* may think that drummer boys sign up to play the drums, but their real function in battle is as stretcher-bearers. Of the fifty-four men and boys in his own company, only thirteen survived Cemetery Ridge. Describing the pain and suffering he saw, Kieffer says earnestly to the readers of *St. Nicholas* that though he had "imagined war so grand and gallant a thing," it is "horribly wicked and cruel" (308). And Kieffer's account of it is perhaps all the more impressive for lacking the consolations so often supplied in fiction.

By the end of his story Harry has survived but has been deeply affected by the almost unbearable duties contracted for in joining the army. His reunion with his family, especially his father, is emotional, and provides the closure they both need, but the reader is left with all the sad statistics Harry had so carefully noted in his little black journals, including the fact that of the thirteen friends afflicted with "war fever" who left from his town, only three returned.

Stories about the Revolution and even the Civil War were distanced a bit in time, but in the nineties, the Spanish–American War provided the occasion for fictional speculations about an urgent call to action drawn from breaking news. One remarkable story, "Chuggins, the Youngest Hero with the Army; A Story of the Capture of Santiago," by H. I. Hancock, recapitulates some of the situations in Kieffer's memoir, but assesses war and soldiering quite differently. "Chuggins" Sperry comes from a long line of soldiers and feels that family tradition demands he should come to his country's assistance in its time of need, though he is only thirteen. The uncle with whom he lives disapproves of the project, so he runs away and manages to get to Cuba, where he finds work in an army camp. Again and again he encounters father figures—reporters, soldiers, even Theodore Roosevelt himself, who insist he shouldn't be there, but they admire his courage so much they can't quite send him home. Like

Harry Kieffer, Chuggins encounters death in some harrowing forms. He comes upon the body of a young soldier who looks as if he had been saying "Hurrah" at the moment someone put a bullet through his forehead. The sight freezes the boy's heart. But Chuggins steels himself, takes the soldier's gun, and joins the Rough Riders in battle. Later he is assigned to a medical detail, contracts yellow fever helping some refugees, and is invalided home. The story includes speculations about the pointlessness of war and a frightening description of the boy's trip to the yellow-fever camp. His uncle's stern view of his running away to join the army is supported by the narrative voice and reiterated at the end of the story. But by then Chuggins has been informally adopted by the doctor he had helped in Cuba and is to be educated for a military career at West Point.

The story was apparently popular with both adults and children. The young protagonist's determination to fight, the result of a lifetime of having heard stories about his heroic forebears, is presented sympathetically, though his oversimplified view of his situation troubles his elders, who express the perplexity and confusion adults feel in wartime when their sons clamor for that "desperate glory" that may bring them to grief. The *St. Nicholas* "Letter-Box" for January, 1899, included a touching letter from a father who had grown up on *St. Nicholas*. His letter was written while he watched his son read the passage about the dead soldier to some other little boys. The boys are crying, but they clearly identify with Chuggins and wish to follow his example. Their father notices their tears and their eager response to the call to youthful valor with a mixture of fatherly concern, sympathy, and admiration that echoes the sentiments of Col. Roosevelt, of whom it had been said: "he knew that such a mere boy had no call or right to be on the firing-line, but such deeds and reasoning as Chuggins offered must perplex a lover of heroes," so all he could do was offer a troubled: "Sperry, I don't know what to say to you." (49).

The epigraphs I have chosen express three ways of thinking about heroic story. The first applauds its ability to inspire readers with noble purposes. The second calls into question the effect of such stories on young readers—especially when the stories are not true. And the third makes a case for the quiet power of the good example of ordinary people, "the heroes and heroines of real life." Heroic legend claims to explain the way things are, the way the world works, so its guidance about how life should be lived carries the full force of received opinion. In retelling stories about heroes like Washington, Columbus, Hale, and the rest, *St. Nicholas* instructed its adult audience about parenting, about handling power, about facing inevitable losses, including the loss of young and promising life. Its younger readers were shown that self-discipline, hard work, and cultivation of their minds were needed if they were to be ready to rise to the defense of home, family, or nation in time of trouble. The heroines of American legend reminded young and old that women could be called upon to serve their country as bravely as their brothers, perhaps with even more resourcefulness and cunning.

But, of course, heroes are by definition exceptional people who rise to extraordinary challenges. How do the messages their triumphs offer apply to the circumstances readers, young and old, are likely to face in daily life? *St. Nicholas* offered its readers an opportunity to think together about what the call to heroic action might mean for fallible human beings like themselves. In formula fictions of rescue and initiation, the readership was reassured that well-nurtured young people could, indeed, draw on reserves of competence and meet unexpected challenges successfully. But if realistic stories of everyday life are to serve as "reformist fantasies," they may be called upon to contest traditional heroic themes and provide their own answers to contemporary "cultural dilemmas" (Myers, "Child's Play" 28). So many of the formulaic fictions concerning heroic action published in *St. Nicholas* between 1873 and 1914 allowed the readership to explore its fears and anxieties as well as its wishes and hopes, and to work through problems presented by the call to heroic action that were elided or neglected in the educational discourse found in editorial material, holiday features, song, and heroic biography—which presented a more traditional model of patriotic valor.

Mothers in despair at demands they could not meet found, in story after story, portraits of good women struggling to cope with situations beyond their control. Fathers distressed by their children's risk-taking behavior were shown that the most carefully made parental plans might set in motion unexpected consequences. Children, impelled by impulse or conscience to disobey parental rules, learned that they were not alone and were encouraged to imagine what might happen, for good or ill, if they dared to act out their dreams. And of course children were shown what it might feel like to be a helpless parent unwilling to send a child into danger, while parents were encouraged to appreciate their children's desire for autonomy and agency. Though the stories were often similar in structure, their many variations allowed readers to appreciate that not all children or parents are alike, and that when difficult circumstances put good people under pressure, what may happen next is neither predictable nor always edifying.

In these stories some obviously appalling things happen: a patriotic American lynch mob breaks into a home, bent on murder; an innocent little boy is shot while waving a futile white flag; a young sailor's hopes of glory bring him a violent death. But some less obvious circumstances might also have given thoughtful readers pause. Earnest parents use their children as pawns in dangerous games with other adults, or risk their children's lives for causes the children never really understand. Children are encouraged to play at innocence in order to manipulate hostile adults; they learn to deceive, to kill. Though the stories suggest that the younger generation's access to power and autonomy is, in many ways, a good thing—children in these stories do brave and kind deeds, overcome adult prejudice, resist oppression—moral dilemmas abound. And nothing is as simple as it looks on the mythic level, because fiction, even formula fiction—when looked at in the mass—can raise powerful questions about "the relation between nurturance and autonomy, connectedness and individuation, child and parent, dependence and dominance, feeling and reason . . . experience and the discursive practices that figure or constitute it" (Myers, "Romancing" 98).

WORKS CITED

Bercovitch, Sacvan. "Games of Chess: A Model of Literary and Cultural Studies." *Centuries Ends, Narrative Means*. Ed. Robert Newman. Stanford: Stanford UP, 1996: 15–57.

"Books and Reading for Young Folk." *St. Nicholas* 28 (Feb. 1901): 360.

"Books and Reading." *St. Nicholas* 28 (March 1901): 456.

Brooks, Elbridge S. "Friends or Foes?" *St. Nicholas* 17 (March 1890): 419–26.

Cloud, Virginia W. "The Black Duck." *St. Nicholas* 22 (April 1895): 452–59.

De Certeau, Michel. *The Writing of History*. Trans. Tom Conley. New York: Columbia UP, 1988.

Demerritt, E. W. "How the Tories Broke up Meeting." *St. Nicholas* 11 (July 1884): 687–90.

Gannon, Susan R. "'The Best Magazine for Children of All Ages': Cross-Editing *St. Nicholas Magazine* (1873–1905)." *Children's Literature* 25 (1997): 153–80.

Hancock, Harrie Irving. "Chuggins, the Youngest Hero with the Army; A Tale of the Capture of Santiago." *St. Nicholas* 26 (Nov. 1898): 39–52.

Jenkins, Charles F. "The Five-Pointed Star." *St. Nicholas* 19 (July 1892): 713–14.

Kelly, R. Gordon. *Mother Was a Lady: Self and Society in Selected American Children's Periodicals, 1865–1890*. Westport: Greenwood, 1974.

Kieffer, Harry M. *Recollections of a Drummer-Boy*. *St. Nicholas* 9 (Nov. 1881 to April 1882): 63–71, 138–40, 307–13, 391–400, 456–63; *St. Nicholas* 10 (June–Oct. 1883): 593–7, 649–53, 754–57, 835–40, 911–19.

McIlvaine, Charles. "A Little Contraband." *St. Nicholas* 17 (Sept. 1890): 966–73.

Myers, Mitzi. "'Anecdotes from the Nursery' in Maria Edgeworth's *Practical Education* (1798): Learning from Children 'Abroad and At Home.'" *Princeton University Library Chronicle* 60.2 (Winter 1999): 220–50.

———. "Child's Play as Woman's Peace Work: Maria Edgeworth's 'The Cherry Orchard,' Historical Rebellion Narratives, and Contemporary Cultural Studies." *Girls, Boys, Books, Toys: Gender in Children's Literature and Culture*. Ed. Beverly Lyon Clark and Margaret R. Higonnet. Baltimore: Johns Hopkins UP, 1999. 25–39.

———. "Romancing the Moral Tale." *Romanticism and Children's Literature in Nineteenth-Century England*. Ed. James Holt McGavran, Jr. Athens: U of Georgia P, 1991: 96–128.

Northrop, Mary S. "A Young Hero." *St. Nicholas* 21 (July 1894): 794–800.

Ogden, H. A. "How a Woman Saved an Army." *St. Nicholas* 25 (Feb. 1898): 335–37.

Olson, Marilynn Strasser. "'When Did Youth Ever Neglect to Bow Before Glory?': *St. Nicholas* and War." *St. Nicholas and Mary Mapes Dodge: The Legacy of a Children's Magazine Editor, 1873–1905*. Ed. Susan R. Gannon, Suzanne Rahn, and Ruth Anne Thompson. Jefferson: McFarland, 2004. 243–75.

Parton, Ethel. "Rhyme of the Tory Tollevers." *St. Nicholas* 28 (Dec. 1900): 105–12.

Price, Lillian L. "Bulb of the Crimson Tulip" *St. Nicholas* 27 (July 1900): 828–33.

———. "Laetitia and the Redcoats." *St. Nicholas* 16 (July 1889): 687–90.

Richards, Laura E. "Molly Pitcher." *St. Nicholas* 27 (June 1900): 718–19.

Seawell, Molly Elliot. *Decatur and Somers*. *St. Nicholas* 21 (May–Oct. 1894): 579–86, 669–77, 767–77, 856–60, 966–71, 1055–64.

Stanton, Elizabeth Cady. "Christmas on the Mayflower." *St. Nicholas* 28 (Nov. 1900): 60–65.

Stephens, John, and Robyn McCallum. *Retelling Stories, Framing Culture: Traditional Story and Metanarratives in Children's Literature*. New York: Garland, 1998.

Warner, Charles Dudley. "Talk about Reading." *St. Nicholas* 18.3 (Jan. 1891): 171–73.

Wiley, S. K. "Maurice and His Father." *St. Nicholas* 23 (July 1896): 707–19.

Woodman, C. H. "Girl Who Saved the General." *St. Nicholas* 5 (July 1878): 577–79.

· 9 ·

Worlds of Girls
Educational Reform and Fictional Form in
L. T. Meade's School Stories

Mavis Reimer

In 1886, when L. T. Meade published *A World of Girls: The Story of a School*, she revived a founding genre of children's literature—Sarah Fielding's *The Governess; or, The Little Female Academy* (1749) usually is identified as the first children's novel—and set the formula for what would become one of the most popular types of adolescent fiction in the last decades of the nineteenth century and the first decades of the twentieth century. Meade herself topped the popularity poll conducted by the magazine *The Girl's Realm* in 1898 ("Six" 431). Despite the size and enthusiasm of her contemporary audience, however, Meade's writing has been ignored and dismissed by the literary establishment, for reasons that are familiar to researchers working with nineteenth-century women's texts: she chose to write in popular rather than in elite forms; she was a professional rather than amateur writer; and she wrote voluminously, publishing close to 300 books during a forty-year writing career.

The assumption that the popular, the professional, and the prolific are synonymous with the culturally conservative underwrites most of the criticism on girls' school stories in general and Meade's work in particular.[1] But, in the case of L. T. Meade, even readers prepared to read character and plot sympathetically often express disappointment in Meade's fiction for girls. While the title of Meade's first novel clearly resonates for women readers and feminist literary critics, several have concluded that Meade's work offers less than it promises. To cite just one example, Kimberly Reynolds, who sets out to explicate the cultural reasons for the relatively low status of girls' books within children's literature in her 1990 study, ends by reinscribing that status: girls' books, she concludes, "justify passivity and self-regulation" (156), and girls' school stories, specifically those written by L. T. Meade, only provide a setting for "new and greater opportunities for self-denial, service and adherence to the established principles of femininity" (135).

The difficulty of reading women's writing about and for girls both accurately and sympathetically was one that Mitzi Myers addressed again and again in her work. In her well-known review of Geoffrey Summerfield's study of eighteenth-century children's literature, for example, she identified one of the problems as "presentism," a critical approach "that orders the past to validate today's needs" ("Wise" 108). Compounding the problem of presentist thought was the long-established tradition of assuming male developmental and narrative patterns to be normative, so that women's texts with girls as protagonists invariably appeared to be flawed. As Myers put it, in this view, "[t]he vibrant child cannot be the mother of a woman; she grows down, not up" ("Dilemmas" 69). There was, however, a way out of the impasse to which presentist and androcentric habits of analysis had brought the study of girls' books—a reading practice that carefully contextualized these books within their cultural and generic histories, a reading practice both advocated and modeled by Myers's work. As Myers herself explained it,

> a central aim is to demonstrate how a work of historical children's literature not only reflects its period's concerns, but how it comments on its social and intellectual milieu, how it tries to answer its era's questions about childhood and especially girlhood, how it functions as a cultural critique of contemporary educational practice and gender definition. But I want to do more than examine the educational ideology of my chosen example, the statement that the text makes; I want also to look at the work's literary structure in relation to its content and to argue that the formal elements by which the meaning is represented replicate that meaning. ("Socializing" 52)

In the essay that follows, my analysis of Meade's school stories borrows much from the method articulated by Myers, as readers noticing the allusion in my subtitle to one of Myers's essays on Maria Edgeworth might have guessed. Reading Meade's school stories within the context of the nineteenth-century debates about the education of girls and women opens the possibility of other conclusions than that Meade's stories only adhered to established principles of femininity. In an 1894 magazine article about Girton College, Meade maintained that it was possible to look back over the disputes of the previous forty years and to conclude that "the girl may be fairly considered to have won in the battle," since the opinion that she had the right to learn Greek with her brother and "to think for herself" no longer was "a fit subject for ridicule" (325). Meade's comment not only assumes that principles of femininity have been a site of struggle in her culture but also sets the terms of the victory she claims in language borrowed from Mary Wollstonecraft and other "rational dames" of the late eighteenth century. In order to explicate Meade's fictional use of the issues surrounding educational reform, I begin by outlining several recurrent motifs in the writings of the feminists and activists concerned with the definition and development of women's education. In doing so, I attempt to articulate, to use Mary Maynard's words, "what these women believed they were doing and the terms in which they discussed and tried to understand their predicament" (222). I then consider Meade's translation of the terms of the educational debates into the narrative strategies and structure of her girls' school stories.

Central to the work of the theorists and activists who battled to reform girls' secondary education and to gain access for women to higher education was an analysis of the implications of the past and present state of girls' schooling. One of the models the educational reformers repeatedly worked against was that of the girl finished at one of the fashionable ladies' academies, which had "flourished since the early eighteenth century" and which "continued to serve the wealthier classes" until the end of the nineteenth century (Vicinus 165). Common complaints against the finishing schools included the mean conditions and unhealthy locations of the schools; the lack not only of physical recreation but, in schools where girls were put into "stays" to shape correct posture, of physical movement at all; the meager food; and the "totally insufficient" provision of fires and bedclothes (Kamm 146). The best-known fictional account of a nineteenth-century girls' school, Charlotte Brontë's depiction of Lowood in *Jane Eyre*, details many of these mean conditions. Although Lowood is not a finishing school, the accounts of school life in the autobiographies of Victorian women authenticate many of Jane's experiences.

The women who became leaders in the educational movements, however, agreed that the material conditions of the finishing schools were secondary manifestations of the primary ill besetting such institutions and the schooling of girls in general. That ill was that, as Emily

Davies put it in 1863, women "have never been instructed in general principles" in their academic education (52). Middle-class girls frequently shared their brothers' instruction in rudimentary knowledge in the home nursery. But it seemed to the educational reformers that this early equality was all too quickly set aside. They complained that, while their brothers moved from instruction in arithmetic to education in algebraic theorems, the girls were stopped when they had learned to do basic sums; while their brothers explored astronomy and navigational theory, girls were taught only "conjuring tricks" with the globes (Beale, *History* 5; Somerville 29); while their brothers surveyed classical philosophy and history, girls were required to memorize pages of such texts as William Pinnock's *A Catechism of Modern History* (Sewell 10); while their brothers mastered the grammatical structures of Greek and Latin, girls were assigned lists of English prepositions to learn, that they "might be saved the trouble of thinking" (Beale, *History* 5) or pages of Johnson's dictionary to repeat (Somerville 22). In short, the feminists observed, at the point where boys moved from the largely rote learning of fundamentals to the examination of underlying principles, girls typically were set lessons to memorize or diverted into domestic duties, religious devotion, and the acquisition of accomplishments.

The habit of memorization, conceded some of the women who went on to educate themselves, played its part in allowing them to build a body of knowledge (Sewell 11; Somerville 54), but, for the most part, girls' education was condemned by such women as desultory, what Francis Power Cobbe called "heterogeneous studies pursued in . . . helter-skelter fashion" (*Life* 68). Intellectual women felt themselves locked out of knowledge which their brothers were given as a right, and they protested their disenfranchisement in metaphors that resonate with Virginia Woolf's image of the barred library in *A Room of One's Own*. Elizabeth Wordsworth, principal of Lady Margaret Hall at Oxford, for example, describes the girls "to be found in the schoolroom, peering . . . into their brothers' books, trying their hands at Greek and Latin . . . picking up crumbs of knowledge from beneath the tables of their male belongings" (qtd. by Battiscombe 41).

Dorothea Beale, Emily Davies, and Frances Mary Buss, the three most influential pioneers of modern education for women, often disagreed on particular issues,[2] but all three concurred in identifying lack of systematic teaching as the basic fault of girls' education in their evidence to the Schools Inquiry Commission in 1865. The Taunton Commission did not intend to examine girls' schools when it began its inquiry but was persuaded to do so by pressure from Emily Davies and her influential friends. When she, Beale, and Buss, among a total of eight women, were called to give evidence to the Commission, they became "the first women ever examined in person as expert witnesses before a royal commission" (Holcombe 22). Annie Ridley, writing of the event in her biography of Buss in 1895, remarks, "In 1865 . . . it was an event to cause a heart-thrill when a woman was summoned, not to meekly receive information, but actually to give it; not to listen, but to speak" (4). The description of girls' schools in the Commission's report, which summarized the schoolmistresses' testimony and the Commissioners' investigations into the schools, was cited repeatedly by reformers in the last decades of the century:

> The general deficiency in girls' education is stated with the utmost confidence, and with entire agreement, with whatever difference of words, by many witnesses of authority. Want of thoroughness and foundation; want of system; slovenliness and showy superficiality; inattention to rudiments; undue time given to accomplishments, and those not taught intelligently, or in any scientific manner; want of organization—these may sufficiently indicate the character of the complaints we have received, in their most general aspect. (548–49)[3]

Margaret Bryant has argued that the educational reformers of the nineteenth century "neither attempted nor wished to alter the framework of society, nor its system of shared values" (118), yet their work often served "radical, even revolutionary, purposes" (119). For the feminists' critique had implications far beyond methodology or curriculum. The traditional diversions of girls—domestic duties, religious devotion, and fashionable accomplishments—all assumed that girls were, to use Françoise Basch's term, relative creatures. The finishing schools emphasized the acquisition of enough elocutionary and musical skills to allow girls to give pleasing drawing room performances; skill in drawing and painting adequate to producing decoration for the home; knowledge of modern languages sufficient for conversing with the guests a father, brother, or husband might bring home; and a graceful deportment and dancing style. In fact, many commentators on education during the nineteenth century agreed with the feminists in scorning the mincing, facile young lady the academies reputedly turned out. Emily Davies claimed that "[t]he young lady of the world is universally condemned. No one will give her a good word" (99). There was, in fact, virtual unanimity among the public voices that the primary purpose of education should be the inculcation or development of good character.

But good character in a daughter showed itself in her willingness to act as ligature in the family, in the dominant cultural view. Mrs. G. S. Reaney demonstrates the logic of this position in *English Girls: Their Place and Power* (1879), one of many advice books published for girls during the nineteenth century. In the happy picture of home with which Reaney begins her book, the notion of the girl as relative creature is taken to such extremes that she is metaphorically dismembered: the "daughter of the house" is her mother's "right hand" and "the darling of her father's heart;" her "voice, ears, and fingers are the willing servants" of her older brothers; her knees and back are offered for baby to ride on; and there is always "an arm to be lent" to an aged grandmother (2–6).

The end of girlhood in this model is not a movement into independent adulthood, but into the ultimately relative position of wifehood. Girls' education was meant to facilitate this movement. The purpose of fashionable finishing schools, wrote an anonymous contributor to *Fraser's Magazine* in 1845, is to have their students gain "wares for the marriage-market" ("Enquiry" 177). Feminist reformers also represented education as a useful preparation for any girl who wished to be a thoughtful housekeeper and mother, but the systematic study they advocated was the study they saw as necessary groundwork for any middle-class girl who might earn her own living as an adult. In a letter written to her future biographer in 1871, for example, Buss spoke of her work as an educator as motivated by her "earnest desire to lighten . . . the misery of women, brought up 'to be married and taken care of,' and left alone in the world destitute" (Ridley 93). In fact, Victorian feminism coalesced as a "revolt against redundancy," according to Martha Vicinus. Notoriously identified as "superfluous" or "redundant," single women "had to tackle their marginal position ideologically, economically, and socially" (12); the reformed boarding schools, Vicinus points out, allowed single women both to earn relatively good salaries as teachers and to live in respectable situations outside the domestic sphere. The examples of these women pioneers clearly "fuelled the ambitions of growing numbers of girls to perform tasks traditionally considered outside their spheres," according to Judith Rowbotham (113). For school was, by definition, a world apart from, even opposed to, home. Contemporaneous critics of girls' schools recognized what contemporary critics of Meade have not seen: schooling a girl outside the home to take up service inside the home is a fundamental ideological contradiction, for school itself is part of the public sphere.

The schools also provided the educators with a place to work out the principles of single, female adulthood. The reformers believed, and said, that to allow girls access to explanations and principles, rather than only facts and rules, was to give them the "power to think for themselves" (Beale, "Schools in the Past" 259). Because "self-government" was the goal of such an education (Davies 148), the new headmistresses dispensed with many of the petty rules of the fashionable schools in favor of articulating what Jane Frances Dove, lecturer at Girton College and later head of St. Leonards School, called "broad principles of conduct" (Meade, "Girls' Schools II," 402). The disciplinary code whose end was giving girls "the power to think for themselves" was a rejection of the view that women only existed to serve the needs of others. Cobbe, in particular, was scornful of "the theory that the final cause of Woman is the service she can render to Man," a theory she dubbed "Woman, considered as Adjective"; she saw her work as based, rather, "on the theory that Woman was created for some end proper to herself," a theory she put under the heading "Woman, considered as a Noun" ("Final Cause" 6).

Self-government proceeded from self-knowledge, a knowledge often imaged by the educational reformers in the same terms Woolf was later to use, as "a room of one's own." For example, Constance Maynard, head of Cheltenham after Beale, contrasted the constricted lives of early nineteenth-century girls, who "suffered grievously from want of breathing space" and "were never for a moment alone," with the girls now at school who know the "virtues in solitude" (1067). Emily Shirreff drew the same contrast: daughters at home, she said, are "without even a quiet room of their own in which they may if they choose enjoy solitude and their own pursuits" (409).

Such reflection promoted the establishment of community rather than mitigated against it. Anne Clough, principal of Newnham College, in 1890 reported that the results of women's colleges could be seen both in the students' personal development—"[t]heir studies have taught them energy and self-control; their examinations have taught them the power of collecting their thoughts rapidly"—and in their corporate life— "[t]hese women have lived together and studied together as friends and comrades; they have learnt to plan and work together" (300). In a talk to the Headmistresses' Association in 1907, an unidentified headmistress suggests the weighty expectations the new teachers had for community life within the schools: "If only every girl would go to school and stay there long enough to learn the corporate virtues, in two or three generations we should realise Utopia" (qtd. by Vicinus 163). This statement represents a high, no doubt an impossibly high, valuation of communal life, but it does not merely reinscribe established principles of femininity by providing new opportunities for self-denial and service. To become a self-disciplined member of a *corps*, to be part of a school body, is to have travelled some distance from being a knee and back for baby or a voice, ears, and fingers in a brother's service.

Meade not only sympathized with, but also publicized, the goals of the educational reformers in her journalistic work. Women's education was one of the central topics addressed by writers in *Atalanta*, the girls' magazine Meade edited for six years after 1887. During the 1890s she herself wrote several series of articles about the new girls' schools and women's colleges, based on visits to Girton College, Somerville Hall, Newnham College, Cheltenham Ladies' College, and Bedford College, among others. Meade reports on the schools in the same terms the reformers use in their writing. She emphasizes, for example, the "cheerful, cosy, and homelike" appointments of the university halls, where every girl has her own "daintily-furnished" apartment ("Somerville" 14, 15). She characterizes the education offered to girls at the new schools as thoughtful and thorough. At Cheltenham, for example, "is to be found the most perfect training for spirit, mind, and body" (283); Girton offers "such a valuable course of training" (327), she concludes, after listing the full slate of subjects in which students can be examined; both Newnham and Girton "give to the students a power of dealing with things in general which cannot be too highly appreciated" (Newnham 529). She insists that school life is not bound up in constraints and rules, but is predicated on girls' honor and thoughtfulness. Girton gives its students "a considerable amount of liberty" outside lecture hours (328); the life at Newnham is arranged so that "[t]here is abundance of time for both work and play," for both "discipline and freedom" (529). At St. Leonards, "[t]he girls are given a great deal of liberty" by Miss Dove despite the objections of some parents (459): "'I trust them fully,' she said. 'I have never had my trust abused'" (460). And she maintains that the schools and colleges teach the values of corporate life. In answer to a question about "the result of life at Girton on the girl mind," Meade reports that one of the principals remarks, "She is taught to be unselfish—in short every quality is sharpened. The sense of comradeship here is splendid" (331). Miss Dove's opinion on the value of school life for girls is that "the opportunity it affords for cultivating a public spirit and for co-operating with other girls is of immense benefit" and that it is "the lack of such opportunities that makes women's lives often so small and petty" (460).

The pictures of schools Meade builds in her boarding school stories follow closely from her documentary accounts. Lavender House in *A World of Girls*, Penwerne House in *The Manor School* (1903), and Fairbank House in *The School Favourite* (1908)[4] are schools that systematically overturn the values and practices of the earlier boarding establishments, as these are represented in the cultural documents of the period, and align themselves with the new style of girls' schools. Unlike the boarding schools described in the autobiographies of Victorian women, the schools of Meade's stories are invariably set in well-proportioned buildings in graciously landscaped grounds. Lavender House, for example, is flanked by lawns and protected by a veritable forest of trees. Mrs. Willis's living and reception quarters boast "a very wide and cheerful hall" with a "handsome encaustic-tiled floor" and a "blazing fire" (7). The "daintily-furnished little" bedrooms of the girls meet the strictest possible hygienic and aesthetic standards, and always have "small bright fire[s]" burning in the grates (9). Fairbank House is "a particularly cheerful, bright-looking house, facing due south, and with a splendid view of the Surrey Downs" (1).

Meade identifies the headmistresses of her fictional establishments as members of the new generation of schoolmistresses by the attitudes to systematic training she gives them. Hester spends her first afternoon at Lavender House enduring "the ordeal of a rather stiff examination" by Mrs. Willis (21), who places her in the third class on the basis of her knowledge of English literature and history, French, German, and general knowledge. In *The School Favourite*, Elizabeth Raleigh's knowledge has been acquired in "a very hap-hazard fashion" (33), and Mrs. Temple feels she must place her "in the lowest class of the Upper School" until she can demonstrate that she has gotten her miscellaneous knowledge "grouped in [her] mind in some sort of order" (35–36).

The headmistresses of Meade's school novels agree with the notion of discipline as the understanding and application of principle. All of them build their behavioral codes around the ideal of honor and the good of the group. Miss Peacock of *The Manor School*, for example, believes that her trust in her students alone will encourage them to live up to her "code of honor" (123). She maintains that "[t]he woman of today can be anything; she can dare anything" and that, in order to "meet that grand future," the "girl of the present day ought to be educated right nobly" (184). Often, the headmistresses in the schools have taken, as a particular favorite, a girl who is neither the brightest, nor the prettiest, nor the richest, nor the best-behaved, but who spiritedly aspires to better things and who is unfailingly committed to the common good.

In creating the idyllic school settings and the demanding but wise characters of the headmistresses in her novels, Meade represents as accomplished fact the ideals for which such headmistresses as Dorothea Beale and Frances Mary Buss were reaching; moreover, she does so in terms that reverse the common complaints against the old-style girls' schools. But it is in reading the school stories for structure that Meade's special achievement becomes obvious. In her plots, Meade exploits the ideological controversies surrounding the purpose of female education and, to borrow Mitzi Myers's description of a similar narrative strategy in one of Maria Edgeworth's short stories, "literalizes new practices of cultural space" ("Child's Play" 35), by creating the school as a new imaginative space for her girl readers.

Among Meade's novels that would fall within the category of school stories are day-school stories, college stories, home schooling stories, and the boarding school stories to which most commentators refer when they speak of Meade's school stories. But whatever the places in which the stories are set, many describe a similar plot movement. An adolescent girl is sent to school (or to college or to be schooled in another home) when her family home is disrupted. Her arrival at the beginning of the story causes a disturbance of established routines and loyalties within the school body or household. She soon finds herself in an untenable situation, her better self prompting her to declare allegiance to one girl or group of girls while she is simultaneously under the secret influence of another, dangerous girl or group. The resolution of the conflict always involves public disclosure of what she has borne in silence for much of the story and, finally, her full integration into the new community. In the most general sense, then, Meade's plots follow the comic pattern identified by Northrop Frye as the "movement from one kind of society to another" (163). With its privileging of youth over age and its hopeful and utopian propulsion, this fiction has been a common choice of writers for children since at least the mid-nineteenth century.

But the opposition of age and youth Frye describes, which is exploited in much children's fiction, is replaced in Meade's stories, most obviously in her boarding school stories, by the opposition between a society administered by men and a society headed by women. Few of Meade's main characters wish to go to school at the opening of the boarding school novels. The girls usually feel themselves expelled from the home of their childhood because their parents are either unwilling or unable to care for them. It is typically their fathers who choose to push them "out into a cold world," as twelve-year-old Hester Thornton in *A World of Girls* puts it (2). Hetty's father has assumed the charge of his two daughters since their mother's death, and he demands a punctilious obedience of Hetty, which she refuses to give him. She is sent to "a first-class school" by him, she believes, to be "reduced to an everyday and pattern little girl" (3–4). It is a fate she determines to resist. Christian Mitford, aged thirteen, of *The Manor School* is sent by her parents to Penwerne House when her father is awarded a diplomatic position in Persia (7). Mr. Mitford has selected the school, his wife reports, because he believes Christian is being spoiled at home and the school has the reputation of being "very severe in tone" (6). Mrs. Mitford, too, expresses the conventional wish that Christian will do her duty (36), but she is far more excited by the accomplishments she anticipates her daughter will acquire: the ability to sing, play, and recite well, "to paint a little," to speak French (and possibly German and Italian) with "a proper accent," to "dance beautifully" (32–33). But Christian has no intention of being turned into "a brilliant, accomplished girl" at what she calls a "severe-discipline school" (33). She has long dreamed of becoming a heroine, "the sort of girl who would do great things" (33), and she seizes this evidence of her parents' "hardness" as a reason to run away from both home and school and to try to make her own way in the world. Fifteen-year-old Elizabeth Raleigh of *The School Favourite* is sent to Mrs. Temple's school when her father, on a "sudden whim," decides she needs "two years' good teaching" in order to "come out as a thoroughly fascinating woman" (14). Like Hester and Christian, Elizabeth warns that the school won't fit her to its pattern easily: "I am rather a wild kind of person, however, and it will take some time to shake me down" (14).

In each of these three novels, the father who selects his daughter's school believes not only that the educational institution will support his goals of reducing her to "a pattern little girl" in preparation for her coming out "a thoroughly fascinating woman," but also that the school will facilitate his daughter's acquiescence to these goals. Each of the fathers, in other words, is confident that he is sending his daughter to one of the finishing schools of the old style that serve, in novelist Sarah Grand's memorable phrase, as "forcing house[s] for the marriage market" (343).

Hester, Christian, and Elizabeth in Meade's novels believe their fathers' representations of school life to be accurate. Each sets off for what she characterizes as the "prison" of school determined not to conform to expectations. But, as I have already argued, the expectations of the headmistresses at the fictional schools are quite different from the fathers' representations of them: the heads expect that girls will realize in their behavior the principles of honesty, industry, and the common good. The conflict in the stories occurs because the main characters, believing they are protesting adult tyranny, refuse to govern themselves according to such principles.

Each wishes to retain for herself the exclusive affection of another girl. In the entangled plots engendered by their selfishness, the girls often see themselves as unable to rectify the situation because to do so would mean exposing their own and others' flouting of the rules of the school. But keeping such secrets finally gives way to the greater call of the community's well-being. The concluding scene of many of Meade's school novels is a tearful public confession by the wrongdoers. Such confession is invariably rewarded with a full and equally emotional forgiveness. The only girls who are banished from the community are the ones who refuse to tell all they know. As Miss Peacock explains to her students, "I do not think, girls, that there is any sin a schoolgirl could commit that I should not forgive if repentance followed" (335). With their confessions and the sympathetic forgiveness of headmistresses and fellow students, Hester, Christian, and Elizabeth are finally reconciled to the schools in which they find themselves.

As contemporary critics observe, however rebellious the main character of a Meade school story is at the outset, she always, sooner or later, capitulates to cultural expectations. The twist of these stories, however, is that the culture Meade creates by realizing the ideals of the educational reformers in her novels is an alternative to patriarchal culture. The rebellious heroine does indeed learn to love school, but the school she learns to love is not the "prison" of a school she railed against in the opening chapters of her story, for the setting of a Meade school novel is precisely *not* the house of the father, but *A World of Girls*.

Meade's stories scored with the audience of girls to whom they were directed, to judge from the available sales information, readers' polls, and contemporary reviews. Reviewing *The Darling of the School* in 1915, for example, the reviewer of the *Huddersfield Weekly Examiner* noted that "we know from actual experience that children will read it with pleasure."[5] The avid readership for Meade's novels might suggest that girls did respond with pleasure to the way in which her characters eluded patriarchal designs. The fact that contemporary critics of the school stories continue to construe them to emphasize the girls' capitulation to convention appears to demonstrate the success of her narrative sleight-of-hand. For Meade's achievement in the school stories is not explicit cultural critique. Indeed, that achievement depends on readers recognizing her negotiation of the conflicting spoken and unspoken interdictions of the culture in which the stories were produced.

Judith Rowbotham and Claudia Nelson have both argued that such ideals as honesty, industry and, above all, selflessness were ideals for both sexes, aspects of the Evangelical definition of good character that schools could be expected to profess. The disciplinary codes developed by the new headmistresses, then, seem comprehensible within the terms of Victorian culture. But, as many Victorian feminists knew, what was actually wanted of girls was not what was said to be wanted. Girls were meant to get husbands. The fact that the dominant Evangelical rhetoric of Victorian society privileged the notion of individual moral character meant only that this goal was not often articulated publicly by the end of the century. In her brilliant and satirical polemic, *Marriage as a Trade*, feminist Cicely Hamilton is particularly scathing about the cultural injunctions to silence:

> The man who has his bread to earn, with hands, or brains, or tools, goes out to seek for the work to which he is trained; his livelihood

depending on it, he offers his skill and services without shame or thought of reproach. But with woman it is not so; she is expected to express unwillingness for the very work for which she has been taught and trained. She has been brought up in the belief that her profession is marriage and motherhood; yet though poverty may be pressing upon her—though she may be faced with actual lack of the necessities of life—she must not openly express her desire to enter that profession, and earn her bread in the only way for which she is fitted. She must stand aside and wait—indefinitely; and attain to her destined livelihood by appearing to despise it. (37)

The "freedom of bargaining to the best advantage" for "the possession of her person," which seems to Hamilton the "logical" approach to treating marriage as a profession for women, is strenuously repressed and made the subject of the legal taboos against prostitution and solicitation (38–39). Rather, a girl is taught to display her "wares" to advantage, to interpret men's consequent interest in her as chivalrous, and to accept such outward deference "in payment for real deference and subjection" (126).

Meade does not lay bare the mechanisms of her culture in a systematic analysis in her school fiction, but she does work to short-circuit the system of exchange Hamilton describes. The concern she expresses in her interviews with headmistresses about "the objects" and ends of "an education so thorough and so stimulating" is not easily set aside ("Girls' Schools II" 463). In her social-realist fiction, such as *A Princess of the Gutter* and *Mary Gifford, M. B.*, Meade shows young women working for remuneration in "the wider world." But, as both Meade and the headmistresses she interviewed knew, there were relatively few appropriate and available vocations for middle-class women in the nineteenth century. By the end of the century, in fact, the protean and resilient notion of girls and women as relative creatures had accommodated itself to the idea of a more intellectual education for girls. While the impetus for the feminists' reforms in education was to prepare women to lead independent lives, for many people, "the principle of educating women to be ornamental wives" was simply replaced by "the principle of educating women to be intellectually capable wives" (185), as Perry Williams has pointed out. The problem of girls' education, in other words, was "managed and contained" by what Winfried Fluck, following Theodor Adorno, calls "the simple device of narrative sequence," in which either-or dilemmas are turned into first-next relationships (41).

It is just such containment that Meade refuses. The conclusions to her school stories are celebrations of the reconstituted school community. In this closure, her texts are unlike texts from other school story traditions. Boys' school stories, such as those by Thomas Hughes, Talbot Baines Reed, and Rudyard Kipling, close with an outline of the fates of their characters in the "sterner after-battle" of life (Reed 8). The eighteenth-century moralists Sarah Fielding and Mary Wollstonecraft conclude their stories about girls at school with families reclaiming their daughters. Meade's contemporaries, Frances Hodgson Burnett and Mary Molesworth, end their school stories with the girls recreating domestic spaces they have lost. Meade, however, refuses to solve the troubling implications of her school stories by writing her heroines past their school days. Rather, she holds open the space she has created—within the school story text, but also within children's literature more generally—for girls to think about girls thinking for themselves.

Meade contests the system Hamilton satirizes, ironically by taking at face value the ideals publicly promoted. Honesty, industry, and selflessness constitute the virtues of the morality espoused by society; it is only through earnest striving to be honestly selfless that the girls of Meade's novels achieve happiness and community. By refusing to pay attention to the hidden messages sent to girls and women—which instruct them to promote themselves by attracting men and besting other women—Meade creates a textual world in which the common good is the real, as well as the rhetorical, goal of girls' lives together.

NOTES

1. See, for example, Isabel Quigly, Mary Cadogan and Patricia Craig, Jacqueline Bratton, and Edith Honig. Gill Frith and Sally Mitchell, to the contrary, offer more contextualized assessments of Meade's writing for girls.

2. Carol Dyhouse contrasts Beale and Buss in terms of the former's religiosity and the latter's secularity (22–28). Joyce Senders Pedersen compares the two headmistresses in similar terms, Beale exemplifying the "saintly" style of authority among headmistresses and Buss exemplifying the "civic-minded" style (254–82). Davies was the principal spokesperson in the campaign to have women's education follow the same courses of study and examination as men's did. Buss agreed with this position. Beale aligned herself, rather, with the position of

Anne Clough, head of Newnham, who hoped that innovations in girls' and women's education might act as a catalyst for the reform of educational practices for boys and men as well. See Ridley 6–9; Holcombe 48; and Beale, "Girls' Schools, Past and Present," 552–53.

3. The reformers more typically cited the section beginning with "Want of thoroughness and foundation" and ending with "want of organization." See, for example, Maria Shirreff Grey's *On the Education of Women* (5) and C. S. Bremner's *Education of Girls and Women in Great Britain* (75). By truncating the quotation of their evidence from the report in this way, the reformers gave the authority of the Commission to their own words.

4. The three boarding school stories with which I work in detail in this analysis exemplify clearly the narrative structures and strategies with which I am concerned. Meade's other school stories make use of variations of these structures and strategies.

5. Review of *The Destiny of the School* used with permission of the trustees of the National Library of Scotland.

WORKS CITED

Basch, Françoise. *Relative Creatures: Victorian Women in Society and the Novel.* New York: Schocken, 1974.

Battiscombe, Georgina. *Reluctant Pioneer: The Life of Elizabeth Wordsworth.* London: Constable, 1978.

Beale, Dorothea. "Girls' Schools, Past and Present." *Nineteenth Century* 23 (1888): 552–53.

———. *History of the Cheltenham Ladies' College 1853–1904.* Cheltenham: "Looker-On" Printing Works, [1919].

———. "Schools in the Past." *Atalanta* 3 (1889–90): 259–61.

Bratton, Jacqueline S. *The Impact of Victorian Children's Fiction.* London: Croom Helm, 1981.

Bremner, C. S. *Education of Girls and Women in Great Britain.* London: Swan Sonnenschien, 1897.

Bryant, Margaret. *The Unexpected Revolution: A Study in the History of the Education of Women and Girls in the Nineteenth Century.* Studies in Education n.s. 10. London: U of London Institute of Education, 1979.

Buss, Frances M. *Leaves From the Notebooks of Frances M. Buss, Being Selections from her Weekly Addresses to the Girls of the North London Collegiate School.* Ed. Grace Toplis. London: Macmillan, 1896.

Cadogan, Mary, and Patricia Craig. *You're a Brick, Angela! The Girls' Story 1839–1985.* London: Gollancz, 1986.

Clough, Anne Jemima. *Women's Progress in Scholarship.* 1890. Rpt. in *The Education Papers: Women's Quest for Equality in Britain, 1850–1912.* Ed. Dale Spender. Women's Source Library. New York: Routledge, 1987. 295–304.

Cobbe, Frances Power. "The Final Cause of Woman." *Woman's Work and Woman's Culture: A Series of Essays.* Ed. Josephine E. Butler. London: Macmillan, 1869. 1–26.

———. *Life of Frances Power Cobbe as Told by Herself.* Posthumous ed. London: Swan Sonnenschien, 1904.

Davies, Emily. *Thoughts on Some Questions Relating to Women, 1860–1908.* Ed. E. E. Constance Jones. Cambridge: Bowes, 1910.

Dyhouse, Carol. "Miss Buss and Miss Beale: Gender and Authority in the History of Education." Hunt 22–38.

"An Enquiry into the State of Girls' Fashionable Schools." *Fraser's Magazine* 31 (1845): 703. Rpt. in *Reform and Intellectual Debate in Victorian England.* Ed. Barbara Dennis and David Skilton. London: Croom Helm, 1987. 176–78.

Fluck, Winfried. "Popular Culture as a Mode of Socialization: A Theory about the Social Functions of Popular Cultural Forms." *Journal of Popular Culture* 21.3 (Winter 1987): 31–46.

Frith, Gill. "'The Time of Your Life': The Meaning of the School Story." *Language, Gender and Childhood.* Ed. Carolyn Steedman, Cathy Urwin, and Valerie Walkerdine. London: Routledge, 1985. 113–36.

Frye, Northrop. *Anatomy of Criticism: Four Essays.* Princeton, NJ: Princeton UP, 1957.

Grand, Sarah. *The Beth Book: Being a Study from the Life of Elizabeth Caldwell McLure.* New York: Appleton, 1897.

Great Britain. School Inquiry Commission. *Report of the Commissioners. Presented to Both Houses of Parliament by Command of Her Majesty.* Vol. I. London: Spottiswoode, [1865].

Grey, [Maria Shirreff]. *On The Education of Women: A Paper Read by Mrs. William Grey at the Meeting of the Society of Arts, May 31st, 1871.* London: Ridgway, 1871.

Hamilton, Cicely. *Marriage as a Trade.* 1909. Detroit: Singing Tree, 1971.

Holcombe, Lee. *Victorian Ladies at Work: Middle-Class Women in England and Wales 1850–1914.* Hamden: Archon, 1973.

Honig, Edith. *Breaking the Angelic Image: Woman Power in Victorian Children's Fantasy.* New York: Greenwood, 1988.

Hunt, Felicity, ed. *Lessons for Life: The Schooling of Girls and Women, 1850–1950.* Oxford: Blackwell, 1987.

Kamm, Josephine. *Hope Deferred: Girls' Education in English History.* London: Methuen, 1965.

Maynard, Constance L. "From Early Victorian Schoolroom to University: Some Personal Experiences." *Nineteenth Century* 76 (1914): 1060–73.

Maynard, Mary. "Privilege and Patriarchy: Feminist Thought in the Nineteenth Century." *Sexuality and Subordination: Interdisciplinary Studies of Gender in the Nineteenth Century*. Ed. Susan Mendus and Jane Rendall. London: Routledge, 1989. 221–47.

Meade, L. T. "English Girls and Their Colleges. Bedford College, and Some Others." *Lady's Pictorial* 23 January 1892: 126–27.

———. "English Girls and Their Colleges. Somerville Hall." *Lady's Pictorial* 2 January 1892: 14–15.

———. "Girls' Schools of To-day I: Cheltenham College." *Strand Magazine* 9 (1895): 283–88.

———. "Girls' Schools of To-day II: St. Leonards and Great Harrowden Hall." *Strand Magazine* 9 (1895): 457–63.

———. "Girton College." *Atalanta* 7 (1893–94): 325–31.

———. *The Manor School*. 1903. New York: Grosset and Dunlap, [1903].

———. *Mary Gifford, M.B.* London: Wells Gardner, 1898.

———. "Newnham College." *Atalanta* 7 (1893–94): 525–29.

———. *A Princess of the Gutter*. 1895. New York: Putnam, 1896.

———. *The School Favourite*. 1908. Chicago: Donohue, [1913].

———. *A World of Girls: The Story of a School*. 1886. Chicago: Donohue, n.d.

Mitchell, Sally. "Children's Reading and the Culture of Girlhood: The Case of L. T. Meade." *Browning Institute Studies* 17 (1989): 53–63.

Myers, Mitzi. "Child's Play as Woman's Peace Work: Maria Edgeworth's 'The Cherry Orchard,' Historical Rebellion Narratives, and Contemporary Cultural Studies." *Girls, Boys, Books, Toys: Gender in Children's Literature and Culture*. Ed. Beverly Lyon Clark and Margaret R. Higonnet. Baltimore: Johns Hopkins UP, 1999. 25–39.

———. "The Dilemmas of Gender as Double-Voiced Narrative; or, Maria Edgeworth Mothers the *Bildungsroman*." *The Idea of the Novel in the Eighteenth Century*. Ed. Robert W. Uphaus. East Lansing: Colleagues, 1988. 67–96.

———. "Socializing Rosamond: Educational Ideology and Fictional Form." *Children's Literature Association Quarterly* 14.2 (Summer 1989): 52–58.

———. "Wise Child, Wise Peasant, Wise Guy: Geoffrey Summerfield's Case Against the Eighteenth Century." *Children's Literature Association Quarterly* 12.2 (Summer 1987): 107–10.

Nelson, Claudia. *Boys Will Be Girls: The Feminine Ethic and British Children's Fiction, 1857–1917*. New Brunswick: Rutgers UP, 1991.

Pedersen, Joyce Senders. *The Reform of Girls' Secondary and Higher Education in Victorian England: A Study of Elites and Educational Change*. New York: London, 1987.

Quigly, Isabel. *The Heirs of Tom Brown: The English School Story*. London: Chatto, 1982.

Reaney, Mrs. G. S. *English Girls: Their Place and Power*. London: Kegan Paul, 1879.

Reed, Talbot Baines. *The Fifth Form at St. Dominic's*. London: Office of *The Boy's Own Paper*. [1887].

Rev. of *The Darling of the School*, by L. T. Meade. *Huddersfield Weekly Examiner* 11 Dec. 1915. DEP 341/646. W & R Chambers Collection. National Library of Scotland, Edinburgh.

Reynolds, Kimberley. *Girls Only?: Gender and Popular Children's Fiction in Britain, 1880–1910*. Philadelphia: Temple UP, 1990.

Ridley, Annie E. *Frances Mary Buss and Her Work for Education*. London: Longmans, 1895.

Rowbotham, Judith. *Good Girls Make Good Wives: Guidance for Girls in Victorian Fiction*. Oxford: Blackwell, 1989.

Sewell, Elizabeth M. *The Autobiography of Elizabeth M. Sewell*. Ed. Eleanor L. Sewell. London: Longmans, 1907.

Shirreff, Emily. *Intellectual Education, and Its Influence on the Character and Happiness of Women*. London: Parker, 1858.

"The Six Most Popular Living Writers for Girls." *The Girl's Realm* Feb. 1899: 431.

Somerville, Mary. *Personal Recollections, from Early Life to Old Age, of Mary Somerville. With Selections from Her Correspondence*. Ed. Martha Somerville. London: John Murray, 1873.

Vicinus, Martha. *Independent Women: Work and Community for Single Women, 1850–1920*. Women in Culture and Society. Chicago: U of Chicago P, 1985.

Williams, Perry. "Pioneer Women Students at Cambridge, 1869–81." Hunt 171–91.

Part 4

REMEMBERING MITZI MYERS

Mitzi Myers
A Memoir (9 October 1939 to 5 November 2001)

Patsy Myers

*B*y her own confession, my sister, Mitzi, was less than enthusiastic about the introduction of a baby sister into her three-year-old world. This is not an unusual reaction for any child about to have a sibling forced upon her, but far from feeling threatened by me, Mitzi viewed me as a bit of a nuisance and a challenge in forbearance.

Assessing the situation as well as she was able, and no doubt observing my raw state, she tolerated me because she decided it might be fun to teach me things since it was obvious I was going to need an education. Thus, our roles were established early on, and I became her first student. It was to remain so for as long as she lived.

Mitzi's footnotes in her later career were legendary, but her intellectual curiosity and reverence for details were both born in her. When I asked questions, she never gave simplistic explanations and always seemed to know any answer replete with the tantalizing bits and pieces that spark creativity and make learning fun. She was far more patient with my limitations than I was, and despite her potentially intimidating intellect, she never lorded her capability over my own. She was a loving sister and a generous, inspirational teacher.

Later she said that books were like children to her, but in the beginning I'm sure they were her allies. A beautiful, brilliant, somewhat introverted girl in a small Texas town in the fifties, Mitzi fueled her own liberation, and that freedom came with the steady realization that restrictions might be placed on her person but that no one would control her mind. I still can see her curled up in a chair in our bedroom reading any and everything she could get her hands on. Once she was grounded by our father for a summertime offense, and he eventually decided to

Figure 10.1.   Childhood picture of Mitzi Myers. Photograph courtesy of Patsy Myers.

offer her an out. "I'll bet you're getting bored just cooped up in here reading." She looked up, smiled demurely, and said, "No, not really," and began reading again. I stood there, eyes bulging, slack-jawed and struck dumb by the courage of her convictions. Our strict father, whom we both fiercely loved and respected, was rarely at a loss, but he realized he'd been outdone, that Mitzi and her books had won.

Figure 10.2. Mitzi Myers at age eighteen or nineteen. Photograph courtesy of Patsy Myers.

Neither my mother nor my father had gone to college, but both had a profound appreciation of education and took enormous pride in their children's accomplishments. When Mitzi was wee, Mother would spread a quilt on the floor and read books to her for hours. At first Mother thought that she had memorized the words, but it became clear that somehow she'd taught herself to read.

And read she did. The librarian at the local Carnegie Public Library, who incongruously gave ballet and tap-dancing lessons there as well, virtually waved her through as she scavenged the shelves for any new fodder. Only once did the librarian call our mother to ask if she knew that Mitzi was reading risque material. Confident of Mitzi's impeccable taste, our mother, to her credit, never flinched or questioned, but now I myself wonder just how risque the book could possibly have been, considering the source and time. The author was more guilty of shabby writing than anything else, I suspect, and Mitzi would have been repelled by that alone. Reading everything taught her how to cull the good from the bad.

So, Mitzi outgrew our hometown and the local library long before she graduated from our local high school and was released to ever widening resources. There was no looking back.

Figure 10.3.   Mitzi Myers. Photograph by Andrea Kane, courtesy Development Communications, Princeton University.

It was at Rice University that she fell in love with Dennis, her future husband, and the eighteenth century. Already drawn to that period, she chose William Godwin for her dissertation, but it was Mary Wollstonecraft with whom she bonded. From Wollstonecraft she progressed to the women she called "her ladies," women who recognized the power of education to provoke changes and betterment, just as Mitzi herself did. In my more petulant moments, I sometimes carped that she knew more about Maria Edgeworth's family than our own, but it was impossible not to share her enthusiasm when she felt such passion. It was her passion for her work that got her through the death of her husband and most of her family and many disappointments and pain.

And when the very books that had sustained her were taken from her by the fire that destroyed her home, it was too much to ask. Not long before her death, the topic of gravestone inscriptions came up, and I asked what she wanted on hers. With her typical black humor she chortled, "She tried." And how hard she *did* try, not even I fully realized until it was too late.

I think of her, I think of all that knowledge and potential gone, lost forever. In honoring her with this collection, we help to keep her intellect, her wit, and her contributions alive. She would have liked that we tried.

The Scholarly Legacy of Mitzi Myers

Gillian Adams with Donelle Ruwe

> Omme tulit punctum qui miscuit utile dulci,
> lectorum delectando pariterque monendo.
> [The one who mixes the useful with the pleasant gets every
> vote by equally delighting and instructing the reader.]
>
> —Horace, *Ars Poetica* lines 343–44

$\mathcal{O}$n 14 November 2001, J. D. Stahl emailed the members of the Children's Literature Association with news of Mitzi Myers's unexpected death from the complications of pneumonia contracted in the aftermath of a fire in her home in Fullerton, California, 13 August 2000. The sad news was carried as well on the child_lit listserve, and there were substantial and well-deserved obituaries in both the *New York Times* (Honan) and the *Los Angeles Times* (McClellan). This article is meant as a tribute to Mitzi and a discussion of the revolutions that she initiated in the field of children's literature criticism.

Editor's note: The core of this essay was authored by Adams and first appeared as "Mitzi Myers, 9 October 1939–5 November 2001" in *ChLA Quarterly* 27.2 (Summer 2002): 88–91. It has been reprinted with the permission of the Children's Literature Association. In addition to minor additions and subtractions of sentences, Ruwe has added substantial material discussing Myers's reviews, affiliation with the UCLA Children's Literature Rare Book Collection, final publications, research on illustrations and Irish literature, and all of the endnotes. Ruwe has added twelve sources to the Works Cited section and removed citations to Myers's publications. For these citations, readers are asked to refer to chapter 12, the comprehensive bibliography of Myers's works compiled by Ruwe.

Mitzi Ouida Myers was born 9 October 1939 in Sulpher Springs, a small town in Northeast Texas. According to her sole survivor and sister, Patsy Myers, from early childhood she was a lover of reading and of books. Mitzi received her bachelor's and master's degrees from East Texas State University, and her Ph.D. from Rice, where she was also a teaching assistant (1962–63). Her research for her dissertation, "Aspects of William Godwin's Reputation in the 1790s," combined with her growing interest in feminist literary criticism, soon led to publications on Harriet Martineau, Hannah More, Mary Wollstonecraft, and other eighteenth- and nineteenth-century women writers.

Mitzi was an assistant professor at the University of California Santa Barbara from 1966 to 1973 but did not make tenure, probably due to her inability to complete the books she was always working on. Given the publication of over 98 scholarly articles, reviews, and edited collections by the time of her death, it would seem that she had more than enough material for several books, particularly one on Maria Edgeworth. Sadly, Mitzi never finished *Romancing the Family: Maria Edgeworth and the Scene of Instruction*, but her extraordinary record of award-winning scholarship on Edgeworth as children's author, pedagogue, political writer, and founder of the Anglo–Irish writing tradition indicate how valuable her book would have been.[1]

After 1973, Mitzi embarked on the tenuous career of a lecturer at a number of academic institutions, such as California Polytech Pomona, California State Fullerton, California State Long Beach, Chapman University, and Scripps College, often simultaneously, and starting in 1980, intermittently at UCLA. She received a number of grants and fellowships; her NEH fellowship (held 1986–87), her Guggenheim (held 1992), along with her 1991 and 1993 research grants from Yale, among others, must have provided a welcome respite from all the driving she had to do.[2] Her beloved husband Dennis Hengeveld died in 1983.

Like most lecturers, she had to teach extensively in writing programs, developing at UCLA curricula for undergraduate basic writing skills, as well as teaching popular courses in children's and young adult literature. And yet, as is often the case with those stuck at the bottom of the academic ladder, she was arguably better known, more widely published, and a more distinguished scholar than many who had tenure at the institutions that she served.

Although Mitzi was never tenured at UCLA, it was at UCLA that she found her scholarly home—or more precisely, she found UCLA's Rare Books and Special Collections.[3] Until the 1980s, Mitzi had been publishing essays on the canonical Georgian era authors Godwin and Wollstonecraft and, as an early feminist, was engaged in reading and reviewing the first important monographs and anthologies in what was then the new field of women's studies. In June of 1982, Mitzi authored her first article in the field of children's literature in a women's history newsletter, "Children's Literature and Women's Studies: Research Opportunities in UCLA's Special Collections." In describing UCLA's world-class collection of early children's books, Mitzi also explained why children's literature should matter to scholars. In so doing, she established the parameters of a research project that she would spend a lifetime completing:

> To describe the nature and range of the material available is to suggest some lines along which scholarly inquiry might proceed, so imperatively do these documents solicit attention from the perspectives of contemporary social historians, family historians, and analysts of literature as ideological construct, the last seeing popular fictions as significant encoders of cultural values, as key agents of socialization. Because they carry out a variety of cultural functions, juvenilia are crammed with clues to attitudes, values, and behavior. They capture the time's trends and anxieties; they encapsulate fashions, lifestyles, psychology and pedagogy. Social movements and philosophical ideas filter down into these books; religious doctrines and moral codes are revealed in their most transparent forms. Most of all, these works show what cultures want of their children and expect of those who tend them. Sometimes juvenilia yield rather sophisticated insights; sometimes they surprise by subtly shifting the conventional formulas expected. Always they raise questions. (2)

This is recognizably Mitzi: the urgency of her voice as she "solicit[s] attention" to children's texts; her keen understanding of how these texts might speak to scholars of different disciplines; her high standards for intellectual rigor in that she insists that the full range of critical approaches be applied to these texts; and last, but not least, her love of daring, vivid language, in her choice of verbs such as "crammed." Mitzi always refused to abide by the masculine code of scholarly writing in which the subjectivity of an author is hidden behind third-person pronouns and dry pronouncements. Mitzi was too excited by the enormous scope of children's literature and the abysmal state of its scholarship to mince words, and her "spirited polemic essays" soon made their mark on the field (Goodenough et al. vi).

It seems that Mitzi's fascination with Maria Edgeworth begins here—for UCLA's unparalleled collection of eighteenth- and nineteenth-century juvenile literature contains books and manuscripts by Maria Edgeworth, approximately 20 percent of the Edgeworth family's library, and the only known complete set of *Early Lessons* (1801). She edited a facsimile edition of the tenth part of *Early Lessons* (1990) and wrote the introduction to Andrea Immel's index of Sarah Trimmer's *Guardian of Education* (1990), both published by the UCLA Department of Special Collections. In interviews and publications, Mitzi continued to be an enthusiastic champion of the collection's opportunities for scholarship in genre and gender (Tennyson 216). It is fitting that the library has established a memorial fellowship in her honor.

Mitzi's career in children's literature began with this 1982 essay on the UCLA special collections. From 1984 on, she gave one or more papers on Georgian children's literature at least once a year, if not at the MLA, then elsewhere. She first came to wide attention with her groundbreaking 1986 essay "Impeccable Governesses, Rational Dames, and Moral Mothers: Mary Wollstonecraft and the Female Tradition in Georgian Children's Books" in *Children's Literature* 14, for which she won the Best Critical Essay Award from the Children's Literature Association. This essay was followed by two essays and two reviews in the *Children's Literature Association Quarterly*. The essays, "'A Taste for Truth and Realities': Early Advice to Mothers on Books for Girls" (1987) and "Socializing Rosamond: Educational Ideology and Fictional Form" (1989), introduced us to Maria Edgeworth, Rosamond, and a totally new way of looking at the notorious Purple Jar story, often anthologized as an example of everything that is wrong with Georgian children's literature by women. The two reviews (1987, 1988) were devastating attacks on Geoffrey Summerfield's *Fantasy and Reason: Children's Literature in the Eighteenth Century* ("Wise Child") and Bette P. Goldstone's *Lessons to Be Learned: A Study of Eighteenth-Century English Didactic Children's Literature* ("Missed Opportunities").

These four pieces made a substantial impact on the way many scholars thought about historical children's literature. Classicists and medievalists know that the fact that a given work is situated more on the instruction end of the continuum between what is pleasant and what is useful does not make it any less literary (n.b. Hesiod and other Greek poets, Dante, Chaucer). Many of us had bought the Romantic idea, which Summerfield's book exemplifies and which seemed to be espoused by the eighteenth-century people at Francelia Butler's first NEH Seminar on Children's Literature (1983), that the works for children written by "that monstrous regiment of women" were boring, unimaginative, and bad for children (who supposedly hated them, in spite of the textual evidence that Mitzi produced that they were read almost to extinction).[4] We were all urged to rejoice when they were supplanted by male-sponsored fairy tales and more "imaginative" works such as *Alice in Wonderland*. Mitzi's impeccable scholarship and convincing explanations of how the works of writers such as Edgeworth and Wollstonecraft were cleverly designed to empower girls to understand the consequences of their actions, govern their own fates, and resist turning into Cinderellas and Sleeping Beauties (the figures that contemporary popular sentimental novels tempted girls to become) totally rewrote our understanding of the eighteenth and early nineteenth century. Mitzi never gave up in her battle against those who indulged in Romantic nostalgia, viewing the child as a literary representation of our lost selves, as her 1992 "Little Girls Lost: Rewriting Romantic Childhood, Righting Gender and Genre," 1999 "Reading Children and Homeopathic Romanticism: Paradigm Lost, Revisionary Gleam" and 1999 "Here's Looking at You, Kid," make clear.[5] The first two essays were published alongside work by Alan Richardson, whom Mitzi appreciated for demonstrating "how influential Romantic childhood has been—and how male-determined" ("Little Girls" 135), but whom she also criticized for not going far enough in his re-envisioning of Romanticized childhood.[6] In Mitzi's eyes, it was not enough to recognize how much of our scholarly language of children's literature comes from the high Romantic, anti-feminine, "culturally conditioned ideology, a tissue of assumptions, prefaces, and perspectives, and not a transhistorical, universal body of truth about childhood" ("Little Girls" 135). Mitzi saw the trap of reading children's literary history as a struggle between the forces of imagination and didacticism, and she demonstrated how inventive, challenging, engaged, and influential "didactic" literature could be.

Mitzi's second review in the *Quarterly*, "Missed Opportunities," is as much about New Historicism as the defects of Goldstone's book, and it is the beginning of the second Myers revolution. Mitzi's review praised New Historicism and accused the old kind of children's literary history of being teleology rather than analytic history (42). Mitzi's manifesto in the review is worth quoting, at least partially:

> A New Historicism of children's literature would integrate text and socio-historic context, demonstrating on the one hand how extraliterary cultural formations shape literary discourse and on the other how literary practices are actions that make things happen—by shaping the psychic and moral consciousness of young readers but also by performing many more diverse kinds of cultural work, from satisfying authorial fantasies to legitimating or subverting dominant class and gender ideologies. (42)

Mitzi then expanded on the "particular attention" that should be paid to ideologies and to issues such as slavery, and she called as well for the examination of "a book's material production, its publishing history, its audiences and their reading practices, its initial reception, and its critical history" (52). To fulfill Mitzi's requirements in every article and book is perhaps too much for mortal scholars, but since she called attention to the misperceptions and misreading caused by not considering a work's context, scholarship in children's literature studies has improved markedly. Certainly studies that emphasize ideology have become increasingly popular. Yet to come is a return to textual criticism with more attention paid to the materiality of a work. Mitzi consistently urged more attention to "rips, dirt, spills, uncensored comments, drawings and scribbles, rude jokes and missing pages—in these 'defacements' we discover the hidden history of childhood" (qtd. in McLellan). Such "defacements" are essential to discovering early children's books as the special issue of the *Children's Literature Quarterly* devoted to medieval children's literature made clear.[7] The hallmark of a Mitzi Myers essay is a fierce and compelling footnoting, as befits a rigorous New Historical scholar. Those of us who followed her work learned to read her essays in stages: a first pass for the essay-proper; a second pass for her astonishingly erudite endnotes that brought together obscure, popular, and multidisciplinary sources; and a final foray into the always formidable list of works cited.

Unlike many children's literature scholars who feel threatened by the close connection between children's literature and education, and who want to distance themselves from education departments, Mitzi felt that educational theory and practice was a vital component in the exploration of the cultural context of a children's book—"pedagogy unites domestic education and public event" ("Erotics" 1995, 3). In her 1989 *Quarterly* article "Socializing Rosamond," Mitzi expounds further on the revolutionary pedagogy of the Edgeworths, father and daughter, an area she was to continue to explore in articles such as "Servants as They Are Now Educated" (1989), "Romancing the Moral Tale" (which received the 1991 Honor Article award from the Children's Literature Association), "Reading Rosamond Reading" (1994), "The Erotics of Pedagogy" (1995), "*Aufklärung für Kinder*" (1995), and "Anecdotes from the Nursery" (1999). For anyone planning to address the development of what we now call "progressive" education, these articles are essential.[8] Mitzi even brought her own hard-won understanding of pedagogy to bear upon her revisionary readings of teacher–student, father–daughter relationships, as in her essay "De-Romanticizing the Subject" (1995):

> As a teacher of writing, I know that successful apprenticeship works not like a master–slave relationship but like the reciprocal economy of gift exchange; as a teacher of children's literature, I recognize that juvenile writing is an inherently transgressive genre, one that insists on writers and readers canny enough to be in two places at once, to play both child and adult. (92)

Mitzi demonstrates how Maria Edgeworth's juvenile fiction "The Bracelets" is a form of feminine life-writing. Edgeworth, Mitzi suggests, uses depictions of teacher–student relationships to form, inform, and reform her father's relationship to his brilliant, desiring and too often neglected daughter. In all her work, as in this essay, Mitzi was acutely aware of gender issues, particularly in regard to adolescent girls, whether she addressed them specifically in articles such as "The Dilemmas of Gender" (1988), "Quixotes" (1989), "Little Girls Lost" (1992), and of course in the special of the *Quarterly* that she edited on Mothers and Daughters (1993–94); or whether they were part of the background, often referred to, in other articles.

Mitzi's final contribution, developed with U. C. Knoepflmacher, to the study of children's literature was the concept of "cross-writing." As

early as 1972 Francelia Butler had claimed that the best children's literature was what she called "shared literature" or "literature of dual appeal"
(Adams, "Francelia" 184–85). Interest in her claim was deflected for
some years by the attempt to define children's literature and to establish
some sort of canon. But in 1987, an MLA conference session, which focused on representing the language of the child in literature, subsequently formed the basis of a 1994 collection of original critical essays,
Infant Tongues: The Voice of the Child in Literature, to which Mitzi contributed. The introduction to the collection by the editors discussed the
instability of the threshold between children's and adult's literature, and
some of the essays moved back and forth across that threshold (Goodenough, Heberle, and Sokoloff). Discussions among the editors and
contributors seem to have resulted in the term "cross-writing," which
grew out of the perception that "a dialogic mix of older and younger
voices occurs in texts too often read as univocal. Authors who write for
children inevitably create a colloquy between past and present selves"
(Myers and Knoepflmacher 1977, vii). A special session at the MLA in
1993, led by Mitzi and U. C. Knoepflmacher, was devoted to texts that
appeal to a child and adult audience, and this session in turn grew into a
special 1997 issue of *Children's Literature* on the subject. Whether critics
address cross-written texts from the standpoint of the audience, as Butler did; or the authors and their intentions (conscious or unconscious),
as more recent critics such as Sandra Beckett have done; or as part of
children's cultural studies, such an approach should not only do much to
clarify the controversies over the definition of children's literature, but
also, as the editors of the special issue hoped, should prove to be "an un-
locker of doors that have shut off and devalued our field" (xv).

After 1995, Mitzi was increasingly interested in the related issues of
Irish politics, women's peace writing, education, and war.[9] In articles
such as "Completing the Union" (1995), "Goring John Bull" (1995),
"Like the Pictures in a Magic Lantern" (1996), "War Correspondence"
(1998), and "Child's Play as Women's Peace Work" (1999), Mitzi demonstrated how even apparently minor works for very young children, such
as Edgeworth's "The Cherry Orchard," can function as a mode of political intervention. Although "war stories are sometimes categorized as
pure adventure or combat zone tales, they are inherently didactic: they
inculcate patriotic moral values or, more often, question the morality of
war" ("Storying War" 2000, 327). What Mitzi wanted to know, given the

war story's focus on masculine adventure and combat, was "How do—or can—women represent revolution?" ("Completing the Union," 1995, 41). Of course women can and do represent revolution, and, as Mitzi proved, they do so in surprising ways and in unexpected places. In essays analyzing Maria Edgeworth's *Ennui, Castle Rackrent*, and *Essay on Irish Bulls*, Mitzi showed how women's storytelling could become a peace-making activity. Edgeworth's female storytelling characters used sharp sarcasm to deflate the warring pretentions of men—in exactly the same way that those Georgian-era female pedagogues that Mitzi so loved re-buked and schooled unruly boys. Ironically, Mitzi the children's literature scholar often argued that literary historians err in seeing Edgeworth as *only* a children's author—and thereby miss the political implications of her many didactic adult novellas, novels, and essays.

Because of Mitzi's unique position—a scholar equally conversant in New Historicism, feminism, children's writing, pedagogical practice, and eighteenth-century literature—she was able to bring one discipline to bear upon another in her own work. She was as ruthless in pinpointing the limitations of others' scholarship as she was generous in enriching the scholarship of others.[10] In critiquing a group of children's books for a feminist journal, she found herself compelled to take not only feminists but also children's authors to task for focusing so much on sending out properly positive messages to young girls that literary quality was given short shrift ("Gender, Genres" 1990). Mitzi's final publications confront and condemn the internet, bad teaching practices, bibliotherapy, and the violence of the world that children must face today. In a review essay and personal memoir, "Little Girls and Boys Lost? Growing Up in Cyber-space," Mitzi addressed what she called the "multiply toxic social envi-ronment" of a "commodified and media-dominated" world that nor-malizes violence and turns children into "sophisticated consumer–kids." She contrasts this toxic world, perhaps too nostalgically, to her own idyl-lic childhood on the outskirts of a small East Texas town, replete with green, secret places, real and imagined. In an interview with Robert Cormier about young adult literature and violence (2000), Mitzi's anx-ious questions and concerns overwhelm her interview subject, and the resulting publication is an odd mixture of Mitzi's ever-expanding and impossible speculations interspersed with Cormier's briefer interjections. Mitzi wanted Cormier to explain the impossible—how to create a poet-ics of memory for children, how to help children become moral adults, why he portrays monstrous subjects, and what is behind the censorship of his works.

One of Mitzi's persistent concerns was to broaden the audience for critical scholarship of children's literature, for too often "people who write about children's literature are mainly read by other people who write about it" ("Erotics" 1995, 6). Mitzi, the inveterate teacher, wanted to change all of that. In the late 1980s she began reviewing children's and young adult literature for the *Los Angeles Times*. Her no-nonsense reviews taught parents and teachers how to think about children's literature: as a literary genre, a popular phenomenon, an historical tradition, and a didactic force. With great *savoir fare*, she compared Judy Blume to Ann Landers (26 Dec. 1987): reading their non-judgmental, supportive works "is an almost universal experience in modern American Life." She sardonically remarked that Eve Bunting "couldn't have turned out more than 100 books for the young if she didn't know her formulas" (9 Jan. 1988). In reviewing Caroline B. Cooney's *Among Friends*, Mitzi explained why so many young adult books use first-person narratives (adolescents can easily identity with a single protagonist's point of view) and how Cooney's use of multiple diaries in *Among Friends* suits teenage readers while also providing a more rounded world view than any single character could supply (6 Feb. 1988). Given Mitzi's scholarly preoccupations, it is no surprise that her review of "ethically enlightened picture books" delved into how similar we are today to eighteenth-century parents: we all select books for children that we believe will enculturate children into the social ethics that we value the most (22 May 1988).

Perhaps her most enduring—or at least most widely disseminated—written legacy will not be her scholarly articles, but her magnificent summary of the history and current status of children's literature for *Encyclopedia Americana* (2000). She examines the functioning of crossover reading and cross-writing over different centuries, demonstrates how children's literature has been shaped by the emergence of the child audience and changing ideas about the psychological dimensions of early literacy, and explores how we evaluate the quality of children's texts. Fortunately, the generous budget of the *Encyclopedia Americana* allowed Mitzi's often dense historical analyses to be leavened by thirty full-color illustrations: many of these illustrations are familiar, such as Kate Greenaway's *Cherry Woman* and Randolph Caldecott's *The Hey-Diddle-Diddle Picture Book*, but others, such as a gorgeously executed 1821 learning game, *The Royal Game of the Dolphin*, are less familiar. Although Mitzi did not publish extensively in the area of children's book illustrations, she was fascinated by images of and for children. She wrote the Foreword to Anne Lunden's book on the reception of picture books (2001), and in 1997 she lectured on pictorial representations of childhood for the UCLA Armond Hammer Museum of Art and Cultural Center.[11]

Mitzi's New Historicist manifesto for the criticism of historical children's literature sets a high standard, one that many children's literature critics may not have the interest, time, or energy to meet. Perhaps only Mitzi could follow through on it to the end. Her dedication and scholarship will be sorely missed. Although we will never know what the next revolution in children's literature studies Mitzi had in mind, her final three, unfinished projects suggest the direction of Mitzi's work: a Norton anthology of children's literature,[12] a multi-volume critical edition of Maria Edgeworth's collected works,[13] and an essay on Maria Edgeworth's favorite childhood character, Rosamond, whom Mitzi always understood to be a projection of Edgeworth. Mitzi's final words about Rosamond can be applied to Mitzi herself: "she has a lot to teach us about female authorship and the intersections of subjectivity with literary and political representation."[14]

NOTES

1. Sentence added by Ruwe.

2. Other fellowships and awards of note include an American Council of Learned Societies Award, NEH summer fellowships, the first Irish American Research Travel Prize, an American Philosophical Society Grant, and Children's Literature Scholarship Awards.

3. The following two paragraphs about the UCLA Children's Literature collection were added by Ruwe.

4. As Gillian Adams notes, Butler's 1983 NEH Seminar was particularly important, for it was the first recognition by the academic establishment that children's literature was a legitimate field of scholarly study (letter to Ruwe). Mitzi was one of the first children's literature scholars to be widely recognized outside the children's literature field, and many of her early articles were republished in prestigious volumes, essay collections, and scholarly editions. These reprints include essays on Harriet Martineau's autobiography (1980), Godwin's *Memoirs* of

Wollstonecraft (1981), and Maria Edgeworth (1988) in *Nineteenth-Century Literature Criticism* (vols 26, 14, 51, respectively); "Reform or Ruin" (1982) in the Norton critical edition of *A Vindication of the Rights of Woman*; "Pedagogy as Self-Expression" (1988) in *Mary Wollstonecraft and the Critics, 1788–2001*; "'Servants as They Are Now Educated'" (1989) in *Feminist Cultural Studies*; and "Sensibility and the 'Walk of Reason': Mary Wollstonecraft's Literary Reviews as Cultural Critique" (1990) in *Literature Criticism from 1400 to 1800*.

5. The rest of this paragraph on Romantic childhood has been added by Ruwe.

6. Richardson's essays are the brief "Childhood and Romanticism" and the lengthier "Romanticism and the End of Childhood." In a special issue of *Nineteenth-Century Contexts* that she guest edited, Mitzi included Richardson's "Romanticism and the End of Childhood" and, one suspects, enjoyed continuing her quarrel with what "Alan Richardson wants to call 'Romantic' childhood" (Introduction 1999, 162). She considers the Romantic ideology masculine, condescending, focused on "spiritualizing narratives," and writing *about* rather than *for* children (163).

7. The rest of this paragraph was added by Ruwe.

8. The rest of this paragraph, not including its final sentence, was added by Ruwe.

9. From this paragraph on, the rest of the essay was authored by Ruwe.

10. At the special session in her honor at the 2002 MLA,"'Rational Dames' and the 'Problematics of Pedagogy': Papers in Memory of Mitzi Myers," the panelists (Susan Gannon, U. C. Knoepflmacher, Judith Page, Alan Rauch, Donelle Ruwe) commented on Mitzi's keen analytical mind and scholarly generosity, her habit of sending packets of useful scholarly articles to her colleagues, and long phone conversations that veered from the personal to discussions of whether the phrase "young adult" could be applied to texts from the Georgian era. Other activities in honor of Mitzi have included a special program sponsored by the Cotsen Children's Library and coordinated by Andrea Immel, "Under Fire: Childhood in the Shadow of War" (9–11 Oct. 2003), and several volumes and special issues of scholarly works dedicated to her (*The Cambridge Companion to Mary Wollstonecraft*, ed. by Claudia L. Johnson, 2002; a special issue of *Women's Writing* on Maria Edgeworth, edited by Maureen O'Connor, 2002).

11. Her talk for the museum, "Pictur'd Morals? Gender, Violence, and History in Children's Literature," addressed "the educating of young readers on the realities of war and violence through children's literature; the reality of childhood play practices and cruelty to animals and the societal reaction to children's aggression" and "gender roles and experiences in children's literature" (White).

12. Mitzi was among the initial team of editors of the *Norton Anthology of Children's Literature*. The team, assembled by General Editor Jack Zipes, included

Gillian Avery, Peter Hunt, Lissa Paul, and Lynne Vallone. The project is continuing under the associate editorship of Lissa Paul and Lynne Vallone.

13. Mitzi was slated to edit four volumes for the Pickering and Chatto twelve-volume series on Maria Edgeworth. Tragically, the fire interrupted her work on the volumes, and she was unable to continue. Marilyn Butler, the primary editor of the volumes, has expressed how important Mitzi was to the project, in particular for her constant flow of letters to the editorial team and her generous sharing of her extensive resources on Maria Edgeworth. Mitzi selected the children's texts to be included and was "inspirational, a true artist, with Endnotes" (Butler, 3 Sept. 2003). All of the volumes published after 2003 are dedicated to Mitzi Myers, and Sue Manley has written a short piece on Mitzi's contributions to be included in the last volume.

14. Myers's unfinished essay, "'Miss Edgeworth's Naughty Girl': or, The Importance of Being Rosamond," is described and quoted extensively in Maureen O'Connor's "Introduction: Our Debt to Mitzi Myers" (2002).

WORKS CITED

Adams, Gillian. "The Francelia Butler Watershed: Then and Now." *Children's Literature Association Quarterly* 25 (1999–2000): 181–90.

———. Letter to Donelle Ruwe. 8 March 2004.

———. "Mitzi Myers, 9 October 1939–5 November 2001." *Children's Literature Association Quarterly* 27.2 (2002): 88–91.

Butler, Marilyn. "Mitzi Myers." E-mail to Donelle Ruwe. 17 July 2003.

———. "Re: Mitzi Myers." E-mail to Donelle Ruwe. 3 Sept. 2003.

Goodenough, Elizabeth, Mark A. Heberle, and Naomi Sokoloff, eds. *Infant Tongues: The Voice of the Child in Literature.* Detroit: Wayne State UP, 1994.

Goodenough, Elizabeth, Andrea Immel, and U. C. Knoepflmacher. "In Memoriam Mitzi Myers." *Lion and the Unicorn* 26.1 (2002): vi–viii.

Honan, William H. "Mitzi Myers, 62, Writer, Editor, and Scholar of Children's Books." *New York Times* (17 Nov. 2001).

McLellan, Dennis. "Mitzi Myers, 62: Literary Scholar." *Los Angeles Times* 13 Nov. 2001: Bll.

O'Connor, Maureen. "Introduction: Our Debt to Mitzi Myers." Special Issue of *Women's Studies* (*The Politics of Reading: Maria Edgeworth*) 31 (2002): 289–97.

Paul, Lissa. "RE: Festschrift in Memory of Mitzi Myers." E-mail to Donelle Ruwe. 1 Feb. 2004.

Richardson, Alan. "Childhood and Romanticism." *Teaching Children's Literature: Issues, Pedagogy, Resources.* Ed. Glenn Edward Sadler. New York: MLA, 1992. 121–29.

———. "Romanticism and the End of Childhood." *Special Issue: Culturing Child-hood*. Ed. Mitzi Myers. *Nineteenth-Century Contexts* 21.2 (1999): 167–89.

Tennyson, G. B. "The UCLA Children's Literature Collection." *Teaching Children's Literature: Issues, Pedagogy, Resources*. Ed. Glenn Edward Sadler. New York: MLA 1992. 212–17.

White, Kelly K. Letter to Mitzi Myers. 7 March 1997. UCLA at the Armond Hammer Museum of Art and Cultural Center, Los Angeles.

· 12 ·

A Bibliography of Mitzi Myers's Scholarly Work

Donelle Ruwe

$\mathcal{T}$he following bibliography is divided into three sections, each of which is organized chronologically. The first section, "Editorial Contributions," identifies Myers's work as guest editor, co-editor, compiler, and organizer of special issues of academic journals. The second section, "Scholarly Articles and Longer Works," lists essays, substantial book reviews, and other substantive works of scholarship authored by Mitzi Myers. The final section, "Book Reviews," lists the shorter book reviews and book notices authored by Myers. Titled book review–articles are listed under "Scholarly Articles." When multiple pieces appear in a single year, they have been alphabetized within the year. Reprints of articles are listed in the same entry as the original publication.

EDITORIAL CONTRIBUTIONS

Co-Compiler, annual bibliography on women and literature. *Women and Literature* 3 (Fall 1975): 33–69.

Guest Editor. "Mothers and Daughters in Children's Literature." Spec. section of *Children's Literature Association Quarterly* 18 (1993–94): 146–76.

Guest Editor. *"Cross-Writing" and the Reconceptualization of Children's Literary Studies.* Spec. issue of *Children's Literature: Annual of the Modern Language Association Division on Children's Literature and the Children's Literature Association* 25 (1997).

Organizer. *Ireland, 1798–1998: From Revolution to Revisionism and Beyond.* Ed. Robert P. Maccubbin. Spec. issue of *Eighteenth-Century Life* 22.3 (Nov 1998): 1–152.

Guest Editor. *Culturing Childhood.* Spec. issue of *Nineteenth-Century Contexts* 21.2 (1999).
Co-Editor with Elizabeth Goodenough. *Violence and Children's Literature.* Spec. issue of *Lion and the Unicorn* 24.3 (Sept. 2000).

SCHOLARLY ARTICLES AND LONGER WORKS

1969

"Aspects of William Godwin's Reputation in the 1790's." Ann Arbor: Dissertation Abstracts International, 1969. 30:2034A–35A (Rice).

1972

"Godwin's Changing Conception of *Caleb Williams.*" *Studies in English Literature, 1500–1900* 12 (1972): 591–628.

1977

"Politics from the Outside: Mary Wollstonecraft's First Vindication." *Studies in Eighteenth-Century Culture* 6 (1977): 113–31.
"You Can't Catch Me: Mary McCarthy's Evasive Comedy." *Regionalism and the Female Imagination* 3.2–3 (1977–78): 58–69.

1979

"Mary Wollstonecraft's *Letters Written . . . in Sweden*: Toward Romantic Autobiography." *Studies in Eighteenth-Century Culture* 8 (1979): 165–85.

1980

"Harriet Martineau's Autobiography: The Making of a Female Philosopher." *Women's Autobiography: Essays in Criticism.* Ed. Estelle C. Jelinek. Bloomington: Indiana UP, 1980. 53–70. Rpt. in *Nineteenth-Century Literature Criticism.* Ed. Janet Mullane and Robert Thomas Wilson. Vol. 26. Detroit: Gale, 1990. 341–46.

"Unfinished Business: Wollstonecraft's *Maria*." *Wordsworth Circle* 11 (1980): 107–14.

"Unmothered Daughter and Radical Reformer: Harriet Martineau's Career." *The Lost Tradition: Mothers and Daughters in Literature*. Ed. Cathy N. Davidson and E. M. Broner. New York: Ungar, 1980. 70–80.

1981

"Godwin's *Memoirs* of Wollstonecraft: The Shaping of Self and Subject." *Studies in Romanticism* 20.3 (1981): 299–316. Rpt. in *Nineteenth-Century Literature Criticism*. Ed. Cherie D. Abbey. Vol. 14. Detroit: Gale, 1987. 88–92.

1982

"Children's Literature and Women's Studies: Research Opportunities in UCLA's Special Collections." *Conference Group on Women's History Newsletter* June 1982: 2–5.

"Reform or Ruin: 'A Revolution in Female Manners.'" *Studies in Eighteenth-Century Culture* 11 (1982): 199–216. Rpt. in *A Vindication of the Rights of Woman: An Authoritative Text*. Ed. Carol H. Poston. 2nd ed. New York: Norton, 1988. 328–43.

1984

"Reading Georgian Women: Pedagogy, Philanthropy, and Power." Abstract of Paper Presented to the North American and Pacific Coast Conferences on British Studies, joint meeting, 23–25 March 1984. *Albion* 16 (1984): 367.

1985

"Domesticating Minerva: Bathsua Makin's 'Curious' Argument for Women's Education." *Studies in Eighteenth-Century Culture* 14 (1985): 173–92.

1986

"Hannah More's Tracts for the Times: Social Fiction and Female Ideology." *Fetter'd or Free? British Women Novelists, 1670–1815.* Ed. Mary Anne Schofield and Cecilia Macheski. Athens: Ohio UP, 1986. 264–84.

"Impeccable Governesses, Rational Dames, and Moral Mothers: Mary Wollstonecraft and the Female Tradition in Georgian Children's Books." *Children's Literature* 14 (1986): 31–58.

1987

"'A Taste for Truth and Realities': Early Advice to Mothers on Books for Girls." *Children's Literature Association Quarterly* 12.3 (1987): 118–24.

"Wise Child, Wise Peasant, Wise Guy: Geoffrey Summerfield's Case against the Eighteenth Century." Rev. of *Fantasy and Reason: Children's Literature in the Eighteenth Century*, by Geoffrey Summerfield. *Children's Literature Association Quarterly* 12.2 (1987): 107–10.

1988

"The Dilemmas of Gender as Double-Voiced Narrative; Or, Maria Edgeworth Mothers the *Bildungsroman.*" *The Idea of the Novel in the Eighteenth Century.* Ed. Robert W. Uphaus. East Lansing: Colleagues, 1988. 67–96. Rpt. in *Nineteenth-Century Literature Criticism.* Ed. Marie Lazarri. Vol. 51. Detroit: Gale, 1996. 108–17.

"Missed Opportunities and Critical Malpractice: New Historicism and Children's Literature." Rev. of *Lessons to Be Learned: A Study of Eighteenth-Century English Didactic Children's Literature*, by Bette P. Goldstone; *The Child as Depicted in English Children's Literature from 1780–1820*, by Sharon Marie Scapple; and *Reading and Righting: The Past, Present and Future of Fiction for the* Young, by Robert Leeson. *Children's Literature Association Quarterly* 13.1 (1988): 41–43.

"Pedagogy as Self-Expression in Mary Wollstonecraft: Exorcising the Past, Finding a Voice." *The Private Self: Theory and Practice of Women's Autobiographical Writings.* Ed. Shari Benstock. Chapel Hill: U of North Carolina P, 1988. 192–210. Rpt. in *Mary Wollstonecraft and the Critics, 1788–2001.* Ed. Harriet Devine Jump. Vol 2. London: Routledge, 2003. 76–91.

"Quixotes, Orphans, and Subjectivity: Maria Edgeworth's Georgian Heroinism and the (En)Gendering of Young Adult Fiction." *Lion and the Unicorn* 13.1 (1989): 21–40.

1989

"'Servants as They Are Now Educated': Women Writers and Georgian Pedagogy." *Essays in Literature* 16 (1989): 51–69. Rpt. in *Feminist Cultural Studies.* Ed. Terry Lovell. Vol 1. The International Library of Studies in Media and Culture. Aldershot, UK: Elgar, 1995. 169–89.

"Socializing Rosamond: Educational Ideology and Fictional Form." *Children's Literature Association Quarterly* 14.2 (1989): 52–58.

1990

"Gender, Genres, Generations: Artist-Mothers and the Scripting of Girls' Lives." Rev. of *Embers: Stories for a Changing World*, by Ruth S. Meyers, Beryle Banfield, and Jamila Gastón Colón; *Books for To-day's Young Readers: An Annotated Bibliography of Recommended Fiction for Ages 10–14,* by Jeanne Bracken and Sharon Wigutoff; *The Lilith Summer*, by Hadley Irwin; *We Are Mesquakie, We Are One*, by Hadley Irwin; *Tatterhood and Other Tales*, ed. by Ethel Johnston Phelps; *Green March Moons*, by Mary Tallmountain; *An Outbreak of Peace*, by Sarah Pirtle; *Morning Breeze: A True Story of China's Cultural Revolution*, by Fulang Lo; *Elizabeth Cady Stanton*, by Martha E. Kendall. *National Women's Studies Association Journal* 2.2 (Spring 1990): 273–81.

Introduction. *The Little Dog Trusty; The Orange Man; and The Cherry Orchard: Being the Tenth Part of Early Lessons (1801).* William Andrews Clark Memorial Library, University of California, Los Angeles. 1990. iii–xiii.

Introduction. *Revolutionary Reviewing: Sarah Trimmer's* Guardian of Education *and the Cultural Politics of Juvenile Literature, An Index.* By Andrea Immel. Occasional Papers 4. Los Angeles: Dept. of Special Collections, U of California–Los Angeles, 1990. vii–xv.

"Sensibility and the 'Walk of Reason': Mary Wollstonecraft's Literary Reviews as Cultural Critique." *Sensibility in Transformation: Creative*

Resistance to Sentiment from the Augustans to the Romantics. Ed. Syndy McMillen Conger. Rutherford: Fairleigh Dickinson UP, 1990. 120–44. Rpt. in *Literature Criticism from 1400 to 1800.* Ed. Marie Lazarri. Vol. 50. Detroit: Gale, 1999. 278–92.

1991

"Romancing the Moral Tale: Maria Edgeworth and the Problematics of Pedagogy." *Romanticism and Children's Literature in Nineteenth-Century England.* Ed. James Holt McGavran, Jr. Athens: U of Georgia P, 1991. 96–128.

1992

"Daddy's Girl as Motherless Child: Maria Edgeworth and Maternal Romance—An Essay in Reassessment." *Living by the Pen: Early British Women Writers.* Ed. Dale Spender. New York: Teachers College, 1992. 137–59.

"Little Girls Lost: Rewriting Romantic Childhood, Righting Gender and Genre." *Teaching Children's Literature: Issues, Pedagogy, Resources.* Ed. Glenn Edward Sadler. New York: MLA, 1992. 131–42.

"Sociologizing Juvenile Ephemera: Periodical Contradictions, Popular Literacy, Transhistorical Readers." Rev. of *English Children and Their Magazines, 1751–1945,* by Kirsten Drotner. *Children's Literature Quarterly* 17.1 (Spring 1992): 41–45.

"Where Did Mary's Mother Come From?" *Children's Literature Association Quarterly* 18.4 (1993–94): 146–47.

1994

"'A Peculiar Protection': Hannah More and the Cultural Politics of the Blagdon Controversy." *History, Gender and Eighteenth-Century Literature.* Ed. Beth Fowkes Tobin. Athens: U of Georgia P, 1994. 227–57.

"Reading Rosamond Reading: Maria Edgeworth's 'Wee-Wee Stories' Interrogate the Canon." *Infant Tongues: The Voice of the Child in Literature.* Ed. Elizabeth Goodenough, Mark A. Heberle, and Naomi Sokoloff. Detroit: Wayne State UP, 1994. 57–79.

1995

"*Aufklärung für Kinder?* Maria Edgeworth and the Genders of Knowledge Genres; or, 'The Genius of Nonsense' and 'The Grand Panjandrum Himself.'" *Women's Writing* 2.2 (1995): 113–40.

"A Comment on 'Women and Nineteenth-Century Fiction' (Review)" *College English* 57.4 (1995): 499–500.

"'Completing the Union': Critical *Ennui*, the Politics of Narrative, and the Reformation of Irish Cultural Identity." *Prose Studies: History, Theory, Criticism* 18.3 (Dec. 1995): 41–77. *The Intersections of the Public and Private Spheres in Early Modern England.* Ed. Paula R. Backscheider and Timothy Dystal. London: Frank Cass, 1996. 41–77.

"De-Romanticizing the Subject: Maria Edgeworth's 'The Bracelets,' Mythologies of Origin, and the Daughter's Coming to Writing." *Romantic Women Writers: Voices and Countervoices.* Ed. Paula R. Feldman and Theresa M. Kelley. Hanover: UP of New England, 1995. 88–110.

"The Erotics of Pedagogy: Historical Intervention, Literary Representation, the 'Gift of Education,' and the Agency of Children." *Children's Literature* 23 (1995): 1–30.

"Goring John Bull: Maria Edgeworth's Hibernian High Jinks versus the Imperialist Imaginary." *Cutting Edges: Postmodern Critical Essays on Eighteenth-Century Satire.* Ed. James E. Gill. Knoxville: U of Tennessee P, 1995. 367–94.

"Moral Majorities? Reconceiving the Literary World We Have Lost." Rev. of *Christian's Children: The Influence of John Bunyan's* The Pilgrim's Progress *on American Children's Literature*, by Ruth K. MacDonald; *The Discovery of Childhood in Puritan England*, by C. John Sommerville; and *Heaven Upon Earth: The Form of Moral and Religious Children's Literature, to 1850*, by Patricia Demers. *Lion and the Unicorn* 19 (1995): 134–44.

"Of Mice and Mothers: Mrs. Barbauld's 'New Walk' and Gendered Codes in Children's Literature." *Feminine Principles and Women's Experience in American Composition and Rhetoric.* Ed. Louise Weatherbee Phelps and Janet Emig. Pittsburgh: U of Pittsburgh P, 1995. 255–88.

"Of Mimicry and (Wo)Man: *Infans* or Forked Tongue?" *Children's Literature* 23 (1995): 66–70.

"Shot from Canons; or, Maria Edgeworth and the Cultural Production and Consumption of the Late Eighteenth-Century Woman Writer." *The Consumption of Culture 1600–1800: Image, Object, Text.* Ed. Ann Bermingham and John Brewer. New York: Routledge, 1995. 193–214.

1996

"'Like the Pictures in a Magic Lantern': Gender, History, and Edgeworth's Rebellion Narratives." *Nineteenth-Century Contexts* 19 (1996): 373–412.

"Portrait of the Female Artist as a Young Robin: Maria Edgeworth's Telltale Tailpiece."*Lion and the Unicorn* 20.2 (1996): 230–63.

"'We Must Grant a Romance Writer a Few Impossibilities': 'Unnatural Incident' and Narrative Motherhood in Maria Edgeworth's *Emilie de Coulanges.*" *Wordsworth Circle* 27.3 (Summer 1996): 151–57.

"When Criticism Comes Alive: Я Toys Us?" Rev. of *When Toys Come Alive: Narratives of Animation, Metamorphosis, and Development,* by Lois Rostow Kuznets. *Children's Literature* 24 (1996): 181–87.

1997

"Canonical 'Orphans' and Critical *Ennui*: Rereading Edgeworth's Cross-Writing." *Children's Literature* 25 (1997): 116–36.

Myers, Mitzi, and U. C. Knoepflmacher. "From the Editors: 'Cross-Writing' and the Reconceptualizing of Children's Literary Studies." *Children's Literature* 25 (1997): vii–xvii.

1998

"War Correspondence: Maria Edgeworth and the En-Gendering of Revolution, Rebellion and Union." *Eighteenth-Century Life* 22.3 (1998): 74–91.

1999

"'Anecdotes from the Nursery' in Maria Edgeworth's *Practical Education* (1798): Learning from Children 'Abroad and At Home.'" *Princeton University Library Chronicle* 60.2 (Winter 1999): 220–50.

"Child's Play as Woman's Peace Work: Maria Edgeworth's 'The Cherry Orchard,' Historical Rebellion Narratives, and Contemporary Cultural Studies." *Girls, Boys, Books, Toys: Gender in Children's Literature and Culture*. Ed. Beverly Lyon Clark and Margaret R. Higonnet. Baltimore: Johns Hopkins UP, 1999. 25–39.

"Introduction. Here's Looking at You, Kid: or, Is Culturing Childhood Colonizing Casablanca." *Nineteenth-Century Contexts* 21 (1999): 157–67.

"Reading Children and Homeopathic Romanticism: Paradigm Lost, Revisionary Gleam, or '*Plus ça Change, Plus C'est La Même Chose*'?" *Literature and the Child: Romantic Continuations, Postmodern Contestations*. Ed. James Holt McGavran. Iowa City: U of Iowa P, 1999. 44–84.

2000

"Literature for Children." *Encyclopedia Americana*. International Edition, 2000. 561–79.

"Little Girls and Boys Lost? Growing Up in Cyberspace." Rev. of *A Tribe Apart: A Journey into the Heart of American Adolescence* by Patricia Hersch. *Michigan Quarterly Review* 39.2 (Spring 2000): 422–33.

"Mary Wollstonecraft Godwin Shelley: The Female Author between Public and Private Spheres." *Mary Shelley in Her Times*. Ed. Betty T. Bennett and Stuart Curran. Baltimore: Johns Hopkins UP, 2000. 160–72.

"My Art Belongs to Daddy? Thomas Day, Maria Edgeworth, and the Pre-Texts of *Belinda*: Women Writers and Patriarchal Authority." *Revising Women: Eighteenth-Century "Women's Fiction" and Social Engagement*. Ed. Paula R. Backscheider. Baltimore: Johns Hopkins UP, 2000. 104–46; 227–52.

"'No Safe Place to Run to': An Interview with Robert Cormier." *Lion and the Unicorn* 24.3 (Sept. 2000): 445–64.

"Storying War: A Capsule Overview" *Lion and the Unicorn* 23.3 (Sept. 2000): 327–36.

2001

Foreword. *Victorian Horizons: The Reception of the Picture Books of Walter Crane, Randolph Caldecott, and Kate Greenaway*. By Anne Lunden. Lanham: Scarecrow Press, 2001. vii–ix.

"Gendering the 'Union of Hearts': Irish Politics Between the Public and Private Spheres." *Studies in Eighteenth-Century Culture* 30 (2001): 49–70.

Myers, Mitzi, Diane Hebley, Gillian Lathey, and Juliet Partridge. "War Stories." *The Cambridge Guide to Children's Books in English*. Ed. Victor Watson. Cambridge: Cambridge UP, 2001. 737–40.

2002

"Mary Wollstonecraft's Literary Reviews." *The Cambridge Companion to Mary Wollstonecraft*. Ed. Claudia L. Johnson. Cambridge: Cambridge UP, 2002. 82–98.

"'Miss Edgeworth's Naughty Girl': or, The Importance of Being Rosamond." Unpublished Paper. Excerpted in Maureen O'Connor. "Introduction: Our Debt to Mitzi Myers." *Women's Writing* 31 (2002): 289–97.

BOOK REVIEWS

Rev. of *Marriage: Fielding's Mirror of Morality*, by Murial Brittain Williams. *Mary Wollstonecraft Journal* 2 (May 1974): 36.

Rev. of *Relative Creatures: Victorian Women in Society and the Novel*, by Françoise Basch. *Concerns: Newsletter of the Women's Caucus of the Modern Language Association* 5 (1 Dec. 1975): 12.

Rev. of *Women & Men/Men & Women: An Anthology of Short Stories*, ed. by William Smart. *Concerns: Newsletter of the Women's Caucus of the Modern Language Association* 5 (25 Sept. 1975): 11.

Rev. of *Yesterday's Woman: Domestic Realism in the English Novel*, by Vineta Colby. *Women and Literature* 3 (Spring 1975): 47.

Rev. of *Unquiet Soul: A Biography of Charlotte Brontë*, by Margot Peters. *Women and Literature* 4 (Spring 1976): 56–57.

Rev. of *Reader, I Married Him: A Study of the Women Characters of Jane Austen, Charlotte Brontë Elizabeth Gaskell, and George Eliot*, by Patricia Beer. *Women and Literature* 5 (Spring 1977): 58–60.

Rev. of *The English Jacobin Novel, 1780–1805*, by Gary Kelly. *Studies in Burke and His Time* 19 (Aut. 1978): 274–77.

Rev. of *Mary Wollstonecraft: An Annotated Bibliography*, by Janet Todd; *Imagining a Self: Autobiography and Novel in Eighteenth-Century England*, by Patricia Meyer Spacks; and *The English Jacobin Novel, 1780–1805*, by Gary Kelly. *Women and Literature* 6 (Fall 1978): 47–50.

Rev. of *What Manner of Woman*, ed. by Marlene Springer. *The Eighteenth Century: A Current Bibliography*. New York: AMS, 1981. ns. 4 (1978): 271–72.

Rev. of *Collected Letters of Mary Wollstonecraft*, ed. by Ralph M. Wardle. *The Eighteenth Century: A Current Bibliography*. New York: AMS, 1983. ns 5 (1979): 610–11.

Rev. of *A Fantasy of Reason: The Life and Thought of William Godwin*, by Don A. Locke. *Eighteenth-Century Studies* 16 (Fall 1982): 77–79.

Rev. of *A Critical Edition of Mary Wollstonecraft's* A Vindication of the Rights of Woman: With Strictures on Political and Moral Subjects, ed. by Ulrich H. Hardt; *English Literature in History, 1780–1830: Pastoral and Politics*, by Roger Sales. *Keats–Shelley Journal* 33 (1984): 231–34.

Rev. of *Feminist Theorists: Three Centuries of Key Women Thinkers*, ed. by Dale Spender. *The Eighteenth Century: A Current Bibliography*. New York: AMS, ns. 10 (1984).

Rev. of *Quiet Rebellion: The Fictional Heroines of Eliza Fowler Haywood*, by Mary Anne Schofield; *Fictions of Feminine Desire: Disclosures of Heloise*, by Peggy Kamuf; *Feminism in Eighteenth-Century England*, by Katharine M. Rogers; and *Mothering the Mind: Twelve Studies of Writers and Their Silent Partners*, ed. by Ruth Perry and Martine Watson Brownley. *Eighteenth-Century Studies* 19 (Spring 1985): 107–10.

Rev. of *First Feminists: British Women Writers, 1578–1799*, ed. by Moira Ferguson. *Tulsa Studies in Women's Literature* 5.2 (Fall 1986): 314–16.

"An Optimistic World According to Blume." Rev. of *Just as Long as We're Together*, by Judy Blume. *Los Angeles Times* 26 Dec. 1987, Home Edition: View 4+.

"A Mixed Message on Morality." Rev. of *Will You Be My Posslq?*, by Eve Bunting. *Los Angeles Times* 9 Jan. 1988, Home Edition: VIEW 5+.

"In Search of Father—and Themselves." Rev. of *Sons from Afar*, by Cynthia Voigt. *Los Angeles Times* 30 Jan. 1988, Home Edition: VIEW 5+.

"High Schoolers Learn about the Meaning of Friendship." Rev. of *Among Friends*, by Caroline B. Cooney. *Los Angeles Times* 6 Feb. 1988, Home Edition: View 5+.

"An Odyssey Through Family Roots Turned Upside Down." Rev. of *Denny's Tapes*, by Carolyn Meyer. *Los Angeles Times* 13 Feb. 1988, Home Edition: VIEW 5+.

"A Message of Hope for the Stricken Ladies in Hiding." Rev. of *Even Pretty Girls Cry at Night*, by Merill Joan Gerber. *Los Angeles Times* 7 May 1988, Home Edition: VIEW 5+.

"Words of Fantasy." Rev of *Mexican Americans*, by Julie Catalano; *The Invisible Hunters*, by Harriet Rohmer, Octavio Chow, and Morris Vidaure; *How We Came to the Fifth World*, by Harriet Rohmer and Mary Anchonodo; *To Hell With Dying*, by Alice Walker; *The Green Lion of Zion Street*, by Julia Fields; *Upside-Downers: Pictures to Stretch the Imagination*, by Mitsumasa Anno; *Six Crows*, by Leo Lionni; *The Lion and the Puppy and Other Stories for Children*, by Leo Tolstoy; *The Light Princess*, by George MacDonald, adapt. by Robin McKinley. *Los Angeles Times* 22 May 1988, Special Section, Children's Books: 10+.

"A Trapped Killer Whale Makes Waves of Conscience." Rev. of *The Hostage*, by Theodore Taylor. *Los Angeles Times* 6 Aug. 1988, Home Edition: VIEW 5+

Rev. of *The Converse of the Pen: Acts of Intimacy in the Eighteenth-Century Familiar Letter*, by Bruce Redford. *Eighteenth-Century Studies* 22.1 (Fall 1988): 84–86.

Rev. of *The Autobiographical Subject: Gender and Ideology in Eighteenth-Century England*, by Felicity A. Nussbaum; *The Sign of Angelica: Women, Writing, and Fiction, 1660–1800*, by Janet Todd. *Women's Review of Books* 8.4 (1991): 20–22.

Rev. of *The Mary Shelley Reader: Containing* Frankenstein, Mathilda, *Tales and Stories, Essays and Reviews, and Letters*, by Charles E. Robinson and Betty T. Bennett. *Keats–Shelley Journal* 41 (1992): 244–45.

Rev. of *The Land of Lost Content: Children and Childhood in Nineteenth-Century French Literature*, by Rosemary Lloyd; *Moral Instruction and Fiction for Children, 1749–1820*, by Samuel F. Pickering, Jr. *Eighteenth-Century Fiction* 6.3 (1994): 303–5.

Rev. of *"My Hideous Progeny": Mary Shelley, William Godwin, and the Father–Daughter Relationship*, by Katherine C. Hill-Miller. *Wordsworth Circle* 26.4 (1995): 258–59.

Rev. of *The World of Hannah More*, by Patricia Demers. *Tulsa Studies in Women's Literature* 16.2 (1997): 397–400.

Rev. of *Through the Northern Gate: Childhood and Growing Up in British Fiction, 1719–1901*, by Jacqueline Banerjee. *Nineteenth-Century Contexts* 21 (1999): 299–304.

Index

Abbott, Alice Balch, 181
academia, children's literature in, vii, 174–75
accomplishments, feminine, 146–47, 203–5, 209
Achilles, 192
Adams, Gillian, xiiin2, 234, 237n4
Addison, Joseph, 184
adolescent literature, 10, 5–36, 42, 52, 155, 199, 208–13, 229, 233, 236, 238n10
Adomeit, Ruth, 4
Adorno, Theodor, 212
advice books, 204
Aesop, 7–8, 20, 33, 56. *See also* Croxall, Samuel; La Fontaine, Jean de
age-appropriate literature, 88, 93–99, 138, 154–55;
Agrippina, 140
Aladdin, 58
Alembert, John le Rond d', 54
Ali Baba, 58
Alice in Wonderland, 231
anti-Jacobinism, 54–56, 137–61
anti-Semitism, 151
Antoinette, Marie, 32
Aristotle, 107n16, 108n18
Arnold, Benedict, 192
Aspects of the Novel, 167–68
Atalanta, 206
Aulnoy, Mme d', 39, 42, 58, 153; as Mother Bunch, 8

Austen, Jane, 80, 117, 132n4, 143, 165
authorship, issues of, 7–8, 154
autobiographies, 207, 233
Avery, Gillian, 239n12

Badger, Charlotte, 158n16
Bagehot, Walter, 167
Baillie, Joanna, 117, 133n9
Bakhtin, Mikhail, 143
Baldwin, R., 30
Balfour, Clara Lucas, 157n14
Ball, Elizabeth, 4
The Ballad of Lucy Whipple, 173
Balzac, Honoré de, 165
Barbauld, Anna Laetitia, 3, 85–111; "An Address," 108n22; "Civic Sermons," 107n16; as classical humanist, 94–96; *Hymns in Prose for Children*, 85–86, 97; *Lessons for Children*, x, 85–86, 88–96, 146; "On Prejudice," 108n23; "On the use of History," 107n14; Palgrave school, 86, 90, 106n7; *Poems*, 103
Barnaby Rudge, 165
Barruel, Abbé Augustin, 141–42
Basche, Françoise, 203
Battiscombe, Georgina, 202
Bauerle, Diane, 17
Beale, Dorothea, 202–3, 205, 208, 213–14n2
Beaumont, Marie Le Prince de, 37, 39, 42, 28–52, 55–60; French

conversational pedagogy, 21; Young Misses' Magazine (*Magasin des enfans*), 5, 29, 42, 49–52, 56. *See also* fairy tales

"Beauty and the Beast," 29, 30

Beckett, Sandra, 234

Bell, Andrew, 158n16

Bentham, Jeremy, 156–57n13

Bentley, Thomas, 102, 108n21

Bercovitch, Sacvan, 179–80

Berquin, Arnold, 21

bibliotherapy, 235. *See also* critical approaches

Blake, William, 69, 85

Blume, Judy, 236

boarding schools. *See* schools

Boreman, Thomas, 72

Borgman, Jim, 173

Bottigheimer, Ruth, 25n1, 52

Bowers, Toni, 108n24

Boy of Winander. *See* Wordsworth, William

Bradley, David G., 157n14

Bratton, Jacqueline, 213n1

breastfeeding, 150

Bremner, C. S., 214n3

Brontë, Charlotte, 201

Brooke, Henry, 81, 82n1

Brooks, Elbridge S., 179

Browning, Elizabeth Barrett, 85

Bryant, Margaret, 203

Bunting, Eve, 236

Burckhardt, Johann Gottlieb, 158n16

Burdan, Judith, 51

Burke, Edmund, 144

Burnett, Frances Hodgson, 213

Burney, Francis, 89

Burton, J., 158n16

Buss, Mary Frances, 202–4, 208, 213n2

Butler, Francelia, 231, 234, 237n4

Butler, Marilyn, 157n11, 239n13

Butts, Dennis, 27n40

Byron, Henry, 61

Cadell, Thomas, 132n5

Cadogan, Mary, 43, 213n1

Caldecott, Randolph, 236

California Gold Rush, 173

Cameron, Lucy Lyttleton, 151

Campe, Joachim Heinrich, 21, 158n16

Canning, George, 144

Carlyle, Thomas, 166

Carroll, Lewis, x, 231

Carter, Elizabeth, 99

catalogue practices in children's literature, 1–28

A Catechism of Modern History, 202

Cato, 184

Certeau, Michel de, 184

Chaffin, Roger, 106n11

Chapone, Hester, 108n22

Chaucer, Geoffrey, 231

children: definitions of, 10, 168; children's literature, definitions of, 11, 234–36. *See also* children's literary history; children's literature genres

children's balls, 158n17

children's literary history, ix, 87–88, 153–55, 165–77, 230–37, 238n4; canon creation, xi, 173–74, 199–200, 231–32, 234; in contrast to high brow literature, 165–77, 199–200; as Manichean, 87, 232; as masculinist, x, xii, 88, 200, 231–32; national practices, 19, 21, 23, 29–66, 165–77. *See also* critical approaches to children's literature; Romantic ideology

children's literature genres: allegory, 80; animal tales, 22, 34–35, 41, 52; Biblical stories, 13, 19, 24n1, 43, 52, 61, 113–30, 133n9, 133n12, 134n16; boy's adventure books, 172–75, 235; catechisms, 107n17, 149,153; children's magazines, 173, 179–98, 206; classic, xi; 171–75; didactic literature, 76–77, 87, 113–16, 118, 231, 235–36; drama, 62–62, 80, 113–36; Eastern tales, 80; fable, 34–35, 41, 43, 46, 61, 80, 101, 119–20; fairy tale (*see* fairy tale);

folktale, 119, 133n13; hero stories and legends, xi, 195; historical fiction, xi, 179–98 (*see also Ivanhoe*); moral tale, 52, 61, 150–51, 235; myth, 119–20; picture books, 236–37, 239n11 (*see also* illustrations); poetry, 150–51; school books, xi, 23, 170–72; school story, xi, 43–45 (*see also* governess stories); boys' school story, 213; girls' school story, 199–217; sentimental literature, 231; travel narratives and geography books, 23. *See also Genre Terms*; formula fiction

Children's Literature Association, 227, 230, 233

The Child's New Play-Thing, 72, 88–90, 94. *See also* Mary Collins

Clancy, Patricia, 49, 50

Clark, Beverly Lyon, vii

Clark, Margaret, 24

class issues in children's literature, xi, 75–78, 117–18, 132n3, 146–47, 151, 168–69

Cliff's notes, 170

Clio, 181

Clough, Anne Jemima, 205, 214n2

Cobbe, Francis Power, 202, 205

Cole, Lucinda, 133–34n14

Colley, Linda, 134n19

Collins, Mary 72

Colman, George, 61

Columbian Exposition, 183

Columbus, Christopher, 179–80, 183, 196

conservatisim, 138, 140–43

Cooney, Caroline B., 236

copyright laws, 171. *See also* imprints

Cormier, Robert, 235–36

Covent-Garden, 54

Cowan, Andrew, 158n16

Cowley, Hannah, 132n5

Crabb, George, 90–92, 94, 97, 101, 106n7

Craig, Patricia, 213n1

Crawford, Mary, 106n11

Crespigny, Lady Mary Champion de, 158n16

critical approaches to children's literature: cultural studies, 231–34; feminist, 104, 120, 133n14, 143–44, 199–204, 211–12, 228–29, 235; language (*see* phonics, schema theory); New Historicist, vi–viii, xi, 200, 232, 235, 237; psycholinguistic, 143; reader response (*see* audience; crossover reading); twentieth-century anxieties, 174–75. *See also* educational theory and practice

cross-writing, xiiin3, 186, 193–94, 234, 236

crossover reading, xi, xiiin3, 179–81, 186–87, 193, 196, 236. *See also* audience

Croxall, Samuel, 140

Cruikshank, George, 169

cultural studies. *See* critical approaches to children's literature

Cushman, Karen, 173

cyberspace, 235

dame schools. *See* schools

Dante, 231

Darrah, Lydia, 180, 184–85

Darth Vader, 183

Darton, F. J. Harvey, 6, 87, 142

Davies, Emily, 201–5, 213n2

Davis, Tracy C., 117, 132n8

Day, Thomas (*Sandford and Merton*), 21

Demerritt, E. W., 188

Dickens, Charles, 165

Dickinson, H. T., 157n11

didactic literature. *See* children's literature genres

Diderot, Denis, 52

Dido, 181

Disraeli, Isaac, 144

Dodge, Mary Mapes, 181

domestic heroine, 121

domesticity, rise of, 67–82

Dorset, Catherine Ann, 22, 26n27

Dove, Jane Frances, 205, 207

Duncan, Joseph E., 176
Duval, Gilles, 25n4
Dyhouse, Carol, 213n1

Edgeworth, Richard Lovell, 107n15, 157–58n16
Edgeworth, Maria, xiiin1, xiiin2, 3, 52–53, 86, 101, 133n12, 157–58n16, 158n22, 200, 208, 225, 228, 230–35, 238n4, 238n10; "The Bracelets," 233; *Castle Rackrent*, 235; "The Cherry Orchard," 234, 237; *Collected Works*, 237, 239n13; *Early Lessons*, 230; *Ennui*, 235; "Essay on Irish Bulls," 235; "The Purple Jar," 230–31
education reform, xii, 67–82, 146, 149–50. *See also* Education Act of 1870
education movements: early childhood education, 71, 169; environmental or organic, ix, 69–70 (*see also* Locke, John); girls' education, 199–217; moral education, 67, 76–80; progressive, 233
Education Act of 1870, British, 169–72
educational theory and practice, ix, xi, 139, 146, 149, 233
Edwardian values, 166–67
Eliot, George, 168
Eliot, T. S., 86
Elliot, Dorice Williams, 134n16, 134n20
enlightenment, ix, xiii, 86; domesticity and mother figures, 94–95, 97; humanism and ethics, 97–99
Epictetus, 99
Evangelicalism, 113–14, 118, 133n8, 140, 143, 145, 147, 150–53, 158n18, 211
Evangeline, 181

fairy tales, ix, 29–66; "Aurora," 50; "Beauty and the Beast," 5, 30, 37, 42, 49, 50, 58, 63n3; "Blue Beard," 29, 30–31, 34–36, 46, 58–61, 63n3, 152; "Cinderella," 34–35, 37, 58, 63n3, 152; "The Discreet Princess" (*see*

L'Hertier); "The Fairy," 34, 37; "Jack and the Bean Stalk," 31; in Jane Johnson's notebooks, 73; "Little Red Riding Hood," 29, 34–37, 58–60, 63n3; "Sleeping Beauty," 37; "The Sleeping Beauty in the Woods," 34; morals in 35–38, 42; in More's *Sacred Dramas*, x; politics of, 133n13, 143, 151–53, 231; "Prince Fatal, and Prince Fortunatus," 50; "Princess Hebe" (*see* Fielding, Sarah); "Petit Poucet," 31, 34; "Puss in Boots," 18, 34; "Riquet a la Houpe," 37–38; "Tale of Three Wishes," 50; versus Christian principles, 53–60
female academy, viii–ix, 61. *See also* schools, girls
feminist approaches to children's literature. *See* critical approaches to children's literature
Fénelon, François, 5–6, 9, 21
Fenn, Ellenor, 3, 73, 82n2, 105n6
Ferris, Ina, 165–65, 175
Feuerbach, Ludwig, 107n18
Fielding, Henry, 79, 132n4
Fielding, Sarah, viii–ix, 3, 44, 60, 213; *The Governess*, 5, 30, 42–53, 55–78, 68, 79–81, 199; "To the Honourable Mrs. Poyntz," 43
fingerprints in book cataloguing, 13–19
Fluck, Winfried, 212
Fontaine, Nicolas, 13, 19, 21
Fontaine, Jean de La, 33, 43. *See also* fables
Fontaine, Jacques, 184
Forbes, Duncan, 175
Ford, Charles Howard, 115, 132n5, 134n18
formula fiction, xi, 179–80, 186–97, 236; boy's military initiation story, 191; girl's rescue story, 187–91. *See also* children's literature genres
Forster, E. M., 167–68
Foucault, Michel, 108n20. *See also* critical approaches to children's literature, New Historicist

Fraser's Magazine, 204
Frederick II of Prussia, 52
Freeman, Lisa A., 132n4, 132n6
Freemasons, 142
French influence on children's
    literature, 36, 39, 42
French Revolution, 53, 86, 127, 141
French and anti-French sentiment. *See*
    Anti-Jacobin
Freud, Sigmund and the reality
    principle, 98, 100. *See also* critical
    approaches to children's literature
Frith, Gill, 213n1
Frye, Northrup, 209
Fussell, Paul, 173
Fyfe, Aileen, 147

G., J. 72, 105n6
games. *See* toys
Gannon, Susan R., 188, 238n10
Garrick, David, 114, 116, 132n5
Garside, P.D., 175
Gay, Penny, 132n5
Gellert, Christian Fuerchtegott, 158n16
gender-bending, 120–27
generational conflict, 186–91, 196–97,
    208–10, 233–34
Genlis, Stéphanie-Félicité, Comtesse
    de, 21, 29, 42, 52–53, 146, 149,
    158n16
Genre Terms, 11, 25n9
Georgian era, x, 143, 230–31, 235,
    238n10
Gettysburg, battle of, 193
Gifford, William, 144
Gilray, James, 144
The Girl's Realm, 199
Godwin, William, 52; as William
    Scolfield, 140, 157n10, 237n4
Goethe, Johann Wolfgang von, 165,
    225, 228–29
golden age of children's literature, x
Goldsmith, Oliver, 68. *See also The*
    Renowned History of Little Goody Two-
    Shoes
Goldstone, Bette P., 230–32
Goodenough, Elizabeth, xiiin2, 230, 234

Goody Two-Shoes. *See The Renowned*
    History of Little Goody Two-Shoes
governess manuals, 42, 44. *See also*
    Beaumont, Mme. de; Fielding, Sarah
governess figures: Mrs. Affable (*see*
    Beaumont, Mme. de); Miss Jenny
    Peace (*see* Fielding, Sarah); Mrs.
    Teachum (*see* Fielding, Sarah);
    Marjorie Meanwell (*see The*
    Renowned History of Little Goody Two-
    Shoes)
The Governess, or The Little Female
    Academy. See Fielding, Sarah
grammar books: Camden, William, 8;
    Lilly, William, 8. *See also* children's
    literature genres, school books
Grenby, M. O., 3, 24, 138, 157n6,
    157n11, 158n19
Grand, Sarah, 210
Granville, Countess of, 34, 37, 56
Greek, study of, 201–2, 231
Greenaway, Kate, 236
Grey, Maria Shirreff, 214n3
Grieder, Theodore Godfrey, Jr., 157n11
Grub Street, 144
Guardian of Education. See Trimmer,
    Sarah
Guillory, John, xii
Gumuchian (*Les Livres de l'enfance*), 25n5

Hale, Nathan, 179–80, 183, 187,
    191–92, 196
Hall, Catherine, 133n8
Hamilton, Elizabeth, 140, 143, 157n16,
    158n17
Hamilton, Cicely, 211–13
Hancock, Harrie Irving, 194
Harland, Marion, 115, 132n5
Harris, James 87–98, 108n19
Harris, John, 157n7. *See also* Newbery
    publishing firm
Hazard, Paul, 105n3
Headmistress' Association, 206
Hearn, Michael Patrick, 33
Heberle, Mark A., 234
heroism, 179–98; domestic, 53, 187–91
Hesiod, 231

history, in children's books, 165–77. *See also* children's literature genres, historical fiction
Hockliffe Project, 24
Hoflund, Barbara, 24, 27n40
Holcombe, Lee, 203, 214n2
Hole, Robert, 157n11, 158n18
home education, 74–80, 202
Honan, William H., 227
Honig, Edith, 213n1
Horace, 227
Howard's End, 168
Huckleberry Finn, 87, 106
Huddersfield Weekly Examiner, 211
Hughes, Thomas, 213
Hunt, Peter, 105n4, 239n12
Hutcheson, Francis, 97–98, 108n19

illustrations, 11, 169; of fairy tales, 58–61
Immel, Andrea, 24, 85, 106n6, 138, 230, 238n10
imprints, 13–19
Inchbald, Elizabeth, 117
Infant Tongues: The Voice of the Child in Literature, 234
Irigaray, Luce, 143. *See also* critical approaches to children's literature
Irish literature, 227–28, 234–35
Isaiah, 119

Jackson, Mary V., 118, 133n11, 142–43
James, R. M., 145
Jauffret, Louis François, 154
Jay, Elisabeth, 132n5
Jenkins, Charles F., 185
Joan of Arc, 181
Johnson, Claudia L., xiiin2, 238n10
Johnson, Edgar, 174–75
Johnson, Jane, 73, 82n1
Johnson, Richard, 7
Johnson, Samuel, 81, 202
Johnstone, Sir Alexander, 133n9
Jones, M. G., 115, 132n5

Kamm, Josephine, 201
Keane, Angela, 133n10

Keate, William, 108n22
Keating, E. H., 61
Kelly, R. Gordon, 186
Kelly, Michael, 61
Kendall, Edward, 158n16
Kieffer, Harry M., 193–95
King Richard, 172
Kipling, Rudyard, 213
Knoepflmacher, U. C., vi, xiiin3, 106n13, 233, 238n10. *See also* cross-writing
Kowaleski-Wallace, Elizabeth, 128
Kraft, Elizabeth, 108n19
Kristeva, Julia, 143

L'Hértier de Villandon, Marie-Jeanne, 31, 39–44, 51, 56–58, 60, 62, 63n1
Lamb, Mary, 79
Lamb, Charles, 6, 30, 78–79
Lancaster, Joseph, 158n16
Landers, Ann, 236
Lane, Harlan, 108n18
Lang, Andrew, 31–33, 36, 63n2. *See also* Perrault, Charles
Laufer, Roger, 25n10
Lawrence, Captain of the *Chesapeake*, 181–82
LeBreton, Anna Letitia, 92
Lemann, Nicholas, 91–92
Leonard Bast novel, 168–71
Lewis, C. S. 151
libraries, children's literature collections in: Bodleian, 72, 82n1, 106n9; Cotsen, xiiin2, 6, 85, 238n10; De Montfort University, Hockliffe Project, 24; Folger Shakespeare Library, 13; Lilly Library, University of Indiana Ball Collection at the, 17, 73; New Bodley, Oxford, the Opie collection, 5, 24; UCLA, vii, 62, 24n2. *See also* catalogue practices
Locke, John, ix, 5, 8, 51, 54, 67–79, 99, 152, 156. *See also* education movements, environmental
Lowe, Robert, 169
Lunden, Anne, 237
Lurie, Alison, 133n13

MacCauley, Mary Ludwig Hays. *See* Molly Pitcher
Manley, Sue, 239n13
Martin, Ellen E., 132n7
Martineau, Harriet, 228, 237n4
Marx, Karl, 97, 103, 107–8n18
masculine bias in approaches to children's literature, ix, xii. *See also* Romantic ideology of the child
Mathias, T. J., 144
Maynard, Constance L, 205
Maynard, Mary, 201
McAleer, John, 132n7
McCallum, Robyn, 180–81
McCalman, Iain, 144
McCarthy, William, 92, 105n3, 106n7, 108n19
McClellan, Dennis, viii, 227, 232
McIlvaine, Charles, 193
McMonnies, Frederick, 183
Meade, L. T., xi, 199–217
Meakin, Annette M. B., 114, 132n5, 133n9
medieval children's literature, 231–32
Medievalism, 176–75
Mellor, Anne, 134n20, 145
Military figures, American and British: Decatur, Stephen, 192; General Francis Marion, "The Swamp Fox," 192; General John Fenwick, 191; General Howe, 184; General Hull, 184; Major Banastre Tarleton, 192; Sir Lawrence Terraine, 192; Somers, Richard, 192. *See also* Hale, Nathan; Washington, George
Milton, John 119, 140, 170–71
miniature books, 88; size of books as referenced in bibliographies, 12–13, 22
Mitchell, Sally, 213n1
Modern Language Association, vii, xivn2, 230, 234, 238n10
Molesworth, Mary, 213
Montagu, Lady Mary Wortley, 39, 49
Montluzin, Emily Lorraine de, 157n11
Moon, Marjorie, 26n27, 142, 157n7

Moore, Roger, 173, 176
moral education, 93–99, 142
More, Hannah, x, 52, 86, 113–36, 144–48, 158n16, 158n17, 158n18; *Cheap Repository Tracts*, 113, 134n16, 144; "The Fatal Falsehood," 116, 132n5; "The Invincible Captive," 116; "Ode to Charity," 131; "Percy," 116; "Preface to the Tragedies," 115–16, 132n5; "The Puppet Show," 132n4; *Sacred Dramas*, 113–36, 157n9; "The Search After Happiness," 113–19, 130, 133n12, 134n18; *Strictures on the Modern System*, 115
Mother Goose, viii, 19, 29, 31–32, 34, 38, 43, 49–50, 58, 61, 153. *See also* Perrault, Charles
mother–educators, 67–82
Murat, Countess of, 39, 42
Myers, Mitzi, vi–xii, 62, 85, 131, 155, 221–25, 227–53; "Anecdotes from the Nursery," 186, 233; "Aufklärung," 233; book reviews, 236; "Canonical Orphans," 118; *Children's Literature* special issue on cross-writing, 234; "Child's Play," 186, 189, 196, 208, 234; "Completing the Union," 234–35; "De-Romanticizing," 133n12; "Dilemmas of Peace and War," 200, 233, 238n4; *Encyclopedia Americana*, xiiin3, 236; "Erotics," 233, 236; Foreword, 237; "From the Editors: Cross-Writing," xiiin3, 106n13, 118; "Gender, Genres," 88, 235; "Godwin's Memoirs," 238n4; "Goring John Bull," 234; "Hannah More's Tracts," 113, 131, 134n14, 145; "Harriet Martineau," 238n4; "Impeccable Governesses," xii, ix, 48, 52, 145, 147, 230; "Introduction. Here's Looking," ix, 145, 147, 232, 238; Introduction to *Revolutionary Reviewing*, 138, 145, 147; "Like the Pictures in a Magic Lantern," 234; "Literature for

Children," xiii; "Little Girls and Boys Lost," 235; "Little Girls Lost," 87, 231, 234; "Miss Edgeworth's Naughty Girl," xiii, 239n14; "Missed Opportunities," 231–32; "Mothers and Daughters," 234; Norton anthology of children's literature, 237, 239n13; "No Safe Place to Run to," vi, xiii, 235–36; "Of Mice and Mothers," 86–87, 93, 98, 106n10; on Georgian era women writers, 30; on Romantic ideology, ix, x, 87; "Pedagogy as Self-Expression," 238; "Pictured Morals," 237; "Quixotes," 234; "Reading Children" ix–x, 231; "Reading Rosamond," 233; "Reform or Ruin," 121, 127, 131, 145–46, 148, 238n4; "Romancing the Moral Tale," 197; "Sensibility and the 'Walk of Reason,'" 238; "Servants as They are Now Educated," 233, 238n4; "Socializing Rosamond," xi, 200, 230, 233; "Storying War," 235; "A Taste for Truth," 52–53, 230; "War Correspondence," 234; "Wise Child," 200, 231

Nangle, Benjamin, 108n21
nationalism and imperialism: in children's books, x, xi, 234–35; in children's theater, x, 114, 119–28, 133n9; in school stories, xi; in Sir Walter Scott's *Ivanhoe*, xii, 166, 170–77. *See also* orientalism
Needleman, Robert, 161n21
Nelson, Claudia, 211
Nero, 181
Nesbit, Edith, 87
New Historicism. *See* critical approaches to children's literature
Newbery Award, 173
Newbery, John, and family of: Carnon, Thomas, son of John Newbery, 6; Newbery, Elizabeth, 17; Newbery, John, 6–8, 12, 17

Newbery, publishing firm of, 6–8, 12, 17, 72, 77, 88, 100, 139, 147, 152, 156n1, 157n7
Northrup, Mary S., 183–84, 186
Norton anthology of children's literature, 237n1, 238n12

O'Connor, Maureen, xiiin1, xiiin2, 238n10, 239n14
O'Keeffe, Adelaide, 150–51
O'Malley, Andrew, 25n8
Ogden, H. A., 185
Olson, Marilynn, Strasser, 185, 192
orientalism, 126–28, 133n9
Orléans, Elisabeth Charlotte d', 32, 37, 56,

Page, Judith, 238n10
Paine, Thomas, 141
The Palace of Enchantment, 57
parent–child conflict. *See* generational conflict
Parton, Ethel, 190
patriotism in children's books, 179–98, 184, 188–89. *See also* Anti-Jacobinism; nationalism
Patroklos, 192
Paul, Lissa, 239n12
Pearson, Jacqueline, 132n3
pedagogical writers, female, x, 86, 87, 93. *See also* rational dames
Pederson, Joyce Senders, 213n1
Perrault, Charles, 153; *Histories, or Tales of Past Times (Histoires ou Contes du tems passé)*, 9, 29–66, 152; publication and sales, 19, 24n1, 25n11. *See also* Mother Goose; Samber, Robert
Philp, Mark, 157n11
phonics versus whole language, 9
Pickering, Samuel, F., Jr., 85, 142, 146, 156n1
Pilchard, Mrs., 21
Pinnock, William, 202
Pirovano, Donato, 18
Pitcher, Molly, 180, 184–85

Planché, James Robinson, 30
play, 71–74, 99–100. *See also* toys
Playfair, William, 157n12
pleasure versus utility, ix–x, 29–66,
    67–82, 99–100, 231
Plotz, Judith, 133n11
Plumb, J. H., 25n3
political economy, 98
political writing as children's literature, xi
Pope, Alexander, 78, 108n22
Praeterita, 167
Price, Lillian L., 189–90
Princess of Cleves, 107n14
printers, 8–11. *See also* Harris, John;
    Newbery, publishing firm;
    publishing practices; Tabart,
    Benjamin
printing practices, 3–28
Protestant revolution, 67
psychological approaches. *See* critical
    approaches to children's literature;
    bibliotherapy
publishing practices: in early books,
    6–24, 165, 232; of *Ivanhoe* editions
    in England and United States,
    170–72; in nineteenth-century book
    series, 169
Purinton, Marjean, 134n15, 134n17

Queen Charlotte, 146
Quigly, Isabel, 213n1

Radcliffe, Ann, 143
rational dames, ix, 52–54, 61 85–111,
    137–61, 201. *See also* Dame schools;
    female academies; Georgian era;
    governess figures
rationalists, 51, 87. *See also* Locke, John
Rauch, Alan, 238n10
realism, 168
Reaney, Mrs. G. S., 204
Reed, Talbot Baines, 213
Reform Act, 169
religion in children's theater, x, 113–36.
    See also children's literature genres,
    Bible stories; Evangelicalism; moral
    tales

Remy, Paul, 50
*The Renowned History of Little Goody
    Two-Shoes*, ix, 67–68, 77–79;
    compared to Dick Whittington, 68,
    77
Reynolds, Kimberly, 199
Richards, Laura E., 185
Richardson, Alan, 87, 108n20, 133n13,
    148, 151, 234, 238n6
Richardson, Samuel, 86, 106n12;
    Aesop, 8; *Pamela*, ix, 67–69, 72–76,
    79–80; *Young Grandison*, 21, 107n15
Ridley, Annie E., 203–4, 214n2
Ritchie, Anne Thackeray, 85
Robbins, Sarah, 106n10
Roberts, William, 157n9, 157n12
Robin Hood, 172
Robinson Crusoe, 21
Robison, John, 157n12
Robley, Ann, 106n8
Rodgers, Betsy, 157n14
Romantic ideology of the child,
    145–49, 231–32, 238n6; definition
    of, ix–x, 87–88, 133n11, 133n12; as
    dichotomizing, 87–88; as
    masculinist, ix–x, 87–88, 133n12,
    231–32, 238n6
Romanticism, 58, 129, 131, 140, 155
Roosevelt, Theodore, 194–95
Roscoe, Sydney, 17, 19
Ross, Betsy, 180, 184–85
Ross, Marlon, 134n20
Rousseau, Jean-Jacques, 52, 54, 79,
    87–88, 93, 108n24, 142, 148–49,
    155, 158n16
Rowbotham, Judith, 204–5, 211
Rowe, Karen, 32
Royal Game of the Dolphins, 237
Ruskin, John 151, 167
Ruwe, Donelle, 52, 149, 157n5,
    157n10

Samber, Robert, 9, 33–43, 49–51,
    56–57, 60–63
Sandner, David, 157n13
schema theory, 94–95
Schiller, Johann Christoph, 115

Schmitt, Cannon, 121, 133n10
schools: boarding schools, 74, 80–81;
    Palgrave, 86, 90, 106n7; dame
    schools, 77–78
schools, girl's and women's colleges:
    Bedford College, 206; Cheltenham
    Ladies College, 205–6; fictional
    accounts of, 207–13; Girton College
    200, 205–7; Lady Margaret Hall at
    Oxford, 202; Newnham College,
    205–6, 213n2; Somerville Hall, 206;
    St. Leonard's School, 205–6. *See also*
    Sarah Fielding's *The Governess, or The
    Little Female Academy*
Schools Inquiry Commission, 203,
    214n3
Schuermann, Mona, 131–32n2
science versus supernaturalism, 114,
    119, 127–31
Scolfield, William. *See* Godwin,
    William
Scott, Iain Robertson, 157n11
Scott, Jerry, 173
Scott, Sir Walter, 165–77, 179
scripture prints. *See* children's literature
    genres, Biblical stories; Sarah
    Trimmer
Scudder, Horace, 182
separate spheres, ideology of the, 131
Seawall, Molly Elliot, 192
Sewell, Elizabeth M., 202
sexuality in children's literature: in fairy
    tales, 35–38, 42; virginity, 171
Shakespeare, William, 165
Shefrin, Jill, 72, 82n2
Shelley, Mary, 134n15
Shenstone, William, 77
Sheridan, Richard, 114
Sherwood, Mary, 53, 79, 148, 151
Shireff, Emily, 205
Siddons, Sarah, 114
Simons, Thomas, 158n16
Sinbad, 58
slavery, 232
Sloane, William, 105n6
Smith, Sidney, 137, 151

Smith, Adam, 98
Smith, Pamela Coleman, 101
Socrates, 179
Sokoloff, Naomi, 234
Somerville, Elizabeth, 141
Somerville, Mary, 202
Spock, Dr. Benjamin, 150, 158n21
Stahl, J. D., 227
Stanton, Elizabeth Cady, 182
Stephens, John, 180–81
Sterne, Laurence, 70
St. Nicholas Magazine, xii, 179–98
Stockton, Frank, 183
Stone, Wilbur Macy, 157n13
Stott, Anne 132n5, 134n20
Straparola, Giovan Francesco, 18–19
suffrage and voting rights, 169
Summerfield, Geoffrey, 85, 87, 99,
    105n4, 142, 200, 230
Suzuki, Mika, 45, 53
The Swiss Family Robinson, 167

Tabart, Benjamin, viii–ix, 29, 39, 50,
    58–61, 157n7
Taylor, Ann, 150–51
Taylor, Isaac, 23
Taylor, Jane, 150–51
Tell, William, 181
Tennyson, Alfred, 169
Tennyson, G. B., 230
theater, children's, x
Tolkien, J. R. R., 151
Tom Thumb's Playbook, 107n17; *The Life
    and Death of Tom Thumb* (*see* Richard
    Johnson)
Townsend, John Rowe, 142; toys, ix,
    22–23, 71–73, 146, 150, 161n21. *See
    also* pleasure versus utility
Trimmer, Sarah, viii–x, 39, 46, 50, 52,
    54, 89, 92, 105n6, 230; *Easy
    Introduction*, 146, 149; *Fabulous
    Histories*, 61; *Guardian of Education*, x,
    23, 29–30, 54–61, 63n3, 137–61;
    Ladder of Learning, 20; *Prints of Scripture
    History*, 7, 61; *Sacred History* 157n9;
    Some Account 141, 146, 156n2, 157n14

Tucker, Robert C., 107n18
Tucker, Nicholas, 151–52, 157n5
Tucker, George Holbert, 132n7
Twain, Mark, 166–67, 172–73. *See also*
    Huckleberry Finn
Twells, Alison, 117
Ty, Eleanor, 143–44

UCLA Children's Literature Special
    Collections, vii, 62, 24n2, 227,
    228–30. *See also* libraries, children's
    literature collections in
utopian literature, 103–4, 206, 209

Vallone, Lynne, 239n12
Vicinus, Martha, 201–4, 206
Victorianism, 134n20, 166
Villeneuve, Gabrielle Suzanne Barbot
    de, 39, 49
violence, 120, 189–91, 195, 197,
    235–36, 239n11
Voltaire, 54
Vriesema, P.C.A., 15

Wakefield, Priscilla, 23
Walpole, Horace, 108n22
war, 234, 235, 238n10, 239n11;
    American Civil War, 193–94;
    American Revolution, 183–86,
    192–94 (*see also* Washington,
    George); Napoleonic wars, 53 (*see
    also* anti-Jacobinism); Spanish-
    American War, 193; War of 1812,
    191; World War I, 173, 176n1;
    World War II, 176n1; war fever,
    183–94. *See also* French Revolution;
    women's peace writing
Warner, Charles Dudley, 179–80,
    182–83
Washington, George, 180–85, 187–91,
    196
Watson, Victor, 82n1
Watts, Isaac, 5, 8
Waverley novels. *See* Scott, Sir Walter

Wedgwood, Josiah, 102, 108n21
Weedon, Margaret, 7
Weems, Parson Mason Locke, 181
Welch, d'Alté, 4, 17
West, Jane, 139, 144, 148, 158n16
White, Kelly K., 238n11
Whittington, Dick, 68, 77, 181
Wilberforce, William, 144
Wild Boy of Aveyron, 108n18
Wiley, S. K., 191–92
Williams, David, 158n16
Williams, Jane, 114, 131n1
Willich, Anthony Florian Madinger,
    158n16
Wills, Deborah, 157n14, 158n20
Wilner, Arlene, 43, 46
Winstanley, William, 72
Wittgenstein, Ludwig, 91, 103, 107n16
Wollstonecraft, Mary, ix, 3, 21, 52,
    79–80, 145, 147, 201, 213, 225,
    228–31, 238n4, 238n10
Wolsey, Cardinal, 141, 147
women's peace writing, 234–35
Wood, Marcus, 143
Woodman, C. H., 191
Woolf, Virginia, 86, 168, 189, 202, 205
Wordsworth, Elizabeth, 202
Wordsworth, William, x, 69, 77, 85,
    87, 97, 148–49, 101, 105n3, 105n5,
    151–52. *See also* Romantic ideology
    of the child
Xenophon, 45, 70

Yarde, D. M., 157n14
Yeats, William Butler, 101
Yonge, Charlotte, 105n1, 172
young adult literature. *See* adolescent
    literature

Zall, P.M., 85
Zarucchi, Jeanne Morgan, 32, 33, 62
Zipes, Jack, 238n12
Zits, 173. *See also* children's literature
    genres, magazines

About the Contributors

Gillian Adams is an independent scholar and a former editor of the *Children's Literature Association Quarterly* and *Children's Literature Abstracts*. She is continuing her research into and publication on ancient, medieval, and early modern children's literature.

Bruce Beiderwell is director of the UCLA Writing Program and was a longtime colleague and friend of Mitzi Myers in her years with the program. He is the author of *Power and Punishment in Scott's Novels* (Georgia 1992).

Ruth B. Bottigheimer, from the Department of Comparative Studies at the State University of New York at Stony Brook, has published *Fairy Tales and Society* (1986), *Grimm's Bad Girls and Bold Boys* (1987), a study of Bibles for children in the Western world (1996), and *Fairy Godfather* (2002). She is currently working on a new history of fairy tales and a bibliography of early books for children in Great Britain.

Julia Briggs is professor of English literature at De Montfort University, Leicester, and Emeritus Fellow of Hertford College, Oxford. She is the author of books on ghost stories and Renaissance literature, as well as a biography of E. Nesbit (*Woman of Passion*, 1987). She co-edited a festschrift for the Opies, *Children and Their Books*, with Gillian Avery, and she is currently co-editing a history of popular books for children with Brian Alderson, Dennis Butts, and M. O. Grenby.

Susan R. Gannon, emeritus professor of literature and communications at Pace University, has served in various capacities on the executive board and other committees of the Children's Literature Association from 1986 to 1995. She has published extensively on the history of children's writing, including articles in *Children's Literature*, *Signal*, *Nineteenth-Century Contexts*, and *Studies in the Literary Imagination*, and has co-edited a collection of essays on *St. Nicholas Magazine* and Mary Mapes Dodge.

M. O. Grenby is a reader in the English Department at the University of Newcastle upon Tyne. He was director of the Hockliffe Project, which was established at De Montfort University in 1999 to digitize and encourage research into pre-1850 British children's books (http://www.cta.dmu.ac.uk/projects/Hockliffe). Dr. Grenby has published several books and articles on children's culture and the political literature of the later eighteenth and early nineteenth centuries, research supported by a 2004 Mitzi Myers Memorial Fellowship at UCLA.

William McCarthy, emeritus professor of English at Iowa State University, is co-editor of *The Poems of Anna Letitia Barbauld* (1994) and *Selected Poetry and Prose of Anna Letitia Barbauld* (2001). He is currently writing a new biography of Barbauld.

Anita Hemphill McCormick is currently working on a biography of Dorothy Wordsworth; she also teaches a children's literature course for UCLA's English Department.

Marjean D. Purinton is professor of English and associate chair of the English Department at Texas Tech University, where she also teaches in the Women's Studies Program and the Comparative Literature Program. She is chair of the executive council of the Texas Tech University Teaching Academy and the author of *Romantic Ideology Unmasked: The Mentally Constructed Tyrannies in Dramas of William Wordsworth, Lord Byron, Percy Shelley, and Joanna Baillie* as well as the forthcoming *Staging Grotesques and Ghosts: Techno-Gothic British Romantic Drama*.

Mavis Reimer is an associate professor of English at the University of Winnipeg, Canada, where she teaches children's literature and Victorian studies. She is the co-author of the third edition of *The Pleasures of Children's Literature*.

Karen E. Rowe, professor of English at UCLA, has published various essays on feminism and fairy tales. Her current book in progress on fairy tale and romantic fictions draws on UCLA's renowned Children's Book Collection, which was a second home for Mitzi Myers. Myers was a longtime research associate at UCLA's Center for the Study of Women, for which Rowe served as founding director; there they shared a commitment to feminist approaches to children's literature, eighteenth-century studies, and folklore.

Donelle Ruwe is assistant professor of English at Northern Arizona University and former associate professor of English at Fitchburg State College. She has published on gender and children's literature from the Romantic era and has been the Fleur Cowles Fellow at the Harry Ransom Research Center of the University of Texas–Austin. She serves on the governing board of the Eighteenth- and Nineteenth-Century British Women Writer's Association.